TRAILBLAZERS

WOMEN TALK ABOUT CHANGING CANADA

JUDITH FINLAYSON

Doubleday Canada

Canadian Cataloguing in Publication Data

Finlayson, Judith
Trailblazers: women talk about changing Canada

Includes index.
ISBN 0-385-25658-2

1. Sex discrimination against women – Canada. 2. Women's rights – Canada.
3. Feminists – Canada – Biography. 4. Women – Canada – Biography.
I. Title.

HQ1455.A3F56 1999   305.42'092'271   C99-931181-6

Jacket photograph by Francisco Cruz/Superstock
Jacket and text design by Susan Thomas / Digital Zone
Printed and bound in the USA

Published in Canada by
Doubleday Canada, a division of
Random House of Canada Ltd.
105 Bond Street
Toronto, Ontario
M5B 1Y3

BVG 10 9 8 7 6 5 4 3 2 1

The author would like to thank the Canada Council for its support.

*For Helen, my mother, and Catherine, my mother-in-law,
the invisible sustainers who prepared the way.*

*And for Meredith, my daughter, who will blaze her own
trail knowing the precedents.*

Contents

ACKNOWLEDGEMENTS

Like all my work, *Trailblazers* was greatly enhanced by the contributions of women across the country. A diverse group from many walks of life, they inspired and supported my efforts to document this chapter in women's history.

Naturally, the most significant contribution was made by the women who agreed to be interviewed for the book. Individually, they gave generously of their time, graciously tolerated my probing and were often candid to a fault. Collectively, their vivid stories provide a unique portrait of contemporary Canada. Regrettably, a number of wonderful stories didn't make it into print due to the practical realities of publishing.

I owe a great debt to the many women who suggested potential subjects. In this regard, I am particularly grateful to Jan Barnsely, Betty Baxter, Kathleen Costello, Mary Eberts, Trish Hennessey, Vicki Jensen, Marilyn Linton, Marg Miekle, Helen Porter, Pat Thom, Saeko Usukawa and Frances Wright, among others.

Once again, my thanks to Barbara Sale Schon for the index, and to Madeline Koch, Anne Marie Prychoda and Lori Bartholomew for their help with transcribing and word processing. The staff at Doubleday Canada also deserves a special mention. The President, John Neale, Editor-in-Chief John Pearce, Managing Editor Christine Innes, and Lesley Grant, who stickhandled the book through the editorial and production process, were exemplary in their various roles. All were a pleasure to work with. I'd also like to thank Don Sedgwick who was involved in the early stages of the manuscript and who provided valuable advice that helped me get the emerging behemoth under control. My editor, Beverly Sotolov, deserves particular mention. Her light but extremely deft touch exemplifies the maxim "she edits best who edits least" and a better book is the result of her efforts.

My family is an important and enriching part of my life. My mother lives on in my memory and over the years, my mother-in-law Catherine Dees has made an inestimable contribution to our lives. I am particularly indebted to my husband, Bob, who has always been a strong support and my beautiful daughter, Meredith, who keep me focused on the essentials.

"Those who are bold enough to advance before the age they live in, and to throw off, by the forces of their own minds, the prejudices which the maturing reason of the world will in time disavow, must learn to brave censure. We ought not to be too anxious respecting the opinion of others."

MARY WOLLSTONECRAFT
A Vindication of the Rights of Woman, 1792

INTRODUCTION

In 1965, sociologist John Porter published *The Vertical Mosaic,* his monumental analysis of Canada's social structure. A groundbreaking work, Porter's book debunked the myth of Canada as a classless society and identified the principal ranking systems, carefully controlled by tightly knit élites, that define the social status of our citizens. Although Porter explored the position of groups such as Jews, francophones, native people, and various ethnic groups, not once did he mention the position of women in this hierarchy of influence and power, an oversight which, to be fair, simply reflected the temper of the times. When his book was published, for instance, just two women had ascended to the rank of cabinet minister in the federal government, Ellen Fairclough in 1957 and Judy LaMarsh in 1963.

Although only a paucity of women had manoeuvred their way through the gatekeepers Porter so carefully chronicled, by the time his book appeared, many more with aspirations were waiting in the wings and poised for action. The seminal Royal Commission on the Status of Women was established in 1967 after activist Laura Sabia, then president of the Canadian Federation of University Women and a key figure in the burgeoning movement for female equality, intimidated Prime Minister Lester Pearson. The government took her threat seriously and were worried that two million women really would march on Ottawa if the government didn't examine women's participation — or lack thereof — in Canadian society. The climate that spawned the commission was a sign of things to come.

About the time that Porter was finalizing his manuscript, Anne Underhill was growing tired after twelve years of battle with the gatekeepers in her chosen field. An astronomer at the Dominion Astrophysical Observatory in Victoria, she accepted a position abroad when she recognized that as a woman she would never be acknowledged as one of Canada's best astronomers. The so-called second wave of feminism began in the 1960s and until its effects were felt, opportunities for women advanced at a snail's pace. As a result, even highly skilled scientists such as Underhill were likely to be excluded from their professional élites simply because of their sex. Despite her credentials, Dr. Underhill recalled that "for the longest time" her main responsibility was to ensure that the observatory had enough photographic plates.

Although pockets of feminist activity have existed throughout the centuries, the greatest progress for women as a group resulted from two relatively recent mass movements. In the mid- to late nineteenth century, women organized around the issue of suffrage and won the vote. In the 1960s, women came together again. At that point, various social forces, such as the availability of contraception, dissatisfaction with traditional domestic roles — on the part of men as well as women — and the growing number of women who entered the paid labour force to fuel the needs of a booming economy, converged to propel a second mass movement towards equality. Inspired by, among other things, best-selling books such as Simone de Beauvoir's *The Second Sex* and Betty Friedan's *The Feminine Mystique*, the birth of broadly based feminist organizations such as the Fédération des femmes du Québec and the Committee on Equality for Women, as well as cutting-edge content in *Chatelaine*, then the country's leading women's magazine under the editorship of Doris Anderson, Canadian women united to overcome discrimination and became, once again, a driving force for social change.

During that heady time, women worked on identifying the social determinants of their secondary status and defining their needs as a group. They also pressured policymakers to institute change on a variety of fronts. But the emergence of a dynamic women's movement did more than propel political reform. It also created opportunities for individual women. Today, Bruna Giacomazzi is one of the highest ranking women in Canadian banking. She readily admits that if it hadn't been for the huge settlement won by her American counterparts, in a 1971 class action suit for gender equality, she wouldn't have nudged her toe in the door of management at Household Finance.

Late in 1970, the Privy Council Office asked Freda Paltiel, then a senior research officer at the Department of Health and Welfare, for her opinion on the recently completed Report of the Royal Commission on the Status of Women. Surprisingly, the government felt that events might have overtaken the commissioners' findings since both legislation liberalizing contraception and the *Divorce Act* had recently been passed. As a wife, mother, and social scientist, Ms. Paltiel didn't share their opinion on the vigour of women's latest gains. "I could see that the report was far ahead of the consciousness of the public and the media at the time and that its recommendations would transform society," she recalled.

The report contained many examples of how women were discriminated against in Canadian society, but that was then. As for now, female opportunity is assumed to be a given and past injustices, if acknowledged at all, are likely swept under the carpet, the dusty remnants of a bygone age. Strangely, that recognition is what motivated me to write this book. In 1995, my book *Against the Current*, which documented the fifty-year migration of women into the paid workforce, was published. An oral history, the book captured the experiences of a wide range of women, and the message that emerged from the interviews was, as I wrote then, "one of quiet determination and perseverance, rather than militancy." Inevitably, though, the inequities surfaced: having to leave jobs they loved because they married; being fired for becoming pregnant; training men who were promoted into management, while they remained in clerical jobs; being paid less than a man for doing the same job; and so on; and so on.

After reading *Against the Current*, a number of young women told me they had "no idea" that women as a group had been discriminated against. Although some had a vague notion that in the past certain restrictions had limited female opportunities, they were ignorant of the forces and events that impelled the movement towards gender equality. Most didn't know that the opportunities *they* take for granted came about mainly because many individual women pushed the envelope, often at great cost to themselves. To a considerable extent, the women profiled in this book and thousands like them were the force behind change that created Canadian society as we know it today.

In recent years, historians such as Gerda Lerner have studied the invisibility of women's heritage and how the generation-to-generation transmission of knowledge does not take place for women, as it does for men, whose experiences are the subject of history. Relegated to the footnotes of the historical record and, therefore, lacking a sense of the continuum of female achievement, women as a group are heard only as a series of isolated voices. As a result, each generation believes in its own uniqueness, unaware that throughout the ages many women have questioned male authority — for instance, the twelfth-century nun Hildergard of Bingen, the first woman to challenge the patriarchal version of creation, and the fifteenth-century French writer Christine de Pizan, the first woman to make her living from her pen. Lacking historical continuity, women are vulnerable to being dismissed as aberrant if critical of the status quo. Without this historical narrative, later generations of women waste time, energy, and resources reinventing ideas that their predecessors have already defined.

Given that those who do not understand history are doomed to repeat it, I decided to document the stories of some contemporary women who blazed the trails, making possible the opportunities younger women now accept as their due. Although women have been trailblazing for centuries on a wide variety of fronts, it's easy to forget that in historical terms, many restrictions limiting women's autonomy were lifted quite recently. Consider, for instance, that in 1966, Dr. Marion Powell broke the law by dispensing birth control, or that the issue of violence against women didn't emerge as a social concern until the mid-1970s. When Judy Erola, then Minister Responsible for the Status of Women, raised the issue of domestic violence in the House of Commons in the early 1980s, some male MPs actually laughed in response.

Change was as slow for women in public life and the workplace as it was in the realm of social issues. Quebec didn't elect a female MP until 1972, when Monique Bégin became the first to achieve that distinction. That year, Sylvia Ostry also became the first deputy minister in the federal civil service. With the exception of the war years, the Steel Company of Canada didn't hire women to work in blue collar jobs until 1980, when Debbie Field became one of the first group to invade that territory.

Social change is incremental, a series of small steps in many different areas that cumulatively and over time transform the way we see the world. If we no longer automatically assume that victims of domestic abuse are the creators of their own misfortune and now take for granted that a woman can effectively sit in the CEO's chair, it is due to the efforts of the women represented in this book — and many others, who for practical reasons have not been included. Each in her own way helped to create the climate of perceived equality women now take for granted by challenging the status quo and chipping away at the stereotypes governing attitudes towards women. Change agents in fact, if not in spirit, they often served as lightning rods for opposition to female equality and many had to draw on courage and initiative they didn't know they had. As a group, they created movement on a myriad of fronts. Many paved the way by being the "first" woman to achieve a particular position; some contributed by advancing the law, others by raising our consciousness about the realities of women's experience. They are trailblazers across the spectrum of society, from public life and the professions to religion, community service, education, and health, to the trades and technology, to the arts and the media.

The women included here are a diverse group from a variety of social, economic, racial, and ethnic backgrounds. Their only commonality is, perhaps, determination. Basically, these are women who refused to take no for an answer. Some were conscious that the burden of being a trailblazer included pressure to perform and were painfully aware that if they fell short, their failure would have a negative impact on the women who followed; for instance Monique Bégin, as one of only five women MPs, recalled, "We always had to be excellent in the name of all women and could never afford an ordinary performance."

Not surprisingly, early life experiences played a predominant role in their character formation. The strong support of at least one parent often endowed trailblazers with the self-esteem and confidence necessary to challenge conventional assumptions about women. Sometimes it was a mother who sent a strong message — or perhaps even a covert one, as revealed in the story of artist Helen Lucas — that she wanted her daughter's life to be better than hers. Equally often it was a father for whom the daughter assumed the role of substitute son. Debunking the Freudian myth that women with a strong motivation to succeed are those who have failed "as women," a significant number of these trailblazers cite the support of husbands and families as integral to their achievements.

Often, their motivation for challenging the status quo was close to the surface. For businesswomen Barbara Rae and Maureen Kempston Darkes it was the image of a single mother struggling to raise a family on women's wages. Geologist Alice Payne was inspired by the image of her father, undoubtedly one of the most colourful and interesting people she knew. Justine Blainey was impelled to take on the gatekeepers of male sport when she recognized that success in hockey was a way of gaining her father's attention.

Loneliness, isolation, sometimes even stigmatization, characterize the experience of trailblazing. Some women — Monique Bégin, Freda Paltiel, Debbie Field, to name three — recognized that their comfort level with being an outsider played a role in their ability to succeed. Denial is a survival skill that some acquired over the years. As pioneering journalist Shirley Sharzer described it, she became "deaf, dumb and blind" to the realities of the workplace by, for instance, failing to get the vulgar jokes exchanged in the newsroom. Reflecting on her career as an MP, former cabinet minister Iona Campagnolo remembered setting out on the campaign "oblivious to the 'Chauvinist Pig' tie my manager proudly wore." Apprenticing carpenter Marcia Braundy had what she described as a "bizarre" reaction to being sexually harassed. "Basically, I tried to pretend it wasn't happening," she recalled.

The "impostor syndrome" — feeling like a pretender in a highly valued role — which psychologists say may afflict successful females, occasionally raised its head. "Deep down I don't think I'm the red hot radical that people portray me to be. I always have that dreaded feeling that somebody will discover I'm a fraud," commented birth control pioneer Marion Powell. But equally common were women with an unshakeable belief in their own abilities — for instance, Jean

Sutherland Boggs, who recalled, "I never gave much thought to being the only woman in the world to head a national gallery. I just assumed I was the best person for the job."

As with any book of this nature, many readers will feel that different women ought to have been chosen. However, it was impossible to include all the women who qualify as trailblazers. That said, my criteria were carefully thought out and I considered a variety of factors in my final selections. Some obvious possibilities, such as Kim Campbell, Canada's first female prime minister; Ellen Fairclough, the first woman to hold a cabinet position in the federal government; Rosemary Brown, the first Black MLA; Senator Sharon Carstairs, the first woman to head an official opposition party; or Roberta Bondar, Canada's first female astronaut, were excluded because they had written their autobiographies within a fairly recent time frame. In these instances and in some situations where potential subjects have received a great deal of media coverage — author Margaret Atwood and journalist June Callwood immediately come to mind — I did not feel that I could add anything significant to the public record.

A number of potential subjects were ruled out because I had interviewed them for *Against the Current* as part of the broad swath of women who worked for pay during a crucial period of social change: journalist Doris Anderson, labour organizer Madeline Parent, Judge Nancy Morrison, lawyer Mary Eberts, and artist Mary Pratt, to name just a few. In some cases, ill health and even death precluded interviews. Florence Bird, the first woman to chair a royal commission in Canada was too ill to see me when I called. The following year she passed away. I was in Montreal preparing to meet with native activist Mary Two Axe Early when she was rushed to hospital and subsequently died. The indomitable Laura Sabia also passed away before I could interview her, and two of the women included in the book, Dr. Marion Powell and Kathleen Shannon, didn't live to see it published.

My objective was to capture the experiences of a wide range of women, thereby highlighting the sweep of social change. As a result, some of my subjects are not well known, nor have they achieved "success" according to our traditional definition of the word. While some may not fit the conventional image of a trailblazer, by bringing various issues to the forefront of public consciousness they have advanced our understanding of what it means to be a woman or have helped to smash gender stereotypes. From the vantage point of creating long-term change for women, involvement as a foot soldier in social movements is as significant as a starring role in public events.

Setting out to document this aspect of Canada's forgotten history I chose, once again, to tell the story in the words of the women themselves. I've long believed that oral history is particularly valid for women because our experiences are so rarely documented. As a journalist, I'm conscious that much of what I do — the questions I ask, the information I deem valuable — has been filtered, like all critical standards, through the prism of male values. Consequently, I tried to minimize my role as an interviewer as much as possible, allowing my subjects to capture the truth of their experience as they saw it, and focused my attention on editing their thoughts and feelings into a coherent whole.

Oral history is very much a collaborative effort and I feel very privileged that these women allowed me to recount their experiences. Their courage in living lives that followed no pattern is exemplary and an inspiration to all women in search of their own destiny.

PART 1

PUBLIC LIFE

"I don't remember making choices deliberately in opposition to the imposed environment. I just remember feeling like an outsider and wanting to do things in my own way."

MONIQUE BÉGIN

On October 30, 1972, Monique Bégin became the first woman to be elected as a Member of Parliament from Quebec. In the years that followed she played key roles in the Trudeau government, most notably as Minister of National Health and Welfare. She is currently Dean of Health Sciences at the University of Ottawa.

E arly in 1967, in response to pressure from women across the country, the Royal Commission on the Status of Women was being formed. The commission's mandate was to examine and report on the status of women in Canada, and to recommend steps that could be taken to ensure equal opportunities for women in all areas of Canadian society. Marc Lalonde, then an aide to Prime Minister Lester Pearson, asked if I would serve as a commissioner. I didn't know what a commissioner was, so I asked him who actually ran the commission's work on a full-time basis and he said, "The executive-secretary." "Then that's the job I want," I said. Months later, I received a call and was interviewed by Florence Bird, the commission chair, and two commissioners, along with sixty-seven other candidates. I got the job.

In April 1967, I left Montreal for Ottawa. The following year we travelled across Canada hearing submissions from women. It was very exciting. As a Quebec woman barely out of my twenties, it was extraordinary to discover the country through women and to realize we were all living the same thing. Although I remember the excitement most of all, the exhilarating sense of solidarity was offset by the terrible situations often reported to us.

It seems incredible today, but in those days the status of women didn't include major issues. Violence against women, for example, was not discussed — not just by the commissioners, but by anybody. I recall a few women, in particular native women in the West, speaking of the violence done to them, but it wasn't seen as a collective women's issue. Violence remained in the personal sphere and was thought to concern individuals. Even those of us on the commission were very much prisoners of how the status of women was officially defined by society.

Although I don't recall talking about it or reading about it, I had a sense that new ways of thinking about women were developing. Of course, the radical feminist movement was bubbling up on campuses across the country, but we didn't know enough about it to define it or to contact the young women involved. The movement was threatening and underground. We were definitely "liberal" feminists, believers in incremental social change.

I think I'd always been a feminist — long before I had any idea what that was. Even as a child I resented the way women were treated, starting with my mother, a very quiet person who, I think, perceived early on that she and my father were totally mismatched but had neither the economic power nor the religious sanction to leave the marriage. I was born in Rome, Italy, in 1936. My family was quite well-to-do, but we lost everything in the war. We were the first immigrants to reside in Notre Dame de Grâce, a much wealthier neighbourhood of Montreal than it is now. Our small flat was located on a modest stretch of street in an island of very well-off people. My father, who had been a sound engineer in the European film industry, changed dramatically after the war, from a *bon vivant* who enjoyed life and easily spent money to someone who was most interested in pursuing a spiritual quest.

Although we never discussed things like money or social class at home — the cultural and the spiritual lives were all that mattered to my father — once I started school I understood that we were different. I knew I was a rebel because I argued with the nuns and was told I was impertinent. I was an avid reader and remember reading *The Iliad* and *The Odyssey* in grade two or three. The teacher told me that reading such books was wrong. She reflected the repressive attitudes in Quebec where books were still censored by the Catholic Church. I read everything I could find — biographies of women aviators and Catherine the Great, as well as the lives of female saints — so I had a sense that women could do great things. But even this little pastime told me I was different from other girls.

I engaged in my first deliberate act of defiance when I was nineteen or twenty. I received a marriage proposal from a young engineer, a French Canadian of Belgian origin, which I refused. I understood that it was a good proposal — whatever "a good proposal" means — but I decided it didn't correspond to anything I had in mind for myself. I had no desire to marry as an end in itself, something my schoolmates had started to do, and this period of my life was particularly painful. I couldn't find my place and felt I didn't belong. Then, on my twenty-first birthday, my father, acting very much like a patriarch, threw me out of the house because I was "questioning his authority."

I wanted to study, but I knew I had to earn money. I perceived that girls could be secretaries, sales-ladies, nurses, or teachers, and since I wanted to study, teaching seemed the better career choice. I loved teaching, but I hated the job. My classes had fifty students and the environment under Duplessis was still rigidly puritanical and clerical. During this period of my life I became very cynical and angry about the Catholic Church as an institution. I couldn't stand its hypocrisy and abuse of power.

I left teaching, got a job as a secretary at the University of Montreal, and started going to school at night. After completing my BA in August 1958, I enrolled in the master's program in sociology as a regular student. It was a dream come true. I saw sociology as liberating, a route into a world where things could be questioned from new perspectives. Ironically, until my final year, the chair of the sociology department was always a priest appointed directly by the archbishop to make sure that the discipline's relativism would not destroy our faith.

There was only one other woman in a class of nine. Among other things, I would organize weekly informal seminars to discuss contro-versial authors. The first book I suggested was Simone de Beauvoir's *The Second Sex*, which had just become available in Quebec — it had been banned by the Catholic Church for ten years after its publication in France. Reading Simone de Beauvoir in those repressive times was a revelation. Her idea that being a woman was something you learned — you weren't born knowing it — was a genuine breakthrough.

I finished my MA, won a small scholarship, and moved to Paris to study for my doctorate at the Sorbonne. After two years, I ran out of money and returned to Montreal, where I started doing various consulting jobs. The Quiet Revolution was in its early stages and the old religious Quebec was rapidly being transformed into a modern lay state. Professional gurus — psychiatrists, sociologists, and so on — were replacing priests, and TV was expanding rapidly. Having a sociologist on panels was the new thing and I appeared on a few TV shows.

Women had won the right to vote in Quebec on April 25, 1940, which meant that 1965 marked the twenty-fifth anniversary. Thérèse Casgrain, who had been instrumental in that struggle, single-handedly decided to celebrate the event. As a young sociologist people had seen on TV once or twice, I was asked to be on the organizing committee. Pushed by Thérèse Casgrain, the committee arranged a celebration at the old Mount Royal Hotel on Peel Street. After the celebration, one of the attendees spontaneously moved that a federation should be created to consolidate all women's groups in Quebec with the ultimate goal of changing Quebec society.

Those were very exciting times. We were like conspirators, meeting at Thérèse Casgrain's home every week or so. In November 1966, we officially founded the Fédération des femmes du Québec, and at our founding convention I was elected first vice-president. We had a lot of work to do. The *Napoleonic Code* was a horror story for women — it was more than being barred from jobs. An entire range of attitudes and practices, including the educational system and family law, limited women's full participation in Quebec society and needed to be changed. Soon we were contacted by women's groups from English Canada who were trying, under the leadership of Laura Sabia, then president of the Canadian Federation of University Women, to obtain a royal commission to examine the status of women. Initially, we were opposed to a royal commission because we didn't think we had time to wait for its report, but eventually we decided to join forces.

Being part of the royal commission was a remarkable experience that I still cherish. When our work was finished in the fall of 1970, I accepted a job as the assistant director in the research branch of the new Canadian Radio-television Commission (CRTC). Those were the great years of the CRTC — the Canadian ownership and Canadian content policies were being developed, and I worked with some remarkable people. Even so, I wasn't happy because I couldn't understand what was expected of me. I think I was supposed to help the research branch fit into the bureaucracy, which bored me to death. At the time I didn't realize I couldn't stand bureaucracies and that I had learned through the royal commission and other research projects about ways to bypass them.

In the spring of 1971, while I was at the CRTC, I received another call from Marc Lalonde, who was still working in the Prime Minister's Office, but now for Pierre Trudeau. I barely knew Lalonde, but his wife had been a colleague in the Fédération. One of our strategies had been to identify men in positions of responsibility whom we thought might be "converted" to feminism. Marc Lalonde was one of them, and that connection paid off for women.

He phoned to say there would be a by-election somewhere in Montreal and the Liberal party wanted me to run. Not only had I never considered politics, I was scared of it. It seemed terribly mysterious and tainted with a bad reputation. However, I found politics fascinating as a subject. I knew our chapter on women in politics in the royal commission report was the weakest. Although we recognized that we needed more women in politics, we couldn't figure out how to analyze their exclusion and correct the situation. In an effort to gain insights into how the political system actually worked, we had talked with women who were actively involved — Flora MacDonald, who was then working for the Conservative party in Ottawa, and Pauline Jewett, who had been elected to Parliament in 1963. But we still didn't get it. Now I can see that we lacked a conceptual framework, an analysis — we applied random concepts like discrimination and lack of affirmative action without seeing how everything fit together. Anyway, even though I had no interest in being a politician myself, I kept pushing other women into politics because I knew that is where the power to change things is located. I suppose part of my reluctance was self-protection. I recognized that I was extremely sensitive, which I perceived as a great vulnerability for anyone interested in public life. So when Marc Lalonde called, I laughingly replied, "Thank you. That's not for me." I should mention that at that point no women MPs had ever been elected from Quebec, although that would never have stopped me.

But Lalonde persisted. In April 1972, he phoned again, saying only that he wanted to see me in the Prime Minister's Office. Since I thought he wanted to discuss implementing the royal commission report, I walked up Parliament Hill with my copy under my arm. I arrived in a room full of senior ministers and their aides. I was asked if I'd run, and instead of laughing, I said I'd take five days to think it over. During that time I realized I wanted to be where the action was so I could speed up the process of change for women. For years I believed that to be my only motivation, but I now know that I also had a more personal, selfish reason. Whenever I get bored, which I never admit to myself, I need a new challenge. That was where I was at with the CRTC; I needed to move into a new arena.

I agreed to run for office on three conditions. I didn't fully understand their significance, but I knew they were critical. First, the riding had to be a safe one. I wasn't sure what a safe riding was, but Flora MacDonald had repeatedly told the royal commission that political parties never put women in safe ridings. Second, I was against tokenism, so I demanded that a minimum of three women from Quebec run. Then, I asked for money because I didn't have much in the way of financial resources and I didn't have business connections.

I was elected an hour before Jeanne Sauvé and Albanie Morin, the other two female candidates from Quebec, and on October 30, 1972, became the first woman MP from the province. I was thirty-six years old, and as one of five women in the House of Commons felt that I was entering foreign territory. Grace MacInnis, who until the election had served as the lone woman MP, was joined by Flora MacDonald and the three Quebec Liberals. Eighteen months later, after my second election in 1974, we were a grand total of nine.

With so few of us, the pressures were great. We always had to be excellent in the name of all women and could never afford just an ordinary performance. Also, male colleagues saw us as women first, rather than as individuals. They would often pay me what they thought was a compliment — "My wife likes you very much." Although I resisted the idea that we were tokens — one sociological theory has it that tokens exist when a group constitutes fifteen percent or less of the dominant group — we certainly qualified. The House of Commons was a boys' club, and with so few of us it was impossible to create a female power base. But we did come close on a couple of occasions when the two or three women in Cabinet put down our collective foot on issues such as rape, prostitution, sexual harassment, or the loss of status for native women.

Being Monique Bégin, MP, was a process of discovery that was quite exhilarating, enhanced by the fact that the 1972 election produced a minority government that lasted a record eighteen months. There were great characters in the House such as David Lewis, Tommy Douglas, John Diefenbaker, Robert Stanfield, and Réal Caouette — which meant the place was very exciting. But it didn't take me long to notice the other side of the coin — the extreme egotism of men and the silly ego games they play. I do not enjoy — and I think many women are like me — men's games, which are basically games of power for the sake of power. I detest competition unless it is for defending ideas or values.

For my first three years in the House, I was a backbencher. It wasn't much of a role for someone who had done bigger things and I found it quite frustrating. In practical terms, we didn't have the means to do the job — no riding offices or secretaries. We even paid the long-distance charges between Ottawa and our ridings ourselves. I thought this was terrible, immediately created a little team in the caucus to work on the issues, and won a support infrastructure for all MPs of the House. I was appointed parliamentary secretary to Allan J. MacEachen, Secretary of State for External Affairs, in 1975. I became Minister of National Revenue in 1976 and Minister of National Health and Welfare in 1977, where I remained until I left politics in 1984.

When I succeeded Marc Lalonde as Minister of Health and Welfare, one journalist wrote that he was "strong" but I was "aggressive." That bothered me for a long time, particularly since Marc Lalonde was no lamb. But the remark was symptomatic of more negative attitudes towards women that often surfaced. I was scandalized and very discouraged by some of the things I heard my fellow MPs say. For instance, soon after I became Minister of Health and Welfare, I had to defend the child tax credit I was creating and was shocked by some of the statements — that women would abuse it and not spend it on children or that native women would use the money to rent planes and fly to North Dakota to drink. The status of women wasn't being attacked — it was women in general who were despised, which I found particularly difficult to accept because this attacks you in your essence. Being a woman is the problem — you're second class.

After spending four years teaching women's studies, I see that this problem is systemic. But while I was in politics I kept concluding I was inadequate. I didn't like women who studied situations for five seconds and then decided something happened because they were female, but I think I went overboard in the opposite direction, questioning and accusing myself. This is very dangerous, but it's something that systems make you do.

I didn't generate any hostility towards myself so long as I remained a backbencher, but once I became a competitor in the eyes of the men, things changed. That was when the slanderous remarks started. Sometimes they came from colleagues with considerable status and prestige. I overheard more than once that I was sleeping with this one or that one to get ahead — which certainly wasn't true — or that I was appointed because I was a woman and the government needed a token. I was also accused of being a publicity hound.

As well, I heard MPs on both sides of the House ridicule women for all sorts of reasons related to appearance. Their comments could be pornographic or just plain mocking. The media was particularly nasty. I gained sixty pounds in six months after being appointed Minister of Health and Welfare and the media started to speculate that I was pregnant. They wanted to know who the father was. When I left politics, the *Globe and Mail* referred to me as "a tubby lady in need of a couturier she didn't have."

Although these concerns might seem petty, they were very hurtful and have a serious undertone. The media play a major role in how women occupying non-traditional roles are perceived. Since girls grow up learning that their appearance is crucial, an unflattering image of a powerful woman can be very damaging because it works to limit their aspirations.

In September 1984, when I was at the peak of my career, I left politics. Despite the problems, I loved my twelve years in office and I lived them to the fullest with great satisfaction. I'm not a fool — I fully understand the temptation of power. Being at the heart of a world attained by few men and even fewer women was a marvellous experience. I toyed very seriously with the idea of running for the leadership of the Liberal party, which some people were pushing me to do. However, I decided against it because I recognized a few basic things about myself. Fundamentally, I knew I did not love power enough to become leader and prime minister. To obtain and keep power for its own sake is a full-time job, and that was not something I wanted to do. How much of that was Monique Bégin the woman and Monique Bégin the human being I don't know, but it was surely both.

It was also clear to me that the Liberal party would be in opposition, and I didn't want to serve as a backbencher again. I'm a builder, not a game player. And I needed a sabbatical to refuel intellectually before setting out on a new adventure. So I called it quits, which I've never regretted, although it wasn't easy to recycle myself as a university professor, nor was it easy to go to the United States.

I left my ministerial office just after the September 4, 1984 election. The following day, I arrived in South Bend, Indiana, to assume my duties as a professor of social policy in the Department of Economics at Notre Dame University. I stayed in Indiana for a year, spent the next year at McGill, and then for four years held the first joint chair in women's studies at Ottawa and Carleton universities. I wish I had done women's studies before I went into politics because some of its intellectual scholarship is wonderful and such analysis would have been very helpful in dealing with that bastion of male power.

Now I'm back in health as dean of health sciences at the University of Ottawa. Here, too, I felt the outsider for some years because I did not complete my doctorate. I have about ten honorary doctorates, but they don't count in the eyes of colleagues. I have the legal authority to be called "Dr.," but I don't use the title because my doctorate wasn't earned. But I did earn the title of Honourable, which I still carry as a former cabinet minister. I use that, not so much for the prestige but to remind women that we can accomplish important things.

People still make comments in an effort to make me feel different. My first impulse is discomfort, but then I realize that unpleasant, uncomfortable feeling is also my strength because it has enabled me to do new things. I've always been different and it's what I know best.

"Today when I teach students I say, 'Sexism is the belief that women need less, deserve less, and are worth less than men.' The Royal Commission on the Status of Women opened our eyes to the extent of that belief and the discrimination that it spawned."

FREDA PALTIEL

In 1971 Freda Paltiel made history when she was appointed Canada's first Coordinator, Status of Women. Educated as a social worker and public health professional, she spent much of her working life, both paid and unpaid, in the voluntary sector prior to beginning her career as a public servant.

In December 1970, I was working as a senior research officer at the Department of Health and Welfare, studying voluntary health organizations in Canada. I had recently completed a study on employed European women with families, and I suppose it was due to that experience that I received a call from the Privy Council Office (PCO) asking me to give an opinion on the newly tabled report of the Royal Commission on the Status of Women. Strange as it may seem, in view of the years it has taken to implement the report's 167 recommendations, one of the concerns was that events might have overtaken the report, as legislation liberalizing contraception and the *Divorce Act* had been passed since the commission had undertaken its work! I took the document home, read it carefully, and was profoundly affected by its revelations.

I could see that the report was far ahead of the consciousness of the public and the media at the time and that implementing its recommendations would transform Canadian society. The document contained many examples of how women were discriminated against. For instance, some women who worked in the civil service had been fired as recently as 1967 because they were married. Only two women, Ellen Fairclough, who was appointed in 1957, and Judy LaMarsh, who was appointed in 1963, had ever served as cabinet ministers at the federal level. In January 1970, there were only four women senators out of a total of 102. I knew there was a job to be done. The question was, how to do it? The traditional bureaucratic process was hardly appropriate to bringing about the necessary institutional change.

When I wrote my report on European women, I studied the Nordic societies and was struck by the fact that a great deal of intellectual debate about sex roles hadn't produced a lot of substantive change. That knowledge made me realize that changing the legislation dealing with actual discrimination would have a much more significant effect than tackling prejudice through prolonged social debate, particularly since Canadians are such law-abiding people. But to achieve that result, this huge report needed to be taken apart and divided into policy clusters, and the process for guiding implementation would have to be opened up and made more participatory.

One of my conditions for agreeing to undertake the role of Canada's first Coordinator, Status of Women, was that in addition to the conventional interdepartmental committee of senior public servants, we establish a working group for each policy cluster, resourced with citizens as well as public servants. Moreover, the members of the public would be paid for their efforts — a radical notion for the time. I also requested an interdepartmental committee constituted mainly of women. That was a little difficult to achieve. When I started, only one or two women had reached the assistant deputy minister level — none was yet a deputy. I compiled a "crib sheet" of all the overqualified women who were training their bosses at the time and asked their surprised deputies if these women could represent their departments. Fortunately, I was able to achieve my objective.

We had a certain amount of clout, because in those days the Privy Council was tiny. Deputy ministers always returned calls to the PCO and I intended to use every bit of this influence to ensure that our issues were at the top of the federal agenda. We worked our heads off. I remember sitting in my office one Christmas, dissolved in tears. They weren't tears of helplessness but tears of absolute fatigue. There weren't enough hours in the day. Most of my colleagues didn't have husbands and children and they couldn't understand why I needed to go home to my family. I took heavy briefcases full of work home every night. Fortunately, my husband was very supportive.

Today, it's hard to believe how thoroughly sexism permeated the social fabric and how much needed to be done to move Canada towards being a more equitable society. For instance, the national housing regulations had to be changed because a married woman's income didn't count when couples applied for a mortgage. When we approached a vice-president of Canada Mortgage and Housing Corporation (CMHC) he told us that since he had daughters, he didn't have any objections, but that making these changes could be complicated. Since our lawyer, Shirley Parks, who worked for CMHC and was also on our interdepartmental committee, had already looked at the matter, we were able to respond quickly and get the regulations changed in 1971.

The extent of legal discrimination was astounding, given the prevailing view that *de jure* discrimination had been eliminated in most democracies and that we were merely dealing with *de facto* discrimination. The *Criminal Code*, which was laced with expressions like "women of previously chaste character," was a nightmare. One of our first tasks was to go through it in its entirety to ensure that these blatantly sexist provisions were deleted. Women couldn't even serve on juries! The idea that a husband and wife were so intertwined that they functioned as a single person was deeply embedded in the common law. That had serious consequences — for instance, a woman couldn't testify against her husband, which goes a long way towards explaining why domestic violence was a non-issue. In those days, the late Muriel Ferguson was in the Senate and she was a great ally. When we couldn't negotiate a timetable to introduce legislation on jury duty, she agreed to introduce the bill in the Senate.

As a civil servant trying to implement such dramatic social change, I had some pretty lively debates at the office. Although they were exciting and creative, they were often quite painful. I remember one colleague asking why I thought I was entitled to both a husband and a job. But the opposition was never enough to discourage me, and although some people tried to undermine me when I determinedly tackled the discriminatory social security system, I didn't let it get me down. All of us have times when we are not fully supported in our work life, but good things were always happening, too.

In 1971, a group of women wanted to have a founding meeting for what became the National Action Committee on the Status of Women (NAC). I felt it was important for the government to hear what women were saying, and since they had no money I contacted the parliamentary assistants of three ministers and asked each ministry to put up $5000. My one condition was that the group invite Florence Bird, who had chaired the Royal Commission on the Status of Women, to be the keynote speaker. That created some problems because women were divided about whether to involve "government people," but Laura Sabia persuaded the group to go ahead on those terms.

In my professional roles, I always tried to be disciplined and caring like my mother, who was a remarkable woman. I think I was a nurturing manager. I never had career ambitions *per se* — for instance, I never wanted to be a deputy minister. I always chose titles that gave me strategic marginality, where I never had power over people but I had the possibility of empowering them, and the mandate to influence major policy decisions.

After I left the Privy Council in 1973, I moved back to Health and Welfare. In 1974 I represented Canada at the World Population Conference in Bucharest. When I arrived I was told that Betty Friedan and a group of women were in town for the NGO forum and they intended to denounce the conference. I recognized that the official document prepared by the U.N. was not gender sensitive, so I jumped in a cab, dashed to the other end of the city, and found Betty Friedan. "You don't know me and I don't know you," I said, "but we both want the same thing — a good plan of action that will work for gender equality. If you have a march, your statement will go out with the fishbones in tomorrow's garbage. But if you'll draft what you want, I'll persuade the official delegates to build it in."

That night Margaret Mead was in front of me in the cafeteria. I don't know how close her vision was to that of Betty Friedan, but I told her what was happening and that it would be wonderful if she could meet with Betty's group because her wisdom was valuable. I also told Helvi Sippila, U.N. Under-Secretary General in charge of the conference, what was happening. The next day, as I walked into the committee meeting, she handed me a piece of paper with a revised text. Luckily I did not read it until after I had made my presentation, as we had succeeded in drafting a much more gender-sensitive version.

In 1979, while at Health and Welfare, I helped to develop the first plan of action to address family violence/wife abuse, an area not covered in the royal commission report. It's hard to believe, but in those days the helping professions were taught that spousal abuse arose from sado-masochistic relationships. The message was that abused women really wanted to be beaten. I could see that the grass roots women's groups were viewing social workers as the problem, not the solution, and I told the Canadian Association of Social Workers (CASW) that this had to be addressed. When CASW established a task force on what they euphemistically called "interspousal violence," they asked me to head it. I did that for two years and during that time was able to do a great deal of work on violence against women. We produced research papers that contradicted the prevailing wisdom that women were willing victims and I travelled across the country bringing grass roots women's groups together with professionals to help them see that violence against women was a form of potentially lethal control over women, not love gotten out of hand, as it was generally perceived. Much of what we planted is only coming to fruition now.

Although I'm a mainstream person who has always believed that change must come from within institutions, I've also worked closely with alternative people, since I wanted to change the mainstream. Because of my background, I've always had some comfort level with being an outsider, and I believe that helped me to see things strategically. I grew up in a Catholic working-class neighbourhood in Montreal and was always the only Jew in my class. My mother was the dominant force in my life. From morning to night she worked with my dad as the inside person in their scrap metal business. I was born a year after my mother came to Canada from Russia, and I was a very wanted child. My two brothers were much older. My mother really believed in me and that gave me the confidence to imagine I could influence events.

If my parents had not been so kind and my mother hadn't believed in me so much, I never would have gone to Queen's University, which I loved. All my mother's friends told her she would lose me because I'd reject my roots. She must have felt she was taking a terrible risk, but she supported my departure because she so much wanted my life to reflect what Canada could offer — the immigrant's dream.

I didn't get scholarships. In fact, I have a vivid memory of my father writing a cheque for my tuition and residence fees. Although there were adequate funds in the account, the manager stopped the cheque when it reached his bank because he was so incensed at a girl going away to university. I was called into the bursar's office at Queen's and it was terribly embarrassing. But Queen's, being the gentle and cordial place it is, immediately offered me a job in the library, cataloguing the Canadiana collection, to help pay for my expenses.

I went to university because I wanted to become educated. I had no conscious career goals and never thought about success. I wanted to contribute, to make a difference. I studied political science and philosophy, which in those days was actually psychology, and later was persuaded to enrol in the McGill School of Social Work. I worked as a social worker at the Children's Memorial Hospital in Montreal practically until the day my son, the first of four children, was born. Then I worked at home for ten years, during which time we moved from Montreal to Winnipeg to Windsor and I was Mrs. Volunteer.

Since four children are very time consuming, those were extremely busy years. But they were also extremely rich ones. I was blessed with a very happy marriage. My husband, who was a political scientist, was an erudite person, with a great passion for justice as well as the finer things in life. At seven o'clock every evening, I'd get out of my pedal pushers and put on a dress. My husband often brought people home for dinner so I could have intelligent conversations with adults in the evenings. Having a companionate spouse meant that I wasn't cut off in the same way that many women were and I was able to have a life beyond diapers.

Like most women of my time, I followed my husband's career. I never had full-time help and my family wasn't around after we left Montreal. For ten years the CBC was my lifeline, especially *Trans-Canada Matinée*. But then that phase of our life suddenly ended. One day, when we were living in Windsor, my husband called and said he had to finish his Ph.D. I thought he'd choose Ann Arbor, Michigan. Instead he announced he was going to Jerusalem. Even though I thought moving to Israel with four children seemed a bit much, I said I'd support him. So we went from being a professional household with a split-level house, a station wagon in the driveway, and four neat little kids to being the family of a graduate student in a faraway land.

The move wasn't easy. But it was wonderful in the sense that it transformed our lives and exposed our children to a world they wouldn't have had in the suburbs of Windsor. As for me, it changed my life. I knew I couldn't be a volunteer *par excellence* any more. Something more needed to be done. I liked and still like being a mother (and grandmother), but as I began to do my own work and develop a consciousness about what was possible, I realized that being a mother is a relationship and not an occupation, as our society has made it.

Soon after we arrived in Jerusalem I started doing voluntary work, and that led to an invitation from a professor of family and social medicine to be a tutor on his teaching team on family health at the university. Eventually, I was invited to set up the Medical Social Services Department. Then I was invited to do a Master of Public Health degree because the Department of Social Medicine wanted me to participate in an epidemiological study. I didn't think I needed it, but I'm so glad I did it, because that knowledge was transformative. Until then my professional perspectives focused on the individual and the family. I didn't know about populations, what epidemiologists call the denominators, an important perspective for policy development. Just as I was about to graduate and write my thesis my husband was offered a job in Canada, so we came back and I had to start all over again.

After our return, I stayed at home for a while because that was what mothers were supposed to do. But before long I was climbing the walls. One evening my husband and I were at a dinner at the home of John Porter, the sociologist and author of the classic study *The Vertical Mosaic*. I was talking about a monograph I had written about the Israel Rheumatic Society when the director of research of the Royal Commission on Health Services, who was sitting across the room, perked up and asked me to meet with him. Subsequently, I was invited to research and write a chapter for the commission, and that marked the beginning of my Canadian career in public policy. I was in my mid-forties when I got my first job in the public service, with the Department of Health and Welfare.

My husband passed away in 1988 and I miss him terribly, although I keep busy with various international projects. Over the years, I've learned that every adult needs three anchors: work, family, and friends. I feel fortunate in the opportunities I have had to serve humankind, in my collegial relationships in Canada and internationally, and in the quality of my friendships and family life. These anchors still sustain me.

"When I was elected to Parliament in 1974, like many of my female colleagues I thought that being a woman and an MP was part of the natural course of things to come. I didn't see myself as belonging to a vanguard — that status was reserved for real trailblazers like Agnes McPhail, Ellen Fairclough, or Judy LaMarsh. My generation saw ourselves as their inheritors."

IONA CAMPAGNOLO

When Iona Campagnolo was elected the first woman president of the Liberal party of Canada in 1982, it wasn't an easy victory. But she comes from a long line of strong women and was fortunate enough to be exposed to some impressive female role models during her formative years. As Canada's first Minister of State for Fitness and Amateur Sport, she established a national profile. Among other commitments, she currently sits on the board of the International Centre for Human Rights and Democratic Development.

I n 1974, I was serving as a municipal councillor — in those days, known as an alderman — in Prince Rupert, B.C. I'd joined the Liberal party in 1967 but kept my political profile as low as possible by working in the background, since being publicly partisan was considered "poor form" for a municipal politician. Just before the nomination meeting for the upcoming federal election, the expected Liberal candidate invited me to lunch to say he wouldn't be running due to his wife's sudden illness. He suggested I seek the nomination and offered to manage my campaign if I won. Since I knew women all over Canada were seeking nominations, I jumped at the chance.

I've always suspected I wouldn't have won that nomination so easily if the party had expected to win. I set out on the campaign oblivious to the "Chauvinist Pig" tie my manager proudly wore and equally blind to the realization that the ferocious pace of campaigning is the life of an elected person. The NDP incumbent had served for many years and I worked fiercely running against Dave Barrett's NDP government in Victoria, rather than the national Tory opposition. Victory came with a near three thousand-vote plurality. I had a lot of help getting there, but my team and I were later amused to notice an interesting transformation. Many people who hadn't helped because they thought I'd lose were now happily taking credit for my election. Several obviously backdated cheques arrived to help with the campaign expenses.

Nationally, the election was an interesting one. An unprecedented number of women were elected — nine in all. Although that seems laughable in today's context, at the time it was considered a genuine victory for women. Feminism was in the air and most of us felt we were equal to the task. In these times of backlash and regression to the political right, it's difficult to envision the sense of freedom and liberation that defined the late 1960s and early 1970s. In that heady atmosphere, we expected that in the years ahead our numbers would quickly swell.

Our emotional euphoria was quickly diminished by practical realities. From a physical perspective, the job was unimaginably punishing — more so for British Columbians. My long trek home on weekends — Ottawa to Vancouver to the north — was difficult and demanding in and of itself. To my surprise, I soon discovered it was regarded as a perk by many of my constituents. I'd spend Saturdays hearing people's concerns and in the evening would usually attend a public event. On Sunday, if I was near to my Prince Rupert home — geographically, Skeena was a huge riding — I tried to spend time with my daughter Jan and her family. My girls now regale their own daughters with hilarious demonstrations of Grandma on such family occasions — asleep in their midst, in lieu of quality time spent doing more productive things. I took many midnight "red-eyes" that arrived in Toronto at seven a.m. I'd change planes, arrive in Ottawa by nine, and go straight to work. When people ask me what it takes to be an MP, my first response is always good health, energetic strength of purpose and a solid sense of who you are.

I was forty-two when I came to Ottawa. My twenty-year marriage had ended and I wasn't a kid in any respect. Women were judged primarily on appearance and many of the old clichés still held sway. Journalist Douglas Fisher wrote that I'd never be taken seriously, as I "looked too good." I gained weight — although not deliberately — and in retrospect regard my increased density and the high-necked outfits I wore as "armour." I remember introducing myself to someone who responded that I couldn't be Iona Campagnolo because she's "a big, heavy, Italian mamma!" Campagnolo is my married name; my ancestors must have rolled in their graves!

My daughter Jan was twenty-one and Jennifer was thirteen when my national public life began. I could never have undertaken those responsibilities as fully as I did without the help of my sister, Marion. She voluntarily left her work as an accountant, came with me to Ottawa, and took on the many unpaid tasks that most of my male counterparts could assume their wives would do. My sister was caregiver to Jennifer, hostess when required, general assistant and intelligent sounding board for me. I owe her a great deal, and my debt is still being repaid.

My male colleagues in Parliament weren't particularly shocked at the number of women colleagues and they weren't unkind to us, although some seemed to feel we weren't permanent and would eventually go back to where we belonged. In general, we believed that our male colleagues were glad to have us there, but the media found us a distinct oddity. My backwoods origins coupled with my gender and my blunt speaking style endowed me with a special curiosity. As with all women in non-traditional positions, there was constant speculation about my private life, which, like Judy LaMarsh before me, I found very annoying.

Veteran parliamentarians, who warned me that a reputation for blunt speech could nip my career in the bud, advised me against the dangers of being too easily understood. In time, I learned that discretion was occasionally advisable and I moderated my outspokenness, although I could never become as obscure as some tasks demanded. At my first caucus meeting, B.C. minister Arthur Laing wisely advised me to keep my field marshal's baton in my kitbag for a while. He meant that if I were ambitious, it would be a good idea not to show it. He also implied that as a new member and a woman, I should expect to be underestimated, which was a powerful weapon.

The House of Commons was then — and continues to be — a predominantly male preserve, and some men vigorously defend that turf against perceived invaders. Real power still eludes most women in political life, but even so, I was quickly accorded a measure of power when I served as parliamentary secretary to the Minister of Indian Affairs and Northern Development, Judd Buchanan. He generously shared issues with me and occasionally allowed me to act on his behalf in some of the difficult matters afflicting aboriginal people and those of the High North — a few of whom I'd known since my elementary school days on the Skeena River. In September 1976, I was invited into the Cabinet as Canada's first Minister of State for Fitness and Amateur Sport. Earlier that year, I'd voted in favour of capital punishment and, as a result, was repeatedly informed that my political life in the Liberal party was at an end. Yet, true to his ethos of being "against the current," Prime Minister Trudeau made me one of the privileged élite. Since I'm known as a lover of the arts, my first response to the appointment was "Why me?" In his indomitable style, the prime minister made an extremely logical argument that since sport was dominated by men, I'd be able to shake it up and begin the process of change. Concluding that there are no small ministries, just small ministers, I accepted the post. During my tenure I wasn't very successful at moving the mountain of prejudice against women in sport, but I chipped away at it. Actually, I loved the job, even though journalist Allan Fotheringham dubbed me the "Czarina of Sport" to general amusement and the adjective "high-profile" seemed permanently attached to my name.

In keeping with my tendency towards blunt speech, I felt compelled to let people know what I considered fair. I took a pro-choice position on reproduction and, as a result, was targeted by the anti-choice movement. I was deemed to be what today's neoconservatives would call a "feminazi." One writer of the day described me as "heretofore uncategorized but presumably radical on all issues." That took me aback since I've always been a philosophical centrist, a moderate and a liberal — not a radical.

In those days, whenever I knew I had to go into battle I made a point of wearing the highest heels I could tolerate. I'm tall, but most men are taller, and staring into a tie-knot is not nearly as satisfying as looking your opponent full in the face. Although I knew I made enemies, I still consider it the price I paid for having a real point of view. I invariably evoked enormous loyalty or fierce animosity in almost equal measure. Gradually, I learned to absorb the scars that go with such polarity as part of the discipline of public life. The great Liberal party strategist, Senator Keith Davey, christened me "a loose cannon on the deck of Liberalism" and, just as poetically, "political gold" and an "eccentric." I bore all these epithets proudly, believing that they were a function of differences based on history, geography, philosophy, and gender. I admired the senator, but my view of Canada was very different from his.

I never doubted Prime Minister Trudeau's intellectual commitment to equality for women, although I often suspect that his "gut" reaction — if he ever admitted to one — might be different. When we disagreed, I was always conscious of the influence of his Jesuit tutors. He had a tendency to answer one question with another, which infuriated me. I wasn't intimidated by him, nor was I infatuated, although I admired him immensely. Perhaps he found me difficult to deal with, too, but when Justice Minister Ron Basford retired, I was named as the first woman to sit on the Priorities and Planning Committee of Cabinet, so I had to conclude that despite our differences, the prime minister and I followed the same path.

My term in Cabinet was difficult because the territory was so foreign. When Monique Bégin and I were sworn in we were only the fourth and fifth women in Canadian history to be so honoured. During Cabinet meetings, Jean Chrétien sometimes fired me a kindly note suggesting that I stop "selling," as my point had already been made. Still, I believe absolutely that women in power make a difference. One example was a debate on proposed *Criminal Code* amendments to make rape within marriage a crime. Monique Bégin, Jeanne Sauvé, and I, along with sixteen of our male colleagues argued the point against twenty male members of Cabinet who found the concept incredible. With Trudeau's help, we won.

The indomitable Senator Thérèse Casgrain, who played an instrumental role in winning the right for Quebec women to vote in provincial elections, became a mentor. When she was elected to head the Quebec New Democrats in 1962, she became the first woman in Canada to lead a provincial political party. Mme Casgrain sought me out early in my parliamentary career. Elegant and refined, she often wore magnificent hats, which she devilishly referred to as "another joy that men don't share." She was an inspiration to many women, and, among other things, taught me that being a Quebec nationalist isn't inconsistent with being a strong and supportive Canadian.

I've been fortunate in the women who influenced my life and still remember them all vividly. I had the unusual experience of spending my adolescence in Prince Rupert, a city with a female mayor. In 1948, Nora Arnold became the first woman in Canada to hold that position. Mrs. Arnold dressed elegantly and was known as "a fine figure of a woman," meaning she was robust. I recall rushing down to the train station with a group of teenage girls to see her return from "exotic" Winnipeg after being named Canadian Woman of the Year. She wore a splendid black suit, heavily decorated with silver foxes. Her sterling silver hair was topped by a graceful black hat. Perhaps most impressive of all was the fact that the men surrounding her addressed her with great respect. It was a new phenomenon and it made a great impression on me.

Although some men have been a positive influence, I see myself as particularly fortunate because I come from a long line of strong women, most immediately my wise and beautiful mother, Rosamond. I'm of Scottish and English ancestry, the eldest of four children, and was born Iona Victoria Hardy in Vancouver in October 1932. Although it was never mentioned, I must have been an unwelcome surprise for my eighteen-year-old mother and my unemployed father, arriving, as I did, in the depths of the Depression. My father told me that while I was still a babe in arms he took me to my first political event — a "relief march" in Vancouver.

My father was a blue collar worker who was seasonally employed at the North Pacific cannery on the Skeena River. When I was young we lived in northern B.C. from April to October and in Vancouver during the winter — a pattern followed by many coastal workers in those days. Unlike many children, I'd spend part of the year at a big Vancouver school in winter and then go north to a one-room school on the river in the spring. I was about ten years old when I first went to work in the cannery during the summers. I earned forty-two cents an hour. In those days it was quite common for youngsters to work long hours, and the money I brought the family was very welcome. As a result, I've always thought of work as a process of discipline that I learned early and that has served me well.

When I was twelve, my parents decided to remain at the cannery year-round with my younger siblings, so my brother, who is twenty months younger than myself, and I moved to Prince Rupert to board and attend school. There I met the memorable Miss Mary Ann Way, with whom I boarded. Then in her sixties, she was short and her iron-grey hair was cut extra-close by a barber — never a hairdresser. A self-described "British spinster," she arrived in Prince Rupert some time after its incorporation in 1910 and supported herself by teaching piano. She acted as a general contractor to build her own house, then supervised the building of several houses, which she sold to supplement her income. She was fierce and opinionated with a towering intellect, although with true British reticence she never discussed her personal life or her feelings. She played Chopin for me and made me learn the rudiments of the piano. She also forced me to read Shakespeare aloud, all the while correcting my river accent. I vividly remember her carefully explaining the inequity of the Salique law presented in the early scenes of *Henry V*, by which the French ensured that a woman would never come to the throne. She assured me that in this — as in all else — the British were marginally superior since once in a great while they did allow a woman to be queen.

Miss Way encouraged me to read widely, to think, to paint, to draw, even to cook. She belonged to a book club and at their bimonthly meetings she and her friends discussed the great books of the time: *The Alexandria Quartet* by Lawrence Durrell, or Rebecca West's *Black Lamb and Grey Falcon*. Wearing my best dress, I'd refill the teacups and pass the sweets. I was allowed to listen but never to speak. As she guided me, Miss Way would mutter, "When I'm through with you, young lady, you will pass muster in the Ascot Circle." After Miss Way's tutelage, meeting Queen Elizabeth II proved easy.

Although no one in my family had ever shown the slightest interest in public life, the seeds of my political career were sown early. In grade nine I was the first girl to run for president of the student council. I established another precedent when I won. In high school I expanded my involvement to include community activism, and at fifteen I served as a school representative on a committee that worked to integrate people displaced by the war who were starting a new life in Canada.

I was one of those typical 1950s pretty girls and since so much of a woman's value was based on appearance, I was encouraged to think of modelling as an alternative to becoming a salesclerk or working in an office. Even then I felt that looks were a weak foundation on which to build a life, so I went to work in the Bank of Montreal. I particularly recall one speech from the manager, who informed us that we were fortunate to be working for the bank. Although we earned very little and were expected to work many hours of unpaid overtime, we could always be assured of respect from the public because we were "bank girls." After two months, I left to work for the local power company and joined the Electrical Workers Union.

Two years later, at twenty, I married. My daughters were born seven years apart, and while they were young I started attending night school to get a real education. My life revolved around my marriage, my daughters, the local theatre group, gardening, and volunteerism. In fact, I became involved in elected politics through the garden club. In 1965, when I was vice-president of the Prince Rupert Garden Club, a group of entrepreneurs wanted to develop the city's last major park into a shopping mall. Naturally, the club was opposed to the development, and since our president had only recently arrived from Holland and was unsure of his English, I became our spokesperson. After a major fight, we succeeded in delaying the development for almost fifteen years.

In the fall of 1966, my garden club friends nominated me for the local school board. I won by a sixteen-vote plurality. A year later, I was elected board chair, a position I held for six years. After the school board, I became a city councillor. Of all politicians, city councillors are the closest to the people, and Prince Rupert's mayor of nearly forty years, Peter Lester, was a master political chess player I could study. From him I learned the hard arts of holding fire, hidden agendas, tactics, and strategy, which was never my strong suit. Even so, I learned how to fight fairly, deal with conflicts, and never to hold a grudge.

Because I've always had to make a living, I've worked at all kinds of things. In the 1960s, I did a women's radio show and interviewed every significant visitor to Prince Rupert, including my parliamentary predecessor. I eventually became station sales manager and by selling commercial time on commission was finally able to make a good income. In those days, radio was in its prime, and there was a great sense of excitement in the air because the rules were changing. I worked with a fine team of people and, even now, can't watch television reruns of the sitcom *WKRP* without feeling nostalgic.

When I went to Ottawa I knew in my heart of hearts that as a British Columbian, a Liberal, a northerner, and a woman, I wouldn't be in government for long. After my defeat in 1979 I returned to broadcasting — to CBC-TV in Vancouver where I hosted a show, interviewing the power wielders of the day. It went well for a couple of years, until I incautiously appeared on the cover of *Chatelaine*. A member of the new government discovered I was still alive and obviously not as destitute and powerless as defeated members ought to be. He raised the issue in the House that it was improper for a former member of the Crown to be employed by the public network unless an appropriate amount of time had passed — presumably we needed to be "cleansed" of the taint of public office. A House of Commons committee concurred, and I was fired. I'm told the *Broadcast Act* now contains a clause to this effect, which is informally known as the Iona clause.

Fortunately, I've been associated with a speaker's agent, who has helped me over this and other such results of my life choices to keep myself financially solvent between jobs. And independent producer Larry Shapiro, one of Thérèse Casgrain's circle, offered me a position as panellist on his PBS world affairs show, *The Editors*. That, too, has helped to sustain me these past twenty years on my own. Even so, my friends are constantly exasperated at my choices of low- or non-paid work. As in all things, being known as a member of a political party has advantages and disadvantages. Its disincentive to potential employers remains a largely unexplored fact of political life — a subject I still find too painful to talk about in any depth. Although I wasn't in the House long enough to earn a pension, people occasionally accost me to express disapproval of my drain on the public purse. I've always earned my living with hard work and will continue to do so for as long as I'm able, whether public or private or in between.

One day in 1982, out of the blue, I received a call from Marc Lalonde, my former colleague. "We are thinking that perhaps Mr. Trudeau may wish to leave within the next few years and we would like to have someone in charge of the party who can carry off the period of inevitable vacuum when he goes. We think it is you."

It was a lovely offer, but there was a downside. Until then, it was a tradition in the Liberal party that presidents served two terms and incumbent presidents were not to be challenged. Norm McLeod was in his first term and perceived to be a "Turner supporter." I, ever ambiguously interpreted, was seen to be one of the "ins" in a party of "ins" and "outs." Few seemed to remember — or care — that John Turner, a British Columbian, had brought me into the party many years before. So when I decided to enter the field the fight was tough and invigorating — made more so since it was perceived to be a diversion to detract attention from a review of Prime Minister Trudeau's leadership, as well as by the fact that I was the first woman to be nominated for the post.

As I say these words, I can see the pictures of all the men who preceded me, beginning with a severe-looking Vincent Massey, who became president of the party in 1932, the year I was born. All but Norm and I were senators. The victory wasn't an easy one, but I must say that I loathe some of the "victim" stories told of such breakthrough events. It's perfectly normal for major change to create concern.

However, the night before the vote, a frenzy of highly personalized, anti-woman sentiment did emerge — primarily generated, perhaps not surprisingly, by members of my own sex. Change threatens people for many reasons and women are not immune to fear of the future if their ground rules suddenly change. Some people chose to see my feminist views on reproductive choice, the place of minorities in our society — and apparently much else about me — as a red flag. During the convention, devastating hand-outs that cast doubt on every aspect of my life and moral character were circulated. Finally, the rumour-mongering and lies reached such a crescendo that I left the floor and retreated to my room. I was so exhausted that — surprisingly — I fell fast asleep. When I woke the next morning I found some misogynous notes from opponents pushed under my door.

I can't say these attacks didn't sting, but the important thing is that they didn't cause me to lose confidence. If I let personal criticism stop me, I'd feel that I was breaking faith with all the women who struggled before me. And political life does have its positive aspects. Although I've never been a member of the inner Liberal establishment, my terms as president were productive.

When I took over as president, the Liberal party of Canada was $2 million in debt. My first objective was to improve our finances and then to reclaim the party operations from the Prime Minister's Office and redemocratize them. The task was more difficult than I'd anticipated. The government and many members seemed reluctant to go into the country and, given the expected departure of Mr. Trudeau, morale was low. These needs were addressed by an enormous number of fund-raising dinners. I became a kind of itinerant "road warrior" passed from riding to riding, from one end of the country to the other. The party's grass roots literally saved its élite! It was exhilarating, exhausting, and ultimately successful. When Prime Minister Trudeau resigned after his famous walk in the snow storm on February 29, 1984, I worked at full power trying to keep us afloat during that dark time.

Unfortunately, some people didn't believe I'd work that hard on behalf of the party with no ulterior motive, although I'd always made it clear that I'd never use the immense goodwill that the process had generated towards me at the constituency level. Still, it was generally believed that I intended to run for the leadership of the party. My friends were bombarded with calls asking them to "talk sense to that woman" and stop me, or from supporters who urged them to encourage me to run. I knew that a female candidacy would be beneficial to the party, but I believed that my eclectic education and lack of formal training in business and finance, combined with my inadequacy in French, precluded my considering the leadership.

So although informal 1984 polls put my numbers at twenty-six percent with John Turner's at twenty-seven percent and Jean Chrétien's at twenty-five percent, I chose not to run. It was enough for me to have been considered. When every hour, for days on end, from all over the country, I received single red roses with messages asking me to run for leader, I was flattered — but only that. I was also fully aware that our party would lose the 1984 election and felt that if such a loss were charged to a woman, it might slow progress for other members of my sex — which, of course, ultimately occurred with Canada's first woman prime minister, Kim Campbell.

Instead of running myself, I chaired — with Remy Bujold — the 1984 leadership convention, which elected John Turner. When I announced the results of the vote, I was fully aware of the audience before me — the party was pretty evenly divided between those who supported John Turner and those who voted for Jean Chrétien. The Turner forces were jubilant and needed little more than congratulations after their sixteen-year wait. My inclination was to say something comforting to the Chrétien forces, whose appearance of dejection — even anger — was obvious. So when I introduced Jean Chrétien, I said he "was second on the ballot, but first in our hearts." It was a ten-second decision that I've never regretted, even though it's been misrepresented and criticized. John Turner was, of course, hurt by my statement, but he knew I supported the elected leader so he forgave me. In 1990, I chaired Paul Martin's campaign for leader with Jean LaPierre.

I served out my final term as president and on the day it ended, November 7, 1986, I walked out of the convention and never looked back. I've always disliked serving in any past capacity and did not serve as past president. Once again, I dusted myself off and started over again. I worked in West Africa for a while and when I returned to Vancouver did a stint on BCTV, filling in for the irascible Jack Webster. It was a petty triumph, since he had once growled that no woman would ever substitute for him.

I've often been asked why I didn't marry again — as if finding just about anyone to support me might be preferable to the need to constantly reinvent myself. I've never considered it. I've had so many fine life experiences that I'd be hard pressed to be an equal partner to anyone, and I'd hardly invite someone I felt very warmly towards to share the daily turbulence of my life. Also, I have my beloved daughters whom, I'm convinced, no stepfather could ever love and protect as their own father does. I feel no sadness at choosing a single life — it suits me very well — and since both my grandmothers lived to nearly a century, I have reason to expect that I might enjoy longevity, which I'm looking forward to.

When I graduated from high school there was no hope that I'd go to university. At that time, it was about a thousand miles by road to Vancouver and I couldn't have raised the kind of money a university education would take. So I've taken enormous pleasure in my appointment as founding chancellor of the new University of Northern British Columbia. By its presence across the vast reaches of the northern part of this province, UNBC ensures that no kid like me will ever be denied an education due to lack of access or means of entry. That gives me great satisfaction.

I also chair the Fraser Basin Council, a coming together of the four orders of Canadian governance and a coalition of interests designed to realize sustainability of the Fraser River and its fourteen major tributaries. In many ways I've come full circle. I began on the Skeena River and I'll probably end with the Fraser River. The water under all those bridges I've passed over is an endless flow. Today, nothing makes me happier than to see young women of skill and courage moving into position to join that continuum.

"I fought against quotas when I was at university, so I find it impossible to support them now. I believe in only one thing — merit."

SYLVIA OSTRY

As Paris-based head of the Department of Economics and Statistics for the Organization for Economic Cooperation and Development and, later, as Prime Minister Brian Mulroney's personal representative for the economic summits, Sylvia Ostry knows what it's like to be a major player in the world of international economics and trade. For over forty years, she has held various academic and bureaucratic roles in Canada, making history in 1972 when she became the first woman to reach the deputy minister level in the federal civil service. The mother of two sons, she is known for her relentless work, commitment to excellence, and high-powered entertaining, done in partnership with her husband, Bernard. At last count she had seventeen honorary degrees and when this interview was conducted, was chairman of the Centre for International Studies at the University of Toronto.

In 1964, ten years after earning my Ph.D. in economics, I became the assistant director of research in the labour division of the Dominion Bureau of Statistics. My job was to set up and run a special unit for research on the labour force, which interested me because I've always loved research, which I had done in the early part of my career. However, for five years, I'd been teaching economics at McGill. Three days a week, I'd rise at dawn and take the early train to Montreal and by 1964 my family situation was as much a factor in my job choice as the opportunity to return to research. On my teaching days I was getting back to Ottawa just in time to give my son Adam his bath, and when my second son, Jonathan, came along, the commuting became impossible.

In those days, most women with children didn't work outside the home, but I didn't feel stigmatized. We lived on Aylmer Road, across the river from Ottawa, next door to a family where both parents were doctors. The mother had stopped practising medicine when the children came along. Our children played together and one day I overheard one of my sons ask the others what their mother did. "What do you mean?" they replied incredulously. "She's at home. She does everything." "You mean she doesn't go out to work? Isn't that funny," my son remarked.

In 1969, I became director of the Economic Council of Canada, and in 1972, when I was appointed chief statistician, I became the first woman to reach the deputy minister level in the federal government. I've never spent much time thinking about being the first woman deputy and on the subject of discrimination, either I was lucky or I was unobservant. In fact, being a Jew was as much of an issue as being a woman at the time. After my appointment was announced, the late Jean-Luc Pepin, my minister, called me into his office.

"Sylvia," he said, "I've received a flood of anonymous letters protesting your appointment. I'm not going to show you any of them. Some are so threatening that I'm giving them to the RCMP. The major theme is that if Trudeau wanted to appoint a woman, why punish Statistics Canada? Many were anti-Semitic as well." He laughed and I laughed and that was that. So although I wasn't aware of it in my day-to-day experiences, there was clearly powerful resentment that a woman and a Jew would reach such elevated levels.

A certain amount of sexism was evident in the media. For instance, when I was appointed chief statistician the *Ottawa Citizen* ran a story with the headline "Blue-Eyed Mother of Two Appointed First Deputy Minister." I thought it was very funny and wrote them a letter saying my eyes are green, not blue. Frankly, I'm ambivalent about the publicity I've received for being the first woman this or that. I think I got these jobs because I was the best qualified person.

The Ottawa community was very lively in the 1970s — whatever you think of Trudeau, he encouraged innovative ideas. Since my husband, Bernard, was a deputy minister, too, and we both worked intensely, the idea of bringing people together from many different areas and having interesting discussions appealed to us. Bernard is much better at planning than I am, and any reputation we have as hosts is due largely to him. We both thoroughly enjoy entertaining, although it's been said that we used our parties to further our mutual ambition.

I've been criticized for being ambitious, but I really don't know what that word is meant to imply. My critics certainly can't mean I'm interested in money, since I've been a public servant all my life. I'm very ambitious in the sense that I believe it's possible to feed into the policy process and make change. Recently, I've been trying to pull together an international group to design a protocol for China's entry into the World Trade Organization. That's extremely ambitious, particularly since I'm not an expert on China, but I don't think the people who have said I'm ambitious have that in mind. They mean it in a narrower sense — that I'm interested in status and the accoutrements of the job. Status *is* useful because it helps you to get things done and allows you to feed into the policy process, but for me or my husband, it's never been a goal in itself.

When I grew up in North Winnipeg in the 1930s, it was a ghetto of largely Jewish immigrants, characterized by an extraordinary emphasis on education and culture. Even though my parents had no money — my father was in the pulp and paper business and he lost everything in the stock market crash of 1929 — it was assumed that my brother and I would go to university. There was never any question about that. It simply reflects what the community valued. I had no sense that being a girl made any difference.

My mother was the strongest influence of all. She'd been a teacher in her native England — her father was a highly skilled craftsman trained in Danzig — and she placed an enormous emphasis on obedience and excellence in school. In those days, almost no married women worked outside the home so, after relinquishing teaching, she channelled her formidable energies into child rearing. I could recite poetry by the age of three and read and write by the time I turned five, so she lied about my age and enrolled me in school a year early. Incidentally, Bernard Ostry, also five, was a classmate.

Growing up, I always had lots of girlfriends, but because I always wanted to be first in class, I wasn't popular with boys. My girlfriends tried to get me to spruce myself up in the hope that someone would take me out, but it didn't seem to work. I don't think I really cared. I was more interested in reading and studying than in make-up, clothes, and dates. When I was fifteen I graduated from high school and entered pre-med at the University of Manitoba. I decided to become a doctor, not because I was particularly interested in medicine, but because I wanted to attack discrimination in the medical school. I thought it would be a very tough thing to do and I've always liked challenges.

At that time the medical school had quotas on the number of women and the number of Jews they'd admit. Two of my Jewish male friends and I decided we'd get the highest marks in the province in pre-med and if they didn't admit us we'd sue. I wasn't doing it for any side. I was doing it to stop a university from discriminating against people on what I believed were irrelevant grounds — sex, race, or religion. I felt merit was all that should matter. When I came first in the class and my friends came second and third, the university decided to admit us.

Unfortunately, I soon became bored by medicine. After completing my first year, I spent the summer in Kingston with my brother, who was in the chemical engineering department at Queen's. Meeting people in other disciplines made me aware that I wasn't getting an education in medical school. I did nothing but study medicine — I never even read a newspaper. My parents were terribly understanding, but the dean was another story. I'd fought to get in and when I dropped out he was livid with rage. I felt terrible, but medicine didn't challenge me.

I was nineteen when I made the switch to economics and transferred to McGill. For a variety of reasons, I also decided to marry a political science student I'd met at Queen's. He was a very nice person, but the marriage didn't work. Although I realized I'd made a mistake early on, the relationship lasted seven years. It was difficult to end because he was so nice and I didn't want to hurt him.

After getting my doctorate, I taught for a while at McGill, then was offered a job at Oxford, which isn't a welcoming place for a colonial. Since I didn't have a lot of friends, and I'd just been divorced, I was lonely in many different ways. I knew that Bernard Ostry was studying at the London School of Economics, so I decided to look him up. Within a year, Bernard and I were married. When I became pregnant with our son Adam, I was in the final stages of a book on labour economics and racing against time. Finally, the head of the institute called me in. "Sylvia," he said. "We think it's time you left. We don't feel we could cope with you giving birth in the senior common room." I left but finished the book just before Adam was born. I read the page proofs in the hospital. In 1959, we decided to return to Canada with our fifteen-month-old son. Bernard got a job with the Social Science Research Council in Ottawa. I took a position teaching economics at McGill, hired a live-in housekeeper, and commuted between the two cities.

In 1979, I got my toughest job, and my favourite simply because it was so tough, when I was appointed head of the Department of Economics and Statistics for the Paris-based Organization for Economic Cooperation and Development (OECD). It was an extraordinary opportunity that came right out of the blue, when the previous head retired after twenty years in the job. My initial reaction was to say no since Bernard was in Ottawa and I'd never do anything to jeopardize my marriage. But Bernard urged me to accept. "This is Sylvia's turn and we'll manage," he said.

Early on in my tenure, the deputy governor of the Bank of England phoned me. "I've just seen an article which is an unbelievable attack on you," he said. He read it to me on the phone and it was very, very nasty. Since it had been leaked from inside the OECD, it was perfectly clear I was not welcome as head of the department. I think I was strongly resented for two reasons: I had no background in international economics and I was female.

Many of the people in the department tried to ensure I wouldn't last very long. My first press conference was the crucial test. I kept asking my staff what the procedure was. Were there briefing notes and so on? They advised me not to worry, just to play it by ear. I finally decided I was on my own. I sat myself down, read all the documents thoroughly, and composed my own briefing notes. I decided on an opening line to initiate discussion and things went very well. If I hadn't done that, I think I would have been finished. I did not believe I was a victim, but depending on my reaction, I could have been. If staff were not providing me with the necessary material I had two options: One was to complain to the secretary-general, Emile van Lennep, but that would have alienated the department. The other was to say, "Drop dead. I'll do it myself and it will be better than you can believe." I chose the second.

I loved the OECD, but the geographical distance was very hard on my marriage so, in 1983, I came back to Canada, as the Deputy Minister of Trade. My husband became the Deputy Minister of Industry in Ontario. Since my predecessor at the OECD had been chief economist for almost two decades, I think they were shocked when I resigned.

Certainly, our marriage is a partnership, although I don't think I thought about that when I married Bernard. He's a remarkable person in his generosity of spirit, which I think is unusual for a man of his generation. He's supportive in every way. Even though it made terrible demands on him, he urged me to take the OECD job because it was too great an opportunity to pass up. I couldn't have accomplished what I did without that support. On a personal level, I don't know what I would have done without him because my drive is to work relentlessly. Thanks to Bernard, I became interested in art, the cinema, and clothes, among other things, and he taught me very well. He's provided me with many interests beyond my work.

While I was at the OECD we were doing a major study on the impact of the oil crisis on energy demands. I was working with a young American who told me that the FBI had a long file on me and that my code name was Pussy Cat. "Tell me what it says," I demanded.

"It says you're inordinately fond of clothes and it describes your wardrobe in great detail."

"That's terrific," I said. "Would you please let them know that if they're planning to bribe me, I only want Armani."

I've never thought about a career as something one plans in terms of advancement. I've always thought about the intrinsic interest of the job and what I would learn from it. I love ideas and the intellectual stimulation of my work. With Bernie's help, both our children have become successful public servants. With his help, I've also learned to relax. I go to the cinema, which I love, and to art galleries. I'm grateful to him for expanding my horizons. Left to my own devices, I'd be so narrow I'd be intolerable — and very frumpy.

"I never gave much thought to being the only woman in the world to head a national gallery. I just assumed I was the best person for the job."

JEAN SUTHERLAND BOGGS

Jean Sutherland Boggs' tenure as the first woman to oversee the National Gallery of Canada is just one of her many significant achievements in the art world, which include developing and building both the new National Gallery and the Museum of Civilization. She has served as senior adviser to the Andrew W. Mellon Foundation in New York, curated the exhibition "Picasso and Things: Still Lifes by Picasso," and written numerous books and articles on art. She has received fifteen honorary degrees and the Order of Canada, and in 1992 was made a companion of the Order of Canada.

I've been asked to come back to Canada to take on a new position three times in my career, and my departure from each position I was holding at the time was highlighted by drama.

In 1962, after working in the United States for many years, I accepted a position as curator at the Art Gallery of Ontario. By that time I was fairly well established. In addition to my book *Portraits by Degas,* I had published numerous articles and had a long history as a teacher. However, I hadn't bought works of art, so that was a new area. Two years after I joined the gallery my lack of experience got me into trouble. The Museum of Modern Art in New York owned two Picassos of the same period and they thought they could spare one, a portrait of a seated women, so I negotiated the sale. I was quite surprised when a powerful member of the board of trustees resigned over the purchase. He disliked the painting intensely — it was too modern for him. The other trustees and Bill Withrow, the director, stood by me, but I think they were relieved when, later that year, I accepted a post at Washington University in St. Louis.

In 1966, the chairman of the National Gallery of Canada visited me in St. Louis to ask if I'd consider becoming the gallery's director. Frankly, this wasn't a creative period in the gallery's history. It was badly housed and understaffed, but it did have the major collection of European art in the country and — as we have often said — the major collection of Canadian art in the world. The staff were professional and often heroic, though somewhat demoralized. All things considered, no job could have tempted me more.

Sure, I was conscious of being the first woman, but that never impressed me very much. The art world was fairly nonplussed so far as I could tell. Comments didn't get more critical than "better to have a good female than a poor male."

I enjoyed being director. Even before I arrived I had a row with the business manager, or whatever he was called, after he wanted me to agree to a budget increase of only five percent a year. I had enough sense to know that this was the time to ask for more and I worked over a weekend in St. Louis to ensure we'd be given a thirty-three percent increase instead. Once I arrived at the gallery I concentrated on building up a staff, of which we were both very proud, with the help of Robert Hubbard, the chief curator, who had spent many distinguished years at the gallery. Pierre Théberge, now director of the Montreal Museum of Fine Arts, was appointed at the same time I was, and therefore I can't take any credit for him. [Subsequent to this interview Théberge was appointed director of the National Gallery.]

There were many different personalities on the curatorial staff and I liked and respected them all. I've been ready to accept a greater range of behaviour and attitudes among people working with works of art than those in more conventional occupations. We were able to make wonderful acquisitions and we continued, as the gallery always had, to buy contemporary Canadian art. We even lifted the earlier prohibition against buying or exhibiting American art.

I never believed in hierarchy and I certainly never believed in being a director who contacted staff only through a chain of command. I also respected people's territory. Although I love installing collections and exhibitions, I never did it as a director. I always left that to the curators. And I never interfered as I've seen other directors do — for instance, taking over in the final stages of an installation and moving things around.

I suppose I'm known as someone who was tough about acquisitions and had high standards of scholarship. I don't know where that confidence came from. It's something I simply seem to have. On reflection, though, I must owe a great deal of it to the training I had at the University of Toronto and Harvard. I wouldn't say I was a particularly self-confident person as a whole, nor am I now, but I seem to be very confident about works of art and artists.

There's nothing in my background to suggest art as a career. My father was a geologist with the International Petroleum Company and I was born in Peru while he was working there. I was nine when I came to Canada — to Coburg, Ontario, which was my family's home. I enjoyed the town, but I suffered Ontario's high-school curriculum, which made me determined to pass my senior matriculation when I was sixteen — as I did, with absolutely no distinction.

When I entered the University of Toronto at age sixteen, I was the youngest girl there. I can't say I knew what art history would be, but in those days you had to decide on your major when you enrolled, which is really rather precipitous. My parents knew Dr. Currelly, who was head of the Royal Ontario Museum, and they sent me to see him. He was very persuasive about the newly founded fine arts department — I was in its third class. Fortunately, I enjoyed it. I wonder if I would have been as enthusiastic if I'd studied paleontology, as my father had suggested.

University was a real coming-of-age for me. Trinity College had an extraordinary dean of women, Mossie Mae Kirkwood, who encouraged us to be creative, inventive, and unconventional. The fine arts department was also very good. Once, during the war, we went to see an exhibition of Italian art in New York, at the Museum of Modern Art, improbably, which included Botticelli's *Birth of Venus*. Seeing such great paintings and being associated with first-rate people who excavated or did research themselves were important parts of my education.

After I graduated in 1942, I went to work at the Art Association of Montreal, now the Montreal Museum of Fine Arts. At that point the association felt they should be more responsible to the public so they hired Arthur Lismer, a member of the Group of Seven, to head an education program. He was a highly intelligent, dynamic, and unconventional man. It's hard to adequately convey a sense of his creative energy, only part of which went into his painting. He made his office into a gathering place in wartime Montreal for artists like Alex Colville and Aba Bayefsky, so I came to know many of them. I was theoretically Lismer's secretary, which meant I did everything from organizing art classes to lecturing in his place if he couldn't make it.

Although Lismer was an extraordinarily generous and kind man — when I turned twenty-one he gave me a small landscape that I still have — I gradually began to realize that our museum was an amateur institution and there was a great deal I didn't know about art. Since Harvard had a famous museum training course, I decided to go there. After passing my general examinations, I was given a fellowship to study in Europe. In those days, the late 1940s, a number of interesting Canadians travelled in and out of Paris — people like Jean-Luc Pepin and Pierre Trudeau, whom I'd known at Harvard — and we had a very good time together. Eventually, I did my dissertation on the group portraits of Degas and, since I had to earn a living, taught at two women's colleges, Skidmore and Mount Holyoke. In the summers I went to France.

The main problem with Mount Holyoke was its geographical isolation. Living in what was essentially a community of women, however admirable and intelligent they were, intensified the isolation. I missed the company of men, and just as I was about to sign a contract committing myself to another three years, I decided to make a change. I ended up in California for nine years, teaching at the University of California at Riverside, which is where I was working when I was approached by the Art Gallery of Ontario.

Four years and two jobs later, I became the first woman director of the National Gallery. I was never aware of being a woman while I was doing the job, but I did receive an extraordinary number of honorary degrees, which I know came about because of my sex. In the late 1960s, some institutions felt they had to award honorary degrees to women and my name would automatically come up. It was really a token and it would be wrong to be too flattered by it.

When I was appointed director I reported to a board appointed by the government, specifically for the National Gallery. This structure had been in place for more than fifty years and it worked very well. Unfortunately, some bureaucrats in the federal government persuaded themselves and, in turn, persuaded Judy LaMarsh, then Secretary of State, that we should follow the Smithsonian in Washington, D.C., as a model and create a Crown corporation as an umbrella for all federal museums. Presumably, this would serve their common good. This had not been made clear when they appointed me.

The National Museums of Canada Corporation was implemented in 1968. It was staffed mainly by civil servants rather than museum people and, as a result, they proved very hard to work with. Another problem with the corporation was that a group of trustees whose primary interest was the welfare of the gallery no longer existed. The new structure meant that all the museums were competing with one another and the National Gallery was often sacrificed to less developed institutions.

The condition of the gallery was another irritant. My staff and I spent over two years working with Professor Abraham Rogatnick of the University of British Columbia to determine the requirements for a new building to house the gallery. These requirements were to form the basis for an architectural competition to be administered by the Department of Public Works. I was never involved in the competition beyond getting the Treasury Board to approve it, nor was I consulted or involved in any way in the decision to abandon the results, which was made when I was outside the country.

I can't tell you the exact moment I decided to resign. I'd been thinking about it for some years, but I was obviously torn, because in spite of the constant battles, I loved the job. Eventually, however, fighting with the bureaucracy became too much, and in the spring of 1976 I left to teach at Harvard. Like many administrators, I thought I'd enjoy returning to teaching and research, but I found it much tougher than I'd expected. I hadn't taught for ten years and during that time, from 1966–76, universities had been completely transformed. I had essentially missed the crucial 1960s. Although I had a lot of reading to do to catch up with academic research, this period was extraordinary in terms of my life because it put me in touch with an entire generation of people I wouldn't have known otherwise, some of whom have gone on to great things in the art world.

In 1982, when I was director of the Philadelphia Museum of Art, I was approached by my old acquaintance from Paris, Pierre Trudeau, who was now prime minister, and asked if I'd come back to Canada to head up the Crown corporation that would build the new National Gallery and the Museum of Man, as it was then called. I agreed to be the CEO and chairman of the board of the new Canada Museum Construction Corporation. We'd choose the sites and the architects and supervise the design and construction of the two buildings. The idea behind a Crown corporation was to remove the project from Public Works so the buildings could be completed in a shorter period of time. My mandate was to complete the project within five years, which was quite an undertaking.

I built a tiny nucleus of a staff, solicited advice about sites, and took my recommendations forward to a special Cabinet committee, which included the prime minister. My next task was to see that the architects were chosen. I visited something like sixty architectural firms in Canada. We asked for very brief submissions from twelve and eventually recommended Moshe Safdie for the new National Gallery and Douglas Cardinal, a Métis, which seemed appropriate (although that was not the reason he was unanimously approved by my board and the museum's board), for the National Museum of Man.

Once construction began, my chief role was monitoring the relationships between the architects and the builders. The tensions were enormous and there was tremendous hostility towards the architects. Being a woman didn't help. People in construction aren't used to taking directions from a woman. They think we don't understand bricks and mortar and don't know how to add or multiply.

I was sixty when the government offered me the job, and I thought it would be a great way to spend the last five years of my career. Unfortunately, I had a rather rude awakening. One day in 1985, a few months after the Conservative government came into power, although I don't think that was the cause, I was called in by the clerk of the Privy Council and told that at two o'clock that afternoon a bill would be passed by the House of Commons cancelling my Order in Council appointment. That would be my last day. To be honest, I don't know what the real reason was. I was given the nonsensical explanation that the Privy Council felt this should be a project administered by the Department of Public Works, although they were never able to incorporate the corporation into Public Works even after I left.

I suppose there are always warnings, but you're never totally prepared to be let go. I knew I was having difficulties with certain things — for instance, convincing the Treasury Board. Possibly, being a woman had something to do with it. With hindsight I see that my basic mistake was in not knowing how to play the game and in being more interested in getting the job done than in politicking. Basically, I was never interested enough in that power game. However, even if I'd wanted to play it, I wouldn't have had time.

I suppose I could have made my departure very nasty, and I should have been more hard nosed about bargaining in Privy Council to ensure I got something in return for my compliance. But I was more concerned about how to handle the next few hours so that nothing would interfere with the construction of both buildings. People had to be told I was no longer head, and everything had to continue operating smoothly — not an easy task, particularly since I hadn't been given a sensible explanation for my termination.

At that point I was already at work on the Degas exhibition that would open the new building, so I continued that project. I also worked as an adviser to Marcel Masse, Minister of Communications, for a year.

Since I left I haven't been idle. I've worked on a number of significant catalogues and exhibitions for various museums around the world and spent two years as a special adviser to the Andrew W. Mellon Foundation in New York, among other things. Over these years, except for periods in Jerusalem and as Kress Professor of the National Gallery of Art in Washington, D.C., I have lived in Canada.

In retrospect, I have never regretted accepting our government's invitation to oversee development of new buildings for the National Gallery of Canada and the Canadian Museum of Civilization. The Museum of Civilization, with its imaginative, curving architecture, is a beacon that draws visitors across the Alexandra Bridge from

Ottawa to Hull and is, at the same time, a building that inhabitants of the Gatineau do take pride in. For the National Gallery, on a more difficult site, Safdie followed our directions to leave the façade of the Roman Catholic cathedral in Ottawa, the Basilica, free. This meant it could be seen even from the MacDonald-Cartier bridge, that other access to Hull. Safdie was also asked to expose the side of the neighbouring War Museum and to provide access to the point that is surmounted by a statue of Champlain, who surveys the Ottawa River he explored. In spite of these accommodations, Safdie was able to provide magnificent views of the Parliament Buildings as visitors enter the gallery and blissful vistas over the Ottawa River to Quebec from the workrooms and offices. In considering these political, social, and aesthetic matters, we did not forget the primary purposes of the two museums and their need for special spaces for exhibitions, for various educational activities, for conservation, for workshops, and for storage. I am proud that I had the energy and determination to take both museums so far that no government was able to turn back.

PART 2

BUSINESS AND LAW

"I guess I never thought of balancing. I really just did it all, which fortunately I was able to do because of my tremendous energy."

BARBARA RAE

Barbara Rae was born in Prince George, B.C. in 1931 and grew up in Edmonton. After starting her career as a secretary, in 1972 she became president of Office Assistance in Vancouver and developed the company into the largest office-help placement firm in western Canada. Although she didn't quite finish high school, in 1975 she became the first woman to graduate from the Executive MBA program at Simon Fraser University. Her career is punctuated by many other important "firsts," among them, first woman appointed to the Vancouver Board of Trade (1972) and first — and to date only — woman chancellor of Simon Fraser University (1987). In 1986, she won the YWCA Woman of Distinction Award for Business, in 1987 she became the first — and, again, only to date — woman to win the B.C. Entrepreneur of the Year Award. In 1993 she was awarded the Order of Canada. She currently sits on the boards of a number of Canadian corporations, including B.C. Telecom, CIBC, Noranda, and Xerox Canada.

I was married young, and in 1952 moved to Vancouver. When I went to work for a brand-new kind of business, temporary help, I think my primary motivation was to get to know the city quickly. Like all young brides, I thought I'd be having a family soon, so the idea of working temporarily was very appealing. Six months after I joined I was asked if I'd run the temp desk and if I'd like to buy shares in the company. That was the biggest break of my life. I've always had a tremendous amount of self-confidence and have never shied away from taking risks. Because I didn't have any money, I borrowed $3000 from the Bank of Montreal to purchase my stock. I quickly moved into management and a partnership. If those things hadn't happened, or if I'd had a child right away as I'd hoped, I probably wouldn't have gone on to a career. In 1953 I became a vice-president and never really looked back.

I loved those years of building the business, even though we worked seven days a week. On weekends we economized by not hiring people — we'd go into our office and do the typing ourselves. The growth and the success of the company were exciting and all-consuming. The downside was that I forgot how to do anything else. I wasn't able to separate the business from life and did things like taking the billing to the beach. My social life completely revolved around the company and my partners.

In those days, my husband didn't mind having a workaholic wife because he was a workaholic, too. The success of the company and the improvement in our financial circumstances were sufficient to energize us both. I've always had tons of energy, which I've become convinced is critical to success. I never ran out of steam, even though I was always doing two jobs — one at the office, the other at home — as well as studying something. For a long time, I didn't realize that many people simply don't have my stamina, but without it challenges aren't reachable.

In 1960, my son, Jamie, was born. That year, as well, my husband, who worked for an oil company, was transferred to Kamloops, which meant I had to leave the company and sell many of my shares. Initially, the change in routine was difficult, but after spending time with my baby I soon realized that being forced to stay home was a blessing in disguise. Within a few months, I was so intrigued with my son and aware of what motherhood was teaching me that wild horses couldn't have dragged me back to the office. If we'd remained in Vancouver, I couldn't possibly have stayed home because I was so focused on the company and its success. In Kamloops, my husband was away all week. The townspeople were familiar with oil company families and knew we were just moving through, so we weren't taken in as members of the community. Fortunately, I discovered a recreational paradise,

Shuswap Lake, where I rented a cabin. My husband would leave Monday morning and the baby and I would leave for the lake a few hours later. In the two years I spent there, I read, studied, and played with my son. Since my dad lived in Kelowna, I was able to get to know him again.

Once we got back to Vancouver I returned to Office Assistance, part-time, to start a marketing and sales department. At that point I did one smart thing — I found a housekeeper. She lived a few blocks away, so if I had to work late she'd take Jamie home for dinner, and if he got sick it wasn't a crisis. She was also good for me, and I kept her with me for twenty-five years. I like my house and garden to be neat and clean, and hiring a housekeeper allowed me to maintain my standards, which benefitted my sense of well-being. Unlike some women, I have no trouble delegating domestic work. Even though I'm not working full-time today, I still have a housekeeper. If my home isn't right, I know I don't focus entirely on whatever task is at hand.

In 1966 I returned to the company full-time. When I joined Office Assistance in 1952, I think I had a vision. I knew I didn't want to go into a steno pool or be a secretary, which given my qualifications was what I could realistically achieve. I grew up in Edmonton and, basically, was raised by my mother and grandmother, since my father had moved to Kelowna, B.C., because of his health. We were supposed to join him, but my grandmother got leukemia so that never happened. The sudden twist our lives took when my parents separated influenced me greatly: all of a sudden it was a struggle to get by and the need for an income was obvious. That experience made me value security and motivated me. Even then I could see that women hit what they now call "the glass ceiling."

My mother had been a high school teacher before she married. After my parents separated, she worked in a traditional female area for a life insurance company, and although she was very clever, the opportunities for advancement simply didn't exist. My aunt, who was only five or six years older than I, had taken all the courses at the bank and worked in the foreign exchange department, but she still couldn't be a manager. So I had a clear understanding of the social and economic restrictions on women. Fortunately, that was balanced by my family, who didn't appear to feel there was any limit to what I could do. That combination opened the world for me. I was highly motivated to break through the barriers that limited women and it never occurred to me that I couldn't do whatever I set my mind to.

I had wanted to be a doctor and planned to go to university, but as the time approached it became clear to me that that wasn't an option because of our economic situation. So I left school at seventeen and started clerking at the Bank of Montreal. It was fun. There were many young women like me, and one weekend when the manager's secretary eloped I seized the opportunity to take over her job. I'd never intended to be a secretary — that was beyond my training at the time — but I bluffed my way into it because it was a way to get a higher salary and to do more interesting things. Luckily, I had enough brashness and confidence to carry it off. Unfortunately, when they discovered I was only seventeen, I had to move back to my old job, since the person in the secretarial position had to sign off on things and that required a minimum age of twenty-one. My response was to quit, which shocked everyone.

At that point, I went to work for Edmonton's town planner. Edmonton was booming, and although I really didn't have the training for the position, I had enough talent to do the job. The planner was brilliant and had a real mystique about him. I found the job interesting, and since he had no interest in managing the department, he gave me a tremendous amount of leeway.

When I joined Office Assistance, those job experiences, combined with my lack of qualifications, were very much in my mind. Since the staff were all women, I understood that they didn't have any mystical intelligence that I was lacking. That meant I felt I could do any of the jobs in the company, which was different from my jobs with male bosses. There were no women in management positions at the bank, and the town planner's expertise was so far beyond my realm of experience that I couldn't imagine doing it.

In 1972 the president and CEO of Office Assistance retired and I became president. Our annual revenues were about $1 million and we had forty full-time employees and 300–400 temps in Vancouver. My first step was to start developing branches. We bought several small companies and began to expand geographically. By the end of the 1980s we had expanded across the West and had 175 full-time staff, around 3000 temps, and annual sales of over $40 million. Frankly, it was very easy. We always made a profit. We were very frugal and if we had to operate on a shoestring we knew how to do it, probably because we were an all-women company.

At Office Assistance, the women were very supportive of one another. There was no reason to behave any differently. I wanted every promotional opportunity for women and we deliberately introduced programs that made it easier for women to work for us. I thought we'd do a better job without men because our benefits and employment conditions could be tailor-made for women. For instance, we pioneered maternity leave, and if staff wished, we allowed them to take extended leaves of eighteen months with the guarantee that they could have their same salaries when they returned. We offered three- and four-day weeks as an option — I guess because we were in temporary help, we had more insight into how easy it was to manage with people not being at work five days a week. Even though July and August were our busiest times, we instituted a policy that mothers of school-aged children could take holidays then since children were out of school.

I was committed to helping women fulfil their career potential while raising families because I felt badly that circumstances were often hard for women. I'd seen many women, including those on career paths, give up wonderful opportunities because they couldn't cope at home. When I got to know the women employed with us, I discovered that I could always find ways to work something out.

Offering our employees higher salaries was a bit of a problem since their pay wasn't determined by us, but by the market. Giving employees the opportunity to buy stock in the company was a way to balance this. We provided no-interest loans to purchase shares and let employees pay back the money over five years. It wasn't that we were more generous — we were different. We started instituting these policies in the late 1960s and were so far ahead of everyone else that we didn't realize how innovative we were. Later, when people started asking me to give speeches and I talked about profit sharing and flex-time policies, businessmen in the audience seemed to think it was corny. There was lack of interest in and understanding of what we were doing, and I was almost embarrassed to let too many people know about it.

Since I had started as a secretary and had no formal education, as the company grew I began to realize I needed some academic credentials to earn the respect of my male peers in business. In 1972 I enrolled in the Executive MBA program at Simon Fraser University. I was the first woman in the program and the only female in a class of sixty. I suppose I should have been intimidated since I didn't have a high school diploma, much less an undergraduate degree, but I did well on the Graduate Record Exam and I was running a fairly substantial company. I simply didn't let any potential feelings of inadequacy get to me. I loved the program and worked very hard. The culture was very male, but I was too busy to let that bother me. I found the world of commerce so fascinating that it took twenty years before I stopped reading business books and picked up a novel.

In those days, feminism was very much in the news, but I wasn't involved with the women's movement. I figured if I gave 150 percent of myself to what I was doing in my own incubator, I'd be making an adequate contribution to women's rights. Now I can see that not being a blatant feminist helped to get me admitted into a lot of male bastions. In 1972, for instance, I became the first woman director of the Board of Trade even though I was youngish, and certainly not one of the men.

In 1976 my husband and I separated. Although my success contributed to the breakup of my marriage, I think my energy level was the major factor. I was a whirling dervish and my husband wanted a more quiet life. As a single woman executive, I was different. I wasn't part of the social stream and I was vaguely aware of the difference in my status. For instance, the men at the Board of Trade seemed to be friends with one another and were involved in a lot of "couples" social interaction that didn't include me. Actually, I was relieved not to be part of that. I was very busy with what I was doing. I wasn't dating and I didn't want to be set up with people. I was well past fifty before I felt comfortable with that group and began to be fully accepted by them. I don't know if acceptance came with the passage of time and my advanced age, or with the change in my marital circumstances. After my husband and I separated, I was single until 1983, but once I remarried I quickly moved into the group and at that point I enjoyed it. The man I married was vice-president of a university and was very much involved in being invited places. Initially, I went as George's wife, but soon the invitations came for me and he started attending events as Barbara's husband.

I suppose my ambition for an element of wealth and security has played a big role in my success. My ability to prioritize and my need to be immersed in what I'm doing have helped me to achieve those goals. I don't just start things — I finish them, and finish them well. I don't get distracted. I have a tremendous ability to focus and I'm never overwhelmed. I can break things into their components and master them. My weakness is taking on too much and trying always to fulfil other people's expectations. I find it hard to say I can't take something on and I haven't figured out why that's the case. Maybe I need to prove to myself that I can do it all.

When I was moving forward in business, there were virtually no women ahead of me, so female mentors were absent. But I'd classify my grandmother as a mentor. She always felt I could do anything and I felt very special with her. When I took over Office Assistance in 1972, I hired a management consultant to help us to expand. He was very interested in us because our ideas about changing the way work is organized were so far ahead of any group he'd worked with and he taught me a lot about organizations. My second husband has also been a great help because he's accepted me as I am. When I was younger, I pretended I was a little different than I am by hiding my light under a bushel, which is something many women do. I think young women in particular tend to play the traditional female role because they're not confident in their femininity. Women are expected to behave dependently, and I tried to project that when it wasn't reality. As I've aged, I've become more comfortable with myself. I've allowed myself to be proud of the fact that I can run the house and run the office.

My only regret is that I didn't have more children. I had four pregnancies, which resulted in two infant deaths and one miscarriage. A family of four children would have been better for both me and my son. Since my family lived in Edmonton when I lived in Vancouver, the company became my family, and siblings would have provided a better balance for my son.

In 1983 a large Swiss company, ADIA, wanted to expand to Canada and approached Office Assistance. At this point, temporary help was becoming global and getting to be big business. Coincidentally, two of the senior shareholding partners in Office Assistance wanted to retire. We sold eighty percent of the company to ADIA. In 1990, the Swiss group sold ADIA to a German group who wanted to own one hundred percent of Office Assistance, and the price was great! I became chairman for a while, before resigning completely from the company in 1995.

After I left the company I was invited to join several corporate boards of directors. Today, directorships are onerous because corporations look to their directors for governance. Most of mine involve travelling from Vancouver to Toronto, so that and volunteer work keep me very busy. We have a lovely place at Whistler. We hike, bike, ski, and invite friends to visit. I love to entertain, to keep house, and to cook. I still have a part-time housekeeper, so she gets things half done and leaves the fun part to me.

Looking back, I really don't think I'd do anything differently. I'm proud of the role I played in building Office Assistance and I think that our image as a highly successful female company has been both valuable and unique.

"Because I was first so often in my career, I was always told I couldn't take the next step. The message was, for example, 'you've become an account manager but don't expect to make senior account manager.' Once I achieved that position, it was assistant vice-president, and so on. I guess part of my personality thrives on challenges. If someone tells me I can't do something, I'm bound and determined to prove them wrong."

BRUNA GIACOMAZZI

As chief credit officer of the Hongkong Bank of Canada, Bruna Giacomazzi is the first woman to achieve that position and one of the highest ranking women in Canada's banking community. The daughter of Italian immigrants who farmed in B.C.'s Lower Mainland, she is unusual for having achieved her objectives without a university degree. In recent years, she has made a commitment to encourage other women, not only within the bank but also within the community, through her involvement in numerous boards of community organizations. Along with former Prime Minister Kim Campbell, she was one of the originators of The Women's National Retreat, a by-invitation-only event for senior women from many walks of life.

My big break came in 1971 when I was hired by the Mercantile Bank as Assistant Manager, Consumer Credit — that is, the number two position of a two-"man" retail credit department. Although there were no female bank managers at the Mercantile, I knew from talking to people that they were a little more *au courant* than Household Finance, where I'd been since 1965.

I'd started as a clerk-typist after taking a secretarial program at a community college. I was determined to do something that interested me, and teaching and nursing — the two obvious options for girls — didn't turn me on. I could have gone to university, but all the women graduates I knew were working as secretaries. It seemed silly to invest all that time for nothing. I figured it might take me longer than the guys to get ahead, but I'd do it anyway.

I grew up on a dairy farm about forty miles east of Vancouver. Being a farm kid taught me many valuable skills and some important lessons that have served me well throughout my career. Certainly, I learned the value of hard work. Also, discrimination was non-existent. When work needed to be done, it didn't matter whether you were the youngest or the oldest, male or female. If you were available, you did it.

I was blessed with loving, industrious parents. My father died twenty-five years ago and my mother, who just turned eighty-nine, is still my mentor and my inspiration. She emigrated from Italy with little education, but she's a wise woman who really believes in fairness and equality. For instance, she tells a story about when we got hot water on the farm. Since it was expensive, my father and my uncle, who were partners, decided it should be reserved for the barn. When common sense and persuasion didn't convince the men, my mother went on strike. She stopped cooking and went to bed until they gave in. There are many stories like that. She fights for what she believes in and I hope I got that quality from her.

When I started at Household Finance, I was full of aspirations. My first goal was to become training supervisor, which took three years. I had to be twenty-one to qualify for the job and shortly after my twenty-first birthday, I was promoted. I learned a lot in that job and, until I got bored, it was a wonderful experience. Monotony really motivates me; once I master a job I want to do something else, which is usually more. That's probably my dominant drive.

In those days, women couldn't be branch managers at Household Finance, but they had another position, credit interviewer, which was the equivalent of an assistant manager position except it didn't lead to the manager's job. I thought I'd become a credit interviewer for a while and hope to change their minds about women. With hindsight, I was pretty naive. I hadn't anticipated that my management skills and abilities would be relegated to a helping role. Because of my training background, I trained the guys who became assistant managers. They made $50 more a month than I did; and since I made only $200, that was a significant amount. I was posted to branches where the new recruits (all male) were sent. I also relieved branches if someone was sick — but nobody was supposed to know this, because it wasn't allowed. I worked for some great guys who were good mentors, but gradually I began to realize there was no way they would change their minds about promoting a woman.

In 1971 the climate suddenly shifted. Women employees of Household Finance in the U.S. brought a class action suit for gender discrimination against the company, and when they won a huge settlement, I was approached and asked if I'd become Canada's first female branch manager. Initially, it seemed wonderful. However, the company blew it when they asked me to take the same two-year training program as the guys I'd been training. It seemed they were trying to delay the inevitable, so when the Mercantile offered me a position equivalent to Household Finance's assistant manager, I was ready to move.

About six months after I joined the Mercantile, the guy who was running the department quit. At his urging, the company offered me his job. Because I would have been the first woman in that role, I was offered a six-month trial with a tiny raise to offset the additional responsibility. However, the deal was I'd have to do my old job, too. I was young and wanted the job so badly I could taste it. I reasoned that it wasn't the first time I'd had to work twice as hard as a man. Six months later, when I knocked on the door to remind management I had succeeded, they gave me the title and another small raise.

In 1975, the bank had an opening as an account manager on the commercial side. One other woman in Vancouver and one in the East were account managers, and although the move was a lateral one for me, it would give me experience in commercial lending. The environment was very intimidating for someone who hadn't gone to university. All the guys had MBAs — there were even a couple of Ph.D.s — and for the first time I began to seriously regret my lack of a university degree. I worried a lot about what I didn't know and was terrified I might fail.

That move was my first big challenge, but I had nothing to lose. I was single. I figured if worst came to worst I could always return to retail or consumer credit. I worked like a dog and took a lot of night school courses — anything that would help me with the financial aspect of the job — and my diligence paid off. In 1976, five years after joining the bank, I was promoted to senior account manager, becoming the first woman to reach that level at the Mercantile. Since then, I've been the first woman in every job I've had.

Over the years, one thing I've learned is how to get along with the guys and talk their language. I wasn't one of the boys in that I tried to be like them — I think I've always been very much a woman — but guys have a different way of getting things done. There's lots of kibitzing and camaraderie and they're a bit less judgemental than women, which helps to build the team.

Anyway, here I was, a senior account manager with account trainees who were a group of MBAs fresh out of university. One, who was struggling with his lack of work experience, I took under my wing and I gained two valuable lessons from him. First, that I had learned things on the job, like how to make decisions, that he hadn't learned in university — in other words, I had "street smarts." The second lesson was accidental. This guy was an account trainee, two levels down from me. One day when I took some papers back to his desk, I noticed his pay slip and discovered he was making almost three times as much as I was! I slept on the information because I've learned you should never take action or make a decision when you're angry or emotional. The next morning I marched into the vice-president's office and calmly relayed my information. The company couldn't give me such a big increase all at once — why I'll never know, since I couldn't get an explanation. Instead, they gave me a raise every six months for the next two years to catch me up.

Although I was advancing steadily in my career, being the most senior woman in the bank didn't protect me from gender friction. One evening the bank held a function at the Vancouver Club to say goodbye to the president and welcome his successor. We were a little short staffed at the time so some junior administrators, including one other woman, were invited to fill the table. By now I'd had some experience with the Vancouver Club. About six months earlier, I'd been invited to a lunch that was quite an eye-opener. Just before noon, the senior vice-president phoned and asked me to go with him. I was very excited since I'd never been to the Vancouver Club before, and I was thrilled he was escorting me. In fact, I was so caught up in positive thoughts that the significance didn't register when we stood outside the fire escape and knocked at the door. It didn't even dawn on me when we got into the freight elevator. I finally began to sense something was amiss when the doors of the elevator opened into the kitchen. We passed the stoves, the sinks, and the men in their white uniforms and chefs' hats and emerged into a comfortable reception area where all my colleagues were waiting. They seemed uncomfortable, probably because they'd been told how I was getting there. I was still in a bit of a daze when they started talking about how terrible the club was because it discriminated against Jewish people, natives, and so on. Not once did they mention women.

Six months later, there I was again. This time I had to go through the side door, which to some was progress. The dinner was very nice and at the end of the meal the senior vice-president indicated — I forget how he put it — that snooker would be played on the third floor and that some of us would have to leave. By now I knew no women were allowed on the third floor, period. I found the other woman and told her we had to go. She didn't realize what was happening, and as the group trooped downstairs she kept asking me why we were leaving. I told her to get her coat and I'd explain later. I knew it wasn't an appropriate time to make a statement.

When the new president came down to say goodbye, he looked worried. He took my hand to shake it and, holding it longer than usual, said, "I'm very, very sorry about this." Although he and I have never discussed the evening, I knew from his body language and the tone in his voice that he was saying this should not be happening.

I hoped I was a first-class lady in how I handled it. "I'm very sorry I have to leave, too," I said pointedly.

The worst part of it was that of the people there, I was one of the most senior. People junior to me were getting a rare opportunity to network with the president, which I was being denied.

The next day the vice-president tried to raise the subject at a staff meeting. I said the experience had been so painful I couldn't talk about it. The story got around, and since we were a close group, people felt badly. Everyone at the dinner sought us out and apologized. Nobody wanted to see that happen and it motivated people to start looking at women's issues in a serious way. After that, things started to change.

Sometimes, not making a statement can work to your benefit. Because of the way I handled the situation at the Vancouver Club, I got the attention of the president. About six months later there was an opening in Montreal for a credit job, and he chose me for the position. It was a tremendous opportunity, which, with hindsight, turned out to be the key catalyst in my career, because it forced me to grow. Prior to moving to Montreal, many of my performance reviews said I needed more confidence in myself. Like many women, I think I suffered from what psychologists describe as "the impostor syndrome," which afflicts some women fulfilling traditional masculine roles. Basically, you believe you don't know what you're doing and fear you'll be exposed. My experience in Montreal allowed me to recognize my competence, and my financial knowledge and expertise grew by leaps and bounds. One incident in particular turned on the lightbulb. I had been asked to prepare a couple of Harvard-style case studies for presentation in a senior credit training course. I was lecturing on a case when I suddenly realized that somebody with a grade twelve education was teaching not only a bunch of MBAs, but also some people in the bank who were much more senior. At that point I finally saw — and, perhaps more importantly, accepted — that I really knew what I was talking about. I wasn't an "impostor."

In 1980, nine years after joining the bank, I was promoted to assistant vice-president. That was an important step, in part because I finally got paid the same as the guys at my level but also because it was an opportunity to demonstrate that I could market the bank. When I'd first started in banking, I was told that I'd never succeed because I couldn't hunt and fish with the guys. One of my customers owned a fleet of boats and one day, about a year after my promotion, the president of the company, his chief financial officer, my account manager, and I made arrangements to go fishing for a day.

Since I grew up on a farm, I knew how to fish. I should have twigged that I was probably the only one with that skill when I saw all the new rods and when the owner of the boat came on deck with a book of instructions. To make a long story short, I had to put all the lines on the rods and bait the hooks because the guys didn't want to touch the live fish. Not only did I catch the lone fish that day, I also had to clean it. I had been told so many times that I'd fail at marketing because I couldn't be part of the male-bonding experiences — like fishing — that I was laughing inside. Sure, I wouldn't go to girlie shows, but there are other ways to build relationships.

Because the Mercantile was a small organization, getting people to move across the country was difficult, which meant that sometimes the right person for a promotion wouldn't get the job because he was so useful where he was. When I say "he," it's because they were all he's in those days. In the early 1980s I sat on a task force which concluded, among other things, that we were losing people in part because we were asking them to stay in jobs where they were needed, rather than providing them with promotional opportunities. So we decided to give qualified assistant vice-presidents the title of vice-president if they had achieved five very specific criteria.

The bank started with three appointments. I should point out that during the life of the task force the other members would often use me as an example of someone who should be promoted when setting the criteria. However, when the appointments were made, I didn't make it, even though I was the only one who qualified on all five criteria. A guy who met only two of the criteria was promoted, which came as quite a shock.

When I started calling people to find out what had happened, I learned he got the title — over the objections of the committee — because he was making noises about leaving the bank and they didn't want him to go. They didn't think I'd leave because I was loyal. That night, I went home and bawled my eyes out. I was very hurt. I had worked so hard and met all their damn criteria, and in the end it didn't matter. It was also embarrassing. Everybody I worked with, including the guy who got the promotion, made a point of apologizing to me.

A year later, when I got the title of vice-president, it didn't have the same impact. In 1985, when the Mercantile was sold to the National Bank, I had some tough decisions to make. I was offered a job, but with reduced responsibilities and downgrading to the title of senior manager, B.C. A few days earlier I'd had lunch with a former colleague who had been out of work for about eight months. He looked like he'd aged about ten years. He strongly advised me to take the job because I'd be in a better position to find another if I was employed. I took his advice, and after what I call my "year of character building," I moved to the Hongkong Bank of Canada, as an assistant vice-president, with the understanding that I'd be a vice-president once it was approved by the board. That commitment was kept.

I don't want to leave the impression that the Mercantile was a terrible employer. My negative experiences reflected the climate of the times and could be duplicated at any corporation. I received great training and was fortunate to work with some wonderful mentors, many of whom I keep in touch with. Most of my memories are very positive.

At the Hongkong Bank I was the first woman assistant vice-president, and my peer group was not particularly welcoming. It took several years to settle in, but once I did, I decided it was time to start making changes for women. The first time I had to fill a branch manager position, human resources developed a list of candidates — all guys whose only experience was on the commercial side. I decided we could do better and, after some digging, came up with a woman who did a wonderful job. She was the first of many women branch managers. Qualified women were being passed over by guys with much less experience, and gender was the only apparent difference. When I left that job, twenty-five percent of our branch managers were female. Although I'm still the most senior woman in the bank, we now have two female senior vice-presidents, and four female vice-presidents, which is pretty good. I've really enjoyed the last couple of years now that I'm not the only woman.

The older I get, the more pleasure I take in destroying myths about women, such as lying about your age. I'm turning fifty this year and I'm proud of it. Like everyone else, I've had my ups and downs, but I've learned some valuable lessons over those years and I'm not ashamed of growing older. That's one reason I decided to come out of the closet about menopause. Although it's no different from any other bodily function, women are supposed to keep it a secret.

When I made the decision not to take hormone replacement therapy, I knew I'd probably have hot flashes, and I worried about how to handle that if one happened during an important meeting. At that point I was still running Special Credit. My job involved negotiating, where body language is important because it tells you a lot about what the other person is thinking. I had my first hot flash during a tough negotiation with three elderly men and a male member of my staff. I could tell they noticed something was wrong and I didn't want them to think they were scoring points — that I was upset and therefore in a weak position. So when one of them stopped talking in midsentence, I said, "Look, I know I'm probably red in the face, but I'm just having a hot flash. I'm going through menopause." Their faces went beet red and they clearly lost their momentum. After that, the negotiating turned into a short session. I don't want to take credit, but from the bank's perspective the meeting was successful.

After it was over, my senior manager asked if I was okay. We had a staff meeting immediately following the negotiation. I told him to go on to it while I went to the washroom to throw some cold water on my face. I guess he told everyone because I could hear laughter as I came down the hall, but when I opened the door there was dead silence. I chose to make a joke about the situation, which worked well. Later, one of the guys gave me a poster that read "I'm Not Having a Hot Flash. It's a Power Surge," which I hung on my office wall. The whole bank knows I'm going through menopause and that's fine. If I was pregnant they'd all know, too. Now all the women in the bank who are either approaching menopause or going through it come to discuss it with me, so I'm mentoring in that area, also.

In 1989, I met my husband. He's a great guy who had been a police officer with the Vancouver police force for twenty years. He's brought balance to my life, he fits in well with my friends and my family, and he's a great support. In fact, I've had two big promotions since we met and I couldn't have handled them as well as I did without his backing. Probably my only regret is that I never had children. When Bob and I got together, we talked about it a lot. He would have made a wonderful father, but I was well into my forties and had a couple of health problems, so it was just too late.

People have asked me what sacrifices I've made for my career. I don't think you make sacrifices. I think you make choices. But sometimes those choices are tough, especially when they have long-term effects. Overall, I'm happy with my choices and I'd change very little if I had to do it all over again — even the experiences that were the most difficult at the time. In the long run, I've learned, the tough lessons bring you the most good because they teach you so much.

"My mother had a tremendous sense of optimism. She used to say 'if you set your goals high enough, you'll ultimately find ways to get there.'"

MAUREEN KEMPSTON DARKES

In 1994, at the age of forty-five, Maureen Kempston Darkes became the first woman president of General Motors Canada. Trained as a lawyer, and the only woman included on the Globe and Mail's *survey of the country's most powerful CEOs, she holds an influential position among Canada's business élite. She credits her success to, among other things, a strong work ethic, a willingness to take risks, and her mother's influence.*

In 1975 I was practising corporate and commercial law with Osler, Hoskin and Harcourt in Toronto. Osler's is an outstanding firm and I thoroughly enjoyed working there, but I was young and thought it would be beneficial to see another side of the law, so when I was offered the opportunity, I joined General Motors of Canada's legal staff. My intention was to stay for a couple of years, then return to a law firm, but since arriving at GM I've never looked back. I love the challenge, the products, and working with the people.

GM is the largest industrial company in Canada, which means I'm able to address complex issues, often with multinational dimensions and global implications. As a bonus, our products are among the most exciting in the world. Everyone is interested in vehicles. Think about what it takes to get a vehicle to market — the engineers, the research and safety scientists, the designers, the product and marketing planners, among many others, as well as the hands-on employees. One of my favourite parts of the job is going to the plants to watch the cars and trucks being built and to share the enthusiasm of our employees as they see a new vehicle take shape.

I certainly didn't set out thinking that one day I'd be president of GM of Canada. Throughout my career, opportunities opened up, and I suppose I've helped that process along by taking risks. After leaving the legal staff, I moved into the tax group. Then I went to New York and worked in GM's worldwide treasury group for a couple of years. When I came back to Canada I went into treasury and then corporate affairs. I was appointed Vice-President, Corporate Affairs and elected to the board of directors in 1991.

Naturally, there have been times when work has disrupted my family life. My husband, Larry, and I have had to adjust our ways of living, particularly during the two years I spent in New York and commuted back and forth. But I always loved the adventure of getting on a road and seeing where it took me. I won't say I didn't worry about failing. I've had some sleepless nights — everybody does — but in the end you've just got to bear down and get through the difficult times. Of course, there's another way of looking at this — without a risk, the reward may not be as great.

I guess I have a lot of self-confidence. I think a great deal of that came from my mother. My father died when I was twelve and his death left my mother with three children to support, which was quite a struggle. Since she didn't have a lot of options, she went back to work as a secretary in a bank. Even with her limited income, she was confident that she could keep the family going. Her "can do" attitude was key to her success. She used to say, "The only time you're beaten is the time you're not there." That was her way of saying, "Wade in, go forward, and make a difference." In many respects, she was an incredible role model.

Work was a positive ideal. My father was an accountant and my parents immigrated from Ireland with a vision of a good life for their children. After my father's death, seeing my mother work as hard as she did to maintain a family on a secretary's income sent a very powerful message. It made me understand from an early age that marriage is not the be-all and end-all for a woman. I recognized the value of self-sufficiency, because nobody knows what the future will bring.

Given our financial situation, my two brothers and I understood clearly that education was our route to a better life. I was a good student who enjoyed school and worked hard. I had two summer jobs to earn money for university and when you work that hard to get an education, you know you've got to make a success of it. I had all kinds of jobs, from playground director to night-time receptionist. On Friday nights and Saturdays I worked at the local community centre, cooking hot dogs and hamburgers and serving soft drinks. I took work where I could get it.

I think I always wanted to achieve. As a child, I used to read adventure books about people accomplishing remarkable things and think how wonderful it would be to do that. The belief in one's ability to achieve was a wonderful aspect of my school years. The teachers encouraged us to do better and better and wouldn't let us get away with mediocre work. I was never told I couldn't do something. I was told, "Here's a challenge — now go and do it." I wanted to get marks as high or higher than the boys and nobody said I shouldn't or couldn't. That spirit carried over into our recreational time. The girls and boys played basketball, volleyball, and hockey together. In the winter we played shinny for hours on end on a rink in our backyard. My brothers used to dress me up in goalie pads and practise shooting pucks at me!

Originally, I wanted to be a history professor, specializing in Canadian studies, but while I was at university the real world caught up with me. I knew there weren't many jobs. In our family it was okay to spend a great deal of time at university, but you couldn't go from living on student loans to old-age pension, so I decided to try law school.

When I enrolled at the University of Toronto's Faculty of Law, I was not among a particularly large group of women, although that was beginning to change. People questioned my decision to embark on another study program. "Why bother?" some asked. "You're just going to get married."

My mother's response was always, "She's going to get educated first."

After I articled, I did corporate and commercial law at Osler's, where Madame Justice Bertha Wilson, the first woman member of the Supreme Court of Canada, was still a practising lawyer. Although she probably doesn't realize it, she was a role model for me, and many others, I'm certain. I looked up to her with great respect and awe. She had an outstanding intellect — greater than anyone with whom I've ever had an opportunity to work. Moreover, if she didn't think the authorities were right, she'd challenge them. I also admired her ability to deal with issues in ways that were businesslike, yet had an element of personal warmth. Being able to observe her, to see her in action and, ultimately, to read some of her judgments, was an inspiration.

When I joined GM there weren't many women in the company. We knew we wanted to attract more — that's just common sense if you want to tap into the best people — but we also recognized that recruiting women would be easier said than done. We knew that women needed the opportunity to relate to other women, to discuss issues among themselves, and to generally develop a sense of belonging to the company. At the same time, management was in need of advice about how to work with the culture of the company to make it more welcoming for women and people from minority groups.

So, about fifteen years ago, I was part of a group that founded the GM of Canada Woman's Advisory Council — a change agent that is active at the policy level. Among other things, the council provides senior management with advice on issues of importance to women, as well as with ideas about how we might resolve those issues and change the company culture. I'm very proud of the work that group has done and continues to do. Over the years, it has been particularly interesting to observe how programs designed to address women's needs often evolve into programs to serve people. Job sharing, for instance. Although it was initially perceived as a woman's issue, job sharing has become a useful tool for men who are contemplating retirement because it offers them a way to ease out of the workplace.

A company with the clout of GM can also act as a catalyst for change outside its own organization. For example, several years ago, I advised the law firms we do business with that we expected to see women and people from visible minorities working on GM cases. This happened and the results were impressive. I always say to women, the goal is not just to do what men have done; the goal is to put your own stamp on something and in so doing to create greater equity for everyone.

I suppose one downside of my job is loneliness. I hope I have an ability to connect with people throughout the organization, but when you're the boss there are times you can't really share everything. Also, the demands of the job are such that you cannot spend as much time as you would like with people on a one-to-one basis. Fortunately, I have a supportive husband and family, which helps a great deal.

I met my husband, who is a lawyer, on our first day of law school. We've been married for over twenty years and I don't think I could do this job without him. When I've had a really rough day, Larry's the person who is always there, and I respect and appreciate that. Sometimes, I'd just like to get away with him for a while, but I don't have as much time as I'd like to do that or to enjoy a social life. We built a cottage up north where my mom and dad had a little log cabin when I was a kid. When I have time, I go up there and enjoy the tranquillity. I like to swim, cross-country ski, and soak up the quietness. I also enjoy connecting with people outside the business. In 1996, I trained with three other women to run a marathon. We had some good fun doing that — I guess I shouldn't say fun, because it was pretty exasperating at times. But it was worth the effort.

I suppose my volunteer activities reflect my interests. I'm an honorary patron of an organization called New Directions, which helps women who have been recently widowed, separated, or divorced. If that group had existed years ago, it would have been a great help to my mother. I know what she went through. I understood that some days she was very lonely and I recognized how hard it was for her to bring up a family on her own. I'm involved with that group because I like to think that in a small way I can give something back to some other women who are going through that pain.

I've been involved, as well, with women's health issues, and not only because they affect me directly. Women are a big part of our customer base and we now employ significant numbers of women, so their health and well-being are crucial to the success of GM. Within the company, I also try to mentor other people. Many people — women and men — helped me to achieve this position by reaching out and providing support when I needed it. I've talked to some women who think mentoring is a sign of weakness because it places women in the traditional role of being "helpers." I don't see that at all. Men help other men and some have helped me. It's the role of senior managers to develop the best people we can.

I know it was of great significance to be the first woman president of GM Canada, but I try not to think about that because the challenges I face are the same whether the president is a man or a woman. Quite frankly, I'm proud to be a woman in this job. If my being in the job can help other women, then I'm proud of that, too. But at the end of the day I set that aside, because my need is to focus on the business and achieve the necessary results, and that has nothing to do with being a man or a woman.

I don't have many regrets, but in the past few years, as I've spent more and more time in the business, I've felt I may not have done as much on the family side as I would have liked. I think that comes with the territory and I have to do a better job of prioritizing. I want to spend more time with my husband — there is so much we want to do together. I enjoyed my mother's company, but she died a little while ago and I wish I'd spent more time with her during those last few years.

In June 1996, my alma mater, the University of Toronto, awarded me an honorary doctor of law degree, which was very exciting. The only sad note was my mother's absence. I felt her loss that day as much as I did on the day she died. I know how important education was to her and how proud she would have been to be there.

"Although my beginnings were very humble, they were also very rich, because they gave me many things that money can't buy — a sense of security, a sense of identity and a sense of cultural connection. They also gave me the ability to dream."

CORRINE SPARKS

When Corrine Sparks was appointed to the Nova Scotia Family Court in March 1987, she became the first Black Nova Scotian to be appointed to the bench and Canada's first Black woman judge. She grew up in a Black community on the outskirts of Dartmouth, attended Mount Saint Vincent University, and graduated from Dalhousie Law School in 1979. In 1999, after the federal government became responsible for appointments to the provincial Supreme Court, Corrine Sparks, by then Nova Scotia's most senior female judge, was not re-appointed to the bench.

A judgeship certainly wasn't something I searched out, and when I consider that now, I feel it had to do with precedents. I didn't dare to dream about being a judge because there had never been a Black judge in Nova Scotia. Back in those days, I also assumed that judgeships went to rich and powerful people, so I didn't think it was within my realm of professional possibilities.

In 1987, I was practising law in Dartmouth with three partners when I received a call from the minister. He was a noted historian who took a special interest in the Black community, and it was common knowledge in the legal community that there was a vacancy on the bench. Although I was aware of the opening, I never saw myself in the role. Actually, I knew of others who were likely candidates for the position.

At the time I had a rather high-profile case, so when the minister asked me to meet with him, I assumed it concerned the case. I packed up my briefcase with relevant material and headed off. I quickly discovered he didn't want to talk about the case at all. He told me that he was considering me for the available judgeship.

Although I'd never aspired to the judiciary, I'd always had a strong desire to succeed. My parents were devoted to their children and they had a great appreciation for education and its ability to open doors, which, I suppose, stemmed from their being denied those opportunities themselves. Today, people say my parents must have been extraordinary — and in the sense that they were instrumental in planting the seeds of ambition, they were. But there were other significant people in my life who caused these seeds to germinate. Certainly, my parents always encouraged me to have a better life, but what does a better life mean when your parents haven't had the benefit of higher education? To them, a better life would have meant being a secretary or perhaps a teacher. I think being a lawyer or a judge was beyond their scope of expectations for their daughter at that time.

When I look back on my childhood, I realize that life must have been very difficult for my parents. However, I wasn't overly aware of that at the time because our home life was stable, secure, and loving. Community life primarily revolved around the church, which, I think, is typical in many Black communities in Nova Scotia. I suppose that led me away from my family, but in a constructive way, since it broadened my experience by providing an opportunity to travel to different churches across the province and to interact with young people from various communities.

As the eldest child in my family, I was constantly told by my parents that I had to set an example for my eight siblings, so I was an industrious and diligent student who always had a part-time job. I loved to learn. I went to the library frequently, and as a result books became a powerful force in my life. Reading exposed me to a world beyond my own little community, and this caused me to dream about possibilities.

I was quiet and shy as a student, and I worked very hard. I knew from an early age that economically I wanted my life to be better than my parents'. I attended a segregated elementary school, and upon reflection realize how educationally deprived the students were. The resources were insufficient — we didn't even have a school library. However, we did have extremely dedicated teachers who appeared to love their work. Despite the material shortcomings, my school years were very positive. I had several teachers, both male and female, who really helped me along the way. Maybe my teachers saw some potential in me that I didn't see myself at the time. In my high school, which was integrated, I had one teacher from India who was a powerful influence. He exposed me to several university libraries in the Halifax–Dartmouth area and nurtured my love of reading.

While I was attending high school, I had this vague idea that I wanted to go to university, but since no one in my family had ever pursued higher education, that wasn't a natural evolution. Although I might have drifted in that direction without the nurturing I received from teachers, their encouragement was pivotal. For example, without my knowledge, the principal of my high school arranged a bursary for me through the local Rotary Club. It represented a lot of money in those days and certainly made attending university much easier. In addition, the Sisters of Charity at Mount Saint Vincent University took a special interest in the local Black women and offered scholarships, one of which I was fortunate enough to receive. Consequently, my years at Mount Saint Vincent were basically debt-free. These days I wonder if I would have been able to complete university if I had not received so much moral and financial support.

Mount Saint Vincent provided me with a very rewarding learning experience. At that time, it was a small, intimate, all-female campus and the Sisters of Charity reached out to all of the students by providing extra educational supports such as tutoring. Perhaps more importantly, they gave young women the sense that we had an individual and a collective destiny. I believe that imbued us with self-confidence. The president at that time, Sister Catherine Wallace, who is now deceased, was an outspoken, elegant, dignified woman, and there was no question she was in charge of the university. The image of such strong, competent women had a powerful effect on me. That was how the world worked — women held leadership positions. Being provided with that role model helped to shape my own self-image.

Being at an all-women university gave me the sense that women achievers were the norm. It wasn't until later that I recognized the monumental challenges that women confront in trying to move beyond gender stereotyping. In a sense my world had always been protected. My mother was strong and encouraging and then I moved into a university setting that was dominated by strong and powerful women. I didn't realize how pivotal those experiences were until much later.

After my attendance at Mount Saint Vincent, the two most appealing options to me were obtaining a master's degree in economics or attending law school. Career ambitions have a lot to do with what you have been exposed to, and since I highly respected many of my teachers, initially I aspired to be a history teacher. While at university, I changed my academic direction. Likely, exposure to the social sciences influenced my decision to change my major from history to economics and political science. Probably, I liked political science more, but coming from a working-class background, economics seemed to offer more career opportunities. After I graduated, I found a position as an investigator at the Human Rights Commission. During my employment there, I began to think about a career in the legal profession. As an investigator, I began to see how the law can facilitate equality.

In 1974, I enrolled in the Faculty of Law at Dalhousie, but I soon began to experience mixed feelings about being there. Only two other Black students were in law, both male. The business of learning law as it was then taught was highly competitive, contrary to the supportive environment at Mount Saint Vincent. With hindsight, I can see that law school was a terribly male-dominated culture and, of course, the adversarial nature of law was difficult for me to come to terms with. Like many of my counterparts, my mind would drift and I'd think about discontinuing my studies. Fortunately, I participated in a study group that provided me with considerable support and encouragement.

In those days, issues like race and gender were rarely mentioned in the classroom. For the most part my classmates were very friendly. Still, some sent a message that Black people didn't belong at law school. One can easily envisage how this could create a sense of frustration and alienation. I also sensed that all eyes were on me and felt pressure to succeed, since a number of local Blacks had entered law school and not graduated.

Back in those days, Dalhousie was one of the most prestigious law schools in Canada and, typically, the students who flocked there came from affluent Canadian families. My classmates were often the sons and daughters of judges, prominent politicians, or powerful business-men. "Where do I fit?" is a question I continually asked myself. Many of my fellow students didn't have to worry about surviving on a student loan or juggling a part-time job. It wasn't that they necessar-ily flaunted their wealth and position or did anything deliberately to make me feel out of place — in fact, I made many good friends at law school, some of whom came from those affluent families — but the vast differences were clear. I had never even been exposed to what they had come to expect from life. They were there in large measure because of what their parents expected of them. I was there primarily because of my own dreams and determination to succeed.

Although Canada holds itself out as an egalitarian society, a class structure certainly exists. This has become very clear to me throughout my career and was highlighted during my tenure on the Canadian Bar Association's Gender Equality Task Force. Political, social, and family connections still matter a great deal in the legal profession. If, like the vast majority of Black people, your opportunities to be involved in the political and economic system have been restricted, the higher you move through the echelons, the more disadvantaged you are. When I was younger, I didn't realize how important one's connections are in terms of one's access to society's highly valued opportunities.

When I graduated from Dalhousie Law School as the first Nova Scotia Black woman, I had no sense of myself as a trailblazer. Being young and looking to my immediate future, my next challenge was to obtain a clerkship and eventually full-time employment. In those days, and perhaps it hasn't changed much, it was very difficult for women to get articling positions. Indeed, I am aware of a number of women who graduated from Dalhousie when I did and had to arti-cle without monetary remuneration. However, in my case, good fortune was on my side and I articled in the City Solicitor's Office for the City of Halifax. I later learned that the city solicitor at the time had employed several other women as law clerks.

In the late 1970s, after I was called to the Nova Scotia Bar, the Alberta oil-and-gas-based economy was booming and there were plenty of employment opportunities in that province. So, along with several of my classmates, I went to Alberta. Although I did not become a member of the Alberta Bar, I was able to obtain employment first as a trust officer and later as a senior executive for an oil and gas company.

My time in Calgary was enjoyable, but I do have one negative memory that is so painful I'll never forget it. One Christmas there was an office party at a downtown hotel, and after parking my car I walked into the lobby alone. A hotel employee stopped me and asked what I was doing there. When I told him I was there for a party, he retorted, "We don't want you or your kind in this hotel." In those days, prostitutes frequented that part of the city and I assumed, correctly, that he was assigning me that designation. We had words, and when I eventually arrived at the party I informed my supervisor, who was outraged and complained to the hotel.

I spent two pleasant years in Alberta, but gradually I realized that I missed the cultural connection with my race, so I moved back to Nova Scotia. Fortunately, a friend from law school had just started a family and wanted to move out of her home office, so we set up a general practice together. We were the first female law firm in Nova Scotia and, as such, were newsworthy. Since we shared goals as legal practitioners, we were able to develop a fine working relationship. However, those were very busy and challenging years. Throughout my years of practice, I made a point of becoming involved in numerous community activities. This developed contacts and the kind of exposure one needs to build a secure practice.

By the time I accepted my appointment to the bench at age thirty-three I had a sense of confidence in my ability to generate a reasonably good living as a lawyer. Mindful of my growing practice and the social isolation that comes with being a member of the judiciary, including possibly distancing from the Black community, I had trepidation about accepting the position. However, the offer of a judgeship usually comes along only once in a lawyer's lifetime. In actual fact, the isolation is real, and since I never married, being a judge is a rather solitary lifestyle. But it has many rewards, not the least of which is the challenge of the work. Until recently, women who have succeeded in the legal profession have pretty much adopted the male paradigm. There have been some notable exceptions, and those are the women I deeply admire and respect.

I strongly believe that one must try to balance one's professional life with hobbies, and I have several. They include a passion for music and the arts, gardening, and exercising. Today, life is so rushed that one must take the time to nurture oneself and find the enchantment in life, which I do through things like gardening. I'm certainly not a homebody, but I enjoy the domestic arts, which for me are part of finding the beauty, peace, and harmony in one's life.

"In the 1950s and 1960s, when I was growing up, Calgary was small and a bit parochial while at the same time strongly influenced by the presence of people who worked for the U.S. oil companies. In my final year of high school I won an essay contest run by the Calgary Lion's Club and the prize was a summer in France. The following year, I won a scholarship and was sent to Algeria on a World University Service study seminar. I hadn't met many people my own age from different parts of the country and travelling with students and professors from across Canada encouraged me to see myself as part of a nation. I also learned about a way of life and a set of political beliefs very different from those I'd grown up with."

LYNN SMITH

In 1991 Lynn Smith became the first woman dean of the Faculty of Law at the University of British Columbia. She has a long history of involvement in social justice issues, particularly as they relate to women. She participated in the two major cases involving pregnancy discrimination heard by the Supreme Court of Canada. She is a winner of the YWCA Woman of Distinction Award and in 1992 was appointed Queen's Counsel.

When I entered law school at the University of British Columbia in 1970, there were fewer than twenty women in a class of 240. The culture was overwhelmingly male and I hung out with a group of male colleagues who became good friends. Years later, one told me that my strong opinions about feminism and other matters had caused them to have doubts about me, but they set them aside when I turned out to be a good student and, presumably, an asset to the study group.

In those days, the law school was an interesting place because it was in transition. A number of new faculty members were raising subjects like the lawyer's role in social change. Women from the Vancouver Women's Caucus, an activist group with which I was involved, were working with other women to organize non-credit women's studies courses at the university. I was invited to give the lecture on women and the law, which proved to be the first of many. But it was probably the most exciting lecture I gave because the experience was so new and the interest was so high.

Atmosphere at the law school was very confrontational. At least one noon-hour session on women and the law turned into a shouting match. Fortunately, other women in the class also questioned some of the ways law was being taught. At least one was considerably more aggressive than I was and I benefited from her militancy.

I had started reading the work of writers such as Simone de Beauvoir in high school and had maintained my interest in feminism while studying philosophy at university in Calgary. After earning an honours degree, I considered doing graduate work but concluded my bent was much more practical. Since I really wanted to explore the possibility of bringing about change, I joined the Company of Young Canadians. After training in Toronto, I was posted to Vancouver and worked with public housing residents, helping them to define their objectives and to organize.

I suppose some of my interest in social issues developed from my working-class background, although my parents weren't involved in politics or community work. My father worked for the same company for over fifty years, first as a salesman and then in a warehouse, and my mother worked in the home. I read avidly and the public library system played an important part in my development — I used to live at the library after school and in the summer months. I attended the academic high school that served Calgary's wealthiest area and felt somewhat different from many of my classmates. At one coffee party the mothers were discussing where their daughters would attend university. They were mentioning places like Smith and Vassar, which were completely foreign to my mother and me. I couldn't have gone to university without scholarships or the public school system.

I was the first woman to article with Shrum, Liddle and Hebenton, now part of McCarthy Tetrault, and partway through my articles I was recruited to be a law clerk for the Chief Justice of British Columbia, John Farris. Since this was the inauguration of the clerking program, I was the first law clerk ever to the Court of Appeal. I think Justice Farris took great pride in the fact that his mother, Evelyn Farris, had worked for years to get the legislation changed so that women could practise law in British Columbia.

In 1973, the year I graduated from law school, I got married to a fellow lawyer. I practised as a barrister, arguing cases in court. My two daughters were born in 1976 and 1979. Of course, juggling a litigation practice with being a wife and mother was a challenge, but like most women, I managed. I also managed to continue my interest in women's issues as a volunteer.

In the late 1970s, I was on the board of an organization called the Vancouver Community Legal Assistance Society (VCLAS). A case came forward involving a woman, Stella Bliss, who had been denied unemployment insurance because she became pregnant and had a baby without meeting the rule that said pregnant women had to work for a particular period of time prior to their delivery date — longer than was ordinarily required — in order to receive unemployment insurance benefits. By that time I had started to teach a credit course in women and the law at the Law Faculty and was asked to come in as co-counsel on a pro bono basis with Allan MacLean, a VCLAS lawyer who knew a lot about unemployment insurance. I said, 'great' and the firm said, 'great' because they liked having lawyers do some pro bono work and they saw this as an important case.

Allan and I argued the case at the Federal Court of Appeal and were unsuccessful. Stella Bliss lost in her argument that she was denied equal protection of the law under the *Canadian Bill of Rights* even though she was able and ready to work and would ordinarily have qualified. She wanted to appeal the decision to the Supreme Court of Canada and VCLAS and other organizations decided to support her. Allan and I continued on the case, but since we were both pretty junior, senior counsel John Nelligan of Ottawa came in to argue the case from our brief. I made my first appearance at the Supreme Court in 1978 as a junior counsel and I don't believe I spoke a word.

Unfortunately, we lost. The court held that it was appropriate to create a special category of benefits for pregnant women, that the discrimination was created by nature, not the statute, and that there was no denial of equal protection of the law since all pregnant persons were treated alike. It was a unanimous decision of all seven members of the court and it was very disappointing. Stella Bliss was outraged and couldn't understand how such a thing could happen. Although the decision provoked a public outcry and was widely criticized in the academic literature, in a sense the loss made me give up for a while. I decided that using the law as a vehicle to promote equality wasn't going to work and that I should do other things.

In 1981, I decided to leave my practice. The decision was related to my children, in particular to one of my daughters who had a health problem. A litigation practice is barely manageable if you have healthy children and a nanny, and although my clients and partners were supportive, it was difficult. My decision was also related to my interests — I'd done more teaching at the UBC Faculty of Law by then, in evidence and family law, as well as women and the law, so when I was offered a position on the faculty I accepted. I enjoyed teaching. I particularly liked the opportunity to study things in depth and to do scholarly writing. I also became involved in some human rights cases, but it was a case I'd done while still in practice that led to a new chapter in my life.

Beth Symes, a Toronto lawyer, was researching a book on women and legal action for the Canadian Advisory Council on the Status of Women. She came across some references to a complaint against a British Columbia judge, the late Judge Bewley, and she phoned me for more information since I'd acted for a coalition of women's groups who had sought to participate in the hearing of the complaint before the Provincial Judicial Council about Judge Bewley's behaviour. In sentencing an individual who had broken into a former girlfriend's home and held her at knifepoint, the judge commented that he couldn't understand what the fuss was about because women don't "get much brains until they're thirty." He suggested that the perpetrator might have killed the woman, but didn't, so what was the harm? The public outcry meant that the complaint was taken very seriously. Judge Bewley was reprimanded but not dismissed from the bench. However, I don't believe he ever sat again as a judge.

My contact with Beth Symes introduced me to a group of women in Toronto who were talking about how to implement the equality provisions in the new *Charter of Rights and Freedoms*. I was in my quiescent, don't-bother-me stage, but I was intrigued and agreed to attend a meeting in Toronto, which was designed to be a round-table opportunity to analyze the Charter's equality guarantees, the arguments that would be made to limit those guarantees, and the impact that other parts of the Charter would have. Remember, the equality rights sections didn't come into effect until three years after the rest of the Charter became law.

Meeting and working with women such as Mary Eberts, Beth Symes, Nancy Jackman, Marilou McPhedran, and others was inspiring. They were extremely capable and focused. It was also exciting because they represented a critical mass. In the B.C. milieu there were very few women lawyers of my vintage with an interest in these areas, whereas in Toronto there were many. Discovering a community of peers from whom I could learn a lot was exhilarating.

Over the next two or three years, my interest in the activist potential of the law was gradually rekindled. I was a founder of the Women's Legal Education and Action Fund (LEAF) because ultimately I decided that women should argue for an interpretation of the Charter that will promote equality — otherwise, it could end up having a reverse effect. During those years, I put a lot of time into LEAF, and in 1986 when another pregnancy discrimination case came along, people were kind enough to say, "Well, of course you'll want to do this."

I said, "Yes I would."

The *Brooks* case was a human rights case from Manitoba, involving some female employees who worked for Canada Safeway and were excluded from receiving company sickness and disability benefits during a period of their pregnancy. The defence was the Supreme Court's decision in *Bliss*, and because of that the women had been unsuccessful at every level in Manitoba. LEAF applied to intervene when the case went to the Supreme Court of Canada. I worked with the case committee to develop the factum, then flew to Ottawa from France, where I was on sabbatical with my family, to argue the case.

When the decision came down, I remember standing by the fax machine and watching the pages come through. It was very exciting.

Not only did we win, but the decision was exactly what we had hoped for. The case was significant for what it said about sex discrimination in general and equality for pregnant women in particular. Chief Justice Brian Dickson, who had also sat on *Bliss*, wrote the majority opinion and explicitly disagreed with *Bliss*. The Supreme Court hasn't overruled itself very often, but did in this case.

I think the dramatic change in the court's approach over the decade between *Bliss* and *Brooks* reflects the relationship between social and legal change. By the late 1980s, pregnancy could be viewed as a necessary and appropriate part of a working person's life that needed to be accommodated rather than penalized. In *Brooks*, the court referred to the increased number of women in the paid workforce. Of course, the presence of two women judges on the Supreme Court of Canada, Bertha Wilson and Claire L'Heureux-Dubé, also made a difference.

In 1990, I was made a full professor in the law faculty and the following year, I was asked to let my name stand for dean. I was reluctant to think about it because I had never seen myself as an administrator, but people seemed to think I could do it and, in a sense, pull the faculty together. When I was offered the post, I obviously felt some responsibility to accept, since a woman had never been in that position before. But I think it would be a mistake to take on something like a deanship only for that reason. After five years, I can say that it takes so much out of your life, you must really want to do it. I've enjoyed it very much — the chance to shape the faculty and the university, to meet a fascinating range of people, to solve difficult and intricate problems, and to work with the profession and the community has been very rewarding.

When I became dean, I think the profession had some doubts about me because I was a known feminist, but I'd be the last person to know that for sure. One or two people have said things like, "It seems to be working out," with a hint of surprise in their voices. In some ways, working within an institution improves my ability to affect change. When you move into a high-status position, people pay more attention to what you have to say.

Looking back, I think if I had it all to do over again I'd be more overt as a feminist. I've probably spent more time regretting what I haven't said than what I have said. I admire people who are willing to take the heat and who speak directly to the issues. However, one can also make a difference by holding back, by picking the points where one intervenes or chooses to be indirect or diplomatic.

With hindsight, I see that my quiescent period was one of the most beneficial times of my professional life. It gave me time to retreat and reflect while I continued to work very hard at the law firm. Because of that time, I feel confident that my record in the profession is solid. I fine-tuned my skills while acquiring a bit of a thick skin, which is very important. I don't want to say I'm the toughest person going — for instance, I could never go into politics — but I can take quite a bit of heat. This is necessary if you're going to be able to carry on in a world where there's still resistance to women as leaders and some hostility to feminism.

During that quiescent period I also developed a good relationship with my daughters. They're very comfortable with having a mother who does what I do, and in some ways they're proud of it. As well, I spent a lot of time with my husband, and our relationship is very important to me. That family support is very grounding and it's crucial. I don't know how people can go out in the world and do battle without it.

"Playing with the girls was okay, but playing with the boys was better, and I wanted part of that."

JUSTINE BLAINEY

Justine Blainey made history when she initiated a four-year legal battle for the right to play hockey on a boys' team that took her all the way to the Supreme Court of Canada. On January 15, 1988, shortly after her fifteenth birthday, she legally played her first game as a girl with an élite Metro Toronto Hockey League team. At the time of this interview she was twenty-three, a first-year student at the Canadian Memorial Chiropractic College, and still one of Canada's top female hockey players.

I f it hadn't been for my brother, David, I wouldn't have wanted to play hockey with the boys. Like many girls, when I was young I enjoyed art, ballet, gymnastics, and figure skating — the usual "feminine" activities. But gradually, I learned that "male" sports were more highly valued. Although I practised skating six days a week, no one wanted to watch me do figure eights, and the only time I had an audience was at the annual carnival. I couldn't help noticing that family members always attended my brother's hockey games, even his practices. Possibly, jealousy of that attention inspired me to hit the ice myself.

I first told my parents I wanted to play hockey when I was eight. My family was very oriented towards education and their immediate response was, "Girls don't do that." At that point I wasn't even allowed to play hockey on the street. It took about two years to convince my family, and during that time my brother, who is only ten months younger than I am, was my greatest support.

I wasn't particularly athletic. Initially, my strongest motivation was getting my dad's attention. Because my parents separated when I was two, time with him was precious. My father was polite and comfortable watching ballet, gymnastics, or figure skating, but I recognized that he really related to hockey. Soon, I started to enjoy the game myself — especially the social aspects, being part of a team trying to achieve a common goal.

By the time I started hockey school I'd been figure skating for six years. I could skate faster than all the boys, until they gave me a puck, but once I mastered stickhandling, I was really hooked. I guess the thing I loved most was the speed of the game. Feeling the wind against my face and hearing the swish of my skates as I raced down the ice were amazing. I also loved being in control of the technique — executing the perfect pass or stopping a one-on-one by a leading scorer. I even enjoyed the bump and grind, the hits, and the smelly sweat of the locker room.

Coaches were soon asking me to play for their teams, and this created problems. Some instructors said, "You can attend the school, but you'll never play in the NHL," or "You'll never play on my team." Sometimes, they wanted me to pretend I was a boy. I heard, "Cut your hair, call yourself Justin, and we'll sign you up." That made me very uncomfortable and I had some bad nights. Because the boys were tough and didn't cry — at least not in public — I kept everything to myself and cried in private. I wanted to prove I was just as tough as they were!

I began playing in a girls' league when I was ten and immediately made the all-star team for players aged ten to fourteen. Although I liked playing with the girls, I could see that my brother was being offered much more. The girls got less ice time, which meant they didn't play as often and their games were usually at inconvenient times. In addition, they had to travel more — as much as five hours to tournaments — whereas the boys rarely played farther than twenty minutes away. I also happen to prefer the boys' game, which is aggressive, fast, and rough. I love a good body-check! I soon realized the boys were more highly valued. They had more sponsorships, larger audiences, and more feedback from society in general.

I was growing increasingly frustrated, so in 1983 I wrote a letter to the newspapers asking for help. My question was, "I can play, but may I?" I had ability, but some rule I didn't understand prevented me from playing. Someone at one of the newspapers contacted a lawyer, Anna Fraser, who took my case. Since I didn't have any money to pay her, she waived her fee.

The case didn't begin until 1985 because I had to wait for the equality section of the *Charter of Rights and Freedoms* to come into effect. Then, the Human Rights Commission refused to accept our complaint because the *Ontario Human Rights Code* explicitly allowed discrimination with respect to sex in sport. In the fall of 1985, we went to the Supreme Court of Ontario and lost.

Being in court was alienating. I remember feeling afraid because I didn't totally understand what was happening. But I believed in my right to play hockey, in Anna, and in my mother and my brother, who were always with me. Some of the boys I played hockey with also supported me throughout the court cases. I wish I could say the same for the girls. I was still playing hockey in the girls' league, but once my legal action began, some — even those who had been my friends — started to resent me. I think they felt put down. My best friend's mother told her not to talk to me because I was a negative influence. The administrators of women's hockey added fuel to the fire by interviewing my teammates and telling them I was ruining women's hockey.

The gossip also affected behaviour in the dressing room. Conversations stopped as soon as I arrived, and when I sat down on the bench everyone got up. Reluctantly, I stopped trusting girls because I felt they were catty and held a grudge. By the time I finished grade seven I had no female friends.

After I lost at the Supreme Court of Ontario, the hockey bosses were very cruel. That evening I arrived for a practice and was told I couldn't participate. We appealed the decision, and when we won at the appeal court on April 17, 1986, I thought the battle was over. Once again I was disappointed. I was getting ready for a game at St. Michael's Arena when a reporter from the *Toronto Star* arrived and told me I couldn't play because the Ontario Hockey Association had persuaded the president of the Metropolitan Toronto Hockey League to change his mind about allowing me to play in the exhibition series.

All I wanted was to be alone with my pain, but I was surrounded by TV cameras. I remember hugging my mom, getting dressed, and cheering the game from behind my team's bench. I probably cheered louder than anyone in the arena, which was full of people, because I felt I had to disguise my feelings. I didn't want to be perceived as a victim. I never had doubts that I was doing the right thing, but that night, for the first time, I began to feel that my dream would never come true for me. Being able to play on a boys' team would be something my daughter could do, if that was her choice. I was thirteen years old and believed I was fighting for the principle of justice, not for myself.

When I started, I had no idea of the obstacles I'd face. The case received a lot of attention, and losing reinforced the belief that I was wrong. Complete untruths — for instance, that I hated women's hockey — were reported, and as I got older, the rumours got worse. When I was thirteen it was said that I made the boys' team because I gave the boys sexual favours. By the time I reached grade nine, I felt I couldn't walk down the hall at school without someone saying negative things. I was very isolated. Worse still, I wasn't even safe. People followed me and chased me in the subway, I was stalked and often received crank calls. Once, the Waterloo police phoned to warn me that a man previously convicted of rape and forcible confinement had been picked up on a minor charge. He had a list of names and addresses in his pocket that included my name and my mother's. Thinking of that incident now, I'm absolutely horrified, but at the time losing my friends hurt more.

Finally, in June 1987 I won at the Supreme Court of Canada and thought my battle was over. Not so. The Ontario Hockey Association fought the decision and I had to go to the Human Rights Commission once again. Fortunately, we won and got court costs, but I still had one more battle. The evening of our victory I phoned my coach, only to be told that he'd given my place to another player — a guy who hadn't even made the team in competitive tryouts. I quickly concluded that he'd been signed the night before so there wouldn't be a place for me. Because of the way the league operates, I had two weeks to find another team.

My brother was very upset. Without even discussing it with me, he phoned the coach and asked if he'd give me a place on the team if one existed. The coach said, "Yes" and my brother said, "Fine, I quit." As a boy, he expected to find another team quickly, but I'd have trouble making the two-week deadline. Things worked out after that. I finally got a chance to play in the boys' league, where I stayed for three and a half years, and my brother found a new and better team.

I loved playing hockey with the boys. Although it was a dream come true, in terms of the game, the problems related to being a girl continued. There were complaints that I was getting too much ice time, and the sexual innuendoes resurfaced. Also, by this time, I was playing with guys who had been socialized differently from those I'd grown up with. Some came from families where girls had a very limited role and they told me they didn't believe I should be on the ice with them. Occasionally, this hostility erupted into violence. I got "run at" a lot, and although I never got hurt seriously, I'd draw a couple of penalties every game because guys were hitting me from behind. Today, they'd be thrown out of the game.

I always had an A average in school, but in the last few years of high school my marks moved up. I don't think I'm brighter than other people, but I've always had a good work ethic. I was an Ontario Scholar, which means my marks were over eighty percent when I left high school. I also received the University of Toronto's National Scholarship, which four to six people from across Canada receive every year. It's a pretty healthy sum, so it enabled me to live in residence and attend the college of my choice.

I graduated with a B.Sc. and entered chiropractic college, which I love. I also volunteer as a hockey coach and do public speaking through FAME [Female Athletes Motivating Excellence]. I'm still playing a lot of hockey, on a women's team that has done very well. I'd like to do some writing, maybe about being a young woman who's not afraid to call herself a feminist, particularly since so many people feel that's unacceptable.

I don't regret my court battle, but it's made me a different person. I'm much stronger than I would have been if I'd followed a more traditional path. Since I've been different myself, I have more sympathy for people who aren't the norm, whether it's because they belong to a minority group or choose to do something unusual. The downside of challenging the status quo is the negative aspects of celebrity.

Last year I did a survey of three high schools, which showed that three times more boys think of themselves as athletes than do girls.

Everyone felt it was unfair that boys receive so much more funding and support, but no one was prepared to make the effort to change things. And, nine years after my court case, I discovered that some schools are still breaking the law by not allowing girls to play on boys' teams even though they qualify in open tryouts.

> "Police work appealed to me because of the variety. I'd hate doing the same thing every day. I like to move on and try different things."
>
> **GERAMY FIELD**

Sergeant Geramy Field is the first woman to head the sexual assault squad in the Vancouver Police Department and to work as a detective on the drug squad in that city. In 1978 she became the first woman in Canada to join a dog squad.

After I joined the police force in 1975, I spent a couple of years in patrol, doing all the things that police officers do — robbery calls, break and enter reports, telling people that somebody has passed away, and so on. But because I don't like doing the same thing for long, I was intrigued by the dog squad. The idea of working with a dog appealed to me and the work, which involves responding to the in-progress calls that get your heart pumping, like a robbery while it's happening, is very active.

Since there had never been any women dog masters before, I recognized I'd have to prove my stuff. I offered to quarry, which involves acting as bait for the dogs that are training. You wear a large leather arm guard, lay a track, and hide until the dog finds you. Most of the time it wasn't scary, but my arms got quite bruised. I remember being afraid the first time I quarried for one dog and master who were notorious — the dog was very tough, with a horrifying bite, and his master gave me a hard time. The bite hurt, but I passed whatever test was there. I didn't wimp out and eventually won the man's respect.

To tell you the truth, I don't think any of the guys on the squad were delighted to have me, but when a vacancy arose I got the position. I was a little naive and didn't realize that the fellow I replaced left because he and the sergeant had a falling out. Since the guys really liked him, there was a lot of animosity towards this girl who was taking his place.

Any specialty squad is a close-knit group. On the dog squad, you work closely with each other, as well as with your dog, and when I arrived I upset the equilibrium. Worse still, I'd been on the force for only three years and it usually takes longer than that to get onto the squad. I didn't realize I was the first woman until after I'd started, and some of the guys made no bones about the fact that my appointment was political. They felt the department was scoring points for having a woman in a non-traditional position. At the time, I didn't think the department would do that. Now, I think, perhaps, they did. However, it turned out all right because I didn't screw up.

The first year had its ups and downs. It was the late 1970s and things that wouldn't happen today were par for the course. In those days, you didn't dare speak out against things — you had to be accepted as one of the boys or you wouldn't make it. Not that the men treated me badly. It was more subtle. A few would make derogatory comments about women, and even though they reassured me that the remarks weren't directed at me, they still hurt. I didn't take the bait and fight back. I kept my frustration inside and concentrated on meeting my objective — proving that I could do the job.

Deep down I knew I could function as well as any of the men and part of me was probably motivated to prove my detractors wrong. In the end, that's what I did. I proved that having my period wouldn't screw up the dog's scent, that I could pick the dog up and put him through a window if necessary, and that I could drive fast in a car chase and not crack up. Eventually, they realized I could perform and accepted me as their equal. They adjusted to the times as they evolved and, I think, proved my belief that when change is gradual, it's more likely to become a more permanent behavioural change as opposed to a temporary adjustment to suit the times. In the long run, I don't believe that making waves is as effective.

I enjoy police work and I suppose I'm lucky because I certainly didn't have a burning desire to join the force. When I was growing up, my vision of a policewoman was a prison matron, which didn't interest me in the least. But the year before I finished university, I ran into a policewoman at the Pacific National Exhibition who told me that women on the force could now do the same jobs as men. That piqued my interest. I was in physical education at UBC, training to be a teacher, and after completing my practicum I concluded that motivating high school girls to be interested in phys. ed. would be a tough job. When I put that together with the realization that as a teacher I'd be seeing the same people and the same set of walls every day, my fate was sealed.

I encountered my first barrier when I applied to the force — not because I'm a woman, but because I was living with my boyfriend. The personnel officer who interviewed me thought this was unacceptable and told me to call back when I got married. I still wasn't married when I graduated, but I called back anyway. I decided if they weren't interested, I'd make them interested. I guess I succeeded, because I was accepted.

That year, there was a fairly big hiring push and close to two hundred people were accepted as recruits. There were twelve women in our class of about ninety. It wasn't as tough as I thought it would be, probably because I was fairly athletic. Running was a big part of our training, as we're trained to chase and catch criminals.

I never saw myself as particularly unusual. In most respects I had a typical middle-class upbringing — a younger brother and a dog. My father, who told me to strive to be different, was a big influence on my life. My mother was a wonderful role model because she had incredible inner strength. As a teenager she was training to be an Olympic swimmer when she developed an ear infection that required mastoid surgery. The operation wasn't done properly and caused her to go deaf. I never realized she was different from the other mothers until I got older. She never complained and always focused on the positive things in life.

My first experience with real police work came when I was still a recruit. I was sent to the east side of Vancouver, the roughest part of the city, with a training officer. Two buddies at the juvenile detention centre had gone crazy with baseball bats and were holding the staff at bay. As I arrived I was told, "You're the rookie. Write down everything that happens." That was disappointing — I wanted to get in on the action. Suddenly the decision was made to go in and arrest the perpetrators. There was lots of screaming and yelling and eventually these two bloodied characters came out. Meanwhile, I was trying to capture all this activity in a report that made sense. I loved it. I thought, this is it, I'm here, I've arrived. Within three years I was on the dog squad.

In 1983 I left the dog squad. There's an unwritten policy that you only stay on a specialty squad for three to five years and, in addition, Sabre, my dog, was slowing down because he'd developed arthritis in his spine and hind legs. I walked the beat on Robson Street for about a year and a half, then I went into CLEU, the Coordinated Law Enforcement Unit. That's a plainclothes surveillance and intelligence gathering unit that deals with organized crime, and it was very interesting work. My first file was pornography-related. Some guys, well known to our vice squad, were putting on a lingerie fashion show and the female officers had to infiltrate the group by pretending to be potential customers with wealthy friends. After that, I wrote my exams and got promoted to corporal, which is the same rank as detective. Once again, I was motivated by the desire to do different things. I wanted to be on the drug squad and in those days, you had to be a detective to do that.

I was the first woman to work on the drug squad as a detective and a full-fledged member of the group, and although they were a tightly knit bunch, I had no problems with the men. I guess by then most of them knew that I had performed well enough on other jobs and wasn't carrying around any issues.

I spent a little over two years on the drug squad, doing everything from street-level buys to cocaine undercover operations. Sometimes I'd work on Granville Mall pretending to be a purchaser, which was difficult because by then I was more than thirty and I had to appear to be a young person trying to buy drugs. I took on a student look — a T-shirt and jeans — as a cover and made notes of how I was dressed because the defence would always ask what I was wearing. On one case that went to trial, the perpetrator described me as wearing a sexy see-through blouse, which wasn't true, and said the only reason that he tried to sell me drugs was because he wanted to have a date with me, the old ploy being that if you're wearing something suggestive it might qualify as entrapment.

I left the drug squad in 1990, and after a few detours, I now work in sexual assault. This is my first women's beat and it's very interesting. It's the first job I've done where I feel I'm actually helping to change people's lives, which at this stage in my career is very satisfying. I was the first woman to run the squad because there aren't many female sergeants. Prior to coming here I had worked on sexual assaults, as anybody would throughout their career — responding to rape calls, taking a sexual assault report, and so on — but I didn't know much about the issues. We handle child abuse and sexual abuse, as well, and recognizing the extent of abuse within the family has been a real eye-opener.

I like the fact that as leader of the squad I can be a bit of a change agent. I've been in a position to push for more training for my officers, I've sat on committees to develop provincewide policies on sexual assault investigations, and I've been able to promote better treatment for victims. Unfortunately, there are still lots of old ideas that need to be changed — protocols in hospitals, for instance. Although the men I work with are extremely sympathetic and good at what they do, I think I have more empathy for a woman who's been sexually assaulted because it's easier for me to imagine how it feels.

In 1978 I got married — to the man I'd been living with for eight years. When I joined the force, he was a fire-fighter but when he saw how much fun I was having, he decided to become a police officer, too. I wasn't particularly pleased when he joined the force — I had my niche and I didn't want him interfering — but it's worked out. Even though I'm a higher rank and earn more money than him, that's fine with him. Neither of us has regular hours and the fact that we don't have kids makes balancing our home life easier. Initially, I didn't want children. I couldn't see how you could have a career as demanding as mine and bring up children well, and my approach was, basically, bring them up well or don't do it. I guess in the back of my mind I thought I might eventually settle down and want kids, but that never happened and now it's too late. At the same time, though, I have a successful marriage and a successful career, and that's a lot to be thankful for.

In the near future, a competition for inspector is coming up and I'm planning to put my hat in the ring. To some extent, that's a function of ego, but I also see things within the department that I'd like to change. Looking back on my career, I think that being a woman has been an advantage. I think it helped me to get noticed and contributed to being offered some interesting positions. I was the right person at the right time because I'm a woman, but I also proved I could do the job.

"I didn't feel being a lawyer was my reason for living, but once I couldn't practise law, that's what I wanted to do. The question was how to get my foot in the door. Since I needed to put food on the table, I decided to start working as a girl Friday in a law firm."

MOBINA JAFFER

In 1978, when she was admitted to the British Columbia Bar, Mobina Jaffer became the first South Asian woman to practise law in the province. She soon became active in the community, particularly around issues of social justice for women. She was the founding president of Immigrant and Visible Minority Women in B.C. and of the West Coast Women's Network, and the only visible minority member of the Canadian Panel on Violence Against Women. A winner of the YWCA Woman of Distinction Award, she was, at the time of this interview, president of the National YWCA and vice-president of the Liberal party of Canada. She ran, unsuccessfully, as a Liberal candidate in the federal elections of 1993 and 1997.

In 1972, when Idi Amin expelled all South Asians from Uganda, my family became refugees. At the time, I was living in London, England, newly married, and had recently received my law degree. After a difficult pregnancy, which required a long hospital stay, I gave birth to my son, Azool, in 1973. During that time we had many hair-raising adventures trying to get various relatives out of Uganda, but finally, in 1975, my family was able to immigrate to Canada.

The transition wasn't easy. My first shock was coming to terms with our new economic reality: although prosperous in Uganda, we had lost everything. When we arrived in Canada, I was also shocked to discover that my legal credentials weren't accepted. Since I'd qualified as a lawyer in England, I had assumed I'd be able to practise in Canada, but when I inquired about joining the British Columbia Law Society, they wouldn't even give me an application form. People advised me to take a secretarial course because they thought I'd never become a lawyer in Canada. But the more they told me I'd never succeed, the more determined I became. The immediate problem was that we were poor and I needed a job. My son was a year old and my husband was having difficulty adjusting.

I knew I couldn't afford to focus all my energy on becoming a lawyer, so I went to secretarial college for a month and learned how to type. Once I felt I had some skills, I went through the phone book, calling law offices to see if they needed secretarial help. That's how I met my current law partner — I got a job working as his girl Friday. Even now, he says I really can't type.

The Honourable Thomas A. Dohm had been a judge and had returned from the British Columbia bench a few years earlier. We got along because, as he tells it, I was the first person who called him asking for a job. He liked that because he admires people with guts. Of course, in my case it wasn't guts. It was naivety; I had no idea how important he was. During the interview he became curious about why someone with a law degree was working as a secretary. When I told him my story, he was outraged. He went directly to the Law Society and demanded that they give me the forms. I filled them out and within ten days my qualifications were assessed.

At the time, it was necessary to become a Canadian citizen to practise law, so I completed the citizenship process while studying for my law exams in the evenings. Managing that with a job, a husband, and a baby wasn't easy, but three years after our arrival in Canada, I was called to the Bar. At that point, I discovered I was the first South Asian woman in B.C. to achieve that status.

One of the reasons my family chose Canada to immigrate to was that we thought it was fair about race. In Uganda we were never the right colour. First, the right colour was white, then, when Idi Amin took over, it became black. We thought Canada would be different, but I soon discovered that race was an issue here, as well. Being brown, a woman, and a lawyer was problematic. In those days there weren't many women in the courtroom, period, and the judges didn't give female lawyers the stature they deserved. Being a woman of colour compounded the problem. When other lawyers were thinking about the trial, I was worrying about potential problems, such as how I'd handle the not unusual situation of having the judge mistake me for an interpreter. But in those days one didn't verbalize such concerns for fear of being identified as a troublemaker. All I wanted was acceptance.

I've been lucky in the sense that once I got over the initial hurdles, I've always had lot of support. My law partner is eighty-one and he's from the old school. He's certainly not a feminist, but when the judges gave me a hard time, he went to bat for me by, for instance, sitting beside me in the courtroom while I conducted a trial.

I decided to practise family law because I quickly realized that issues of Asian culture and divorce weren't being addressed, and that was another eye-opener. Most of my clients were immigrant women, many of whom came to me because they thought I spoke Punjabi. At that point I didn't know the language — I learned to understand it in Canada. But working with these women made me aware of my relative position of privilege. Unlike them, I hadn't received negative messages about being a woman when I was growing up, and I was shocked by what I saw. I couldn't believe how many of my clients were subjected to violence and how difficult their struggles were.

My family is well-educated and politically progressive — my father was the first South Asian elected to the Ugandan Parliament and my mother was the first South Asian woman in East Africa to attend university. It took me a long time to realize how broad-minded they were. I never received messages that there were differences between women and men. Seeing such terrible situations in my practice motivated me to become involved in women's issues. That was a big step, because until then the political issue I had been most concerned about was race. Since I took the equality of women as a given, I'd never worried about the implications of gender. But working as a lawyer, I discovered that being a woman could be as great a barrier to fulfilment as race. My clients told me stories about being physically abused and sexually assaulted, which shocked and horrified me. Over the years, a number of clients have lost their lives, which made me feel hopelessly powerless.

At some point, I can't say exactly when, I decided not to become a fast-track lawyer. I didn't want to work twenty-four hours a day and devote all my energies to moving ahead in my career. I wanted to focus on issues that were important to me — race and gender — and to be active in areas of social justice. I also wanted to have a family life and to be involved in the community.

I started in the 1980s by becoming involved in mainstream women's issues. First, I joined a women's network, which was a good step. Getting to know other women helped to ease my sense of isolation. It also made me aware of how much I enjoy the company of women and the way we process things. I soon branched out. In 1985, I became the first president of Immigrant and Visible Minority Women of B.C. and in 1991 I was appointed chair of the British Columbia Task Force on Family Violence. The following year, I became a member of the Canadian Panel on Violence Against Women. As the only woman of colour on the panel, I was in an extremely difficult position. It was said that I couldn't represent the interests of all women of colour, which was certainly a valid criticism. But I felt that I could accomplish more by being on the inside than if I resigned to make a statement about the underrepresentation of women of colour. I firmly believe that change happens only when you're sitting at the table. One representative is better than none.

Around that time, the British Columbia Law Society mounted a task force on gender in the legal profession. No women of colour were asked to sit on it and I became an advocate on behalf of women from the visible minority population. The problem was that many people within the profession thought gender took precedence over race as an issue, and I paid a price by being identified as someone who wasn't a team player. That was a very difficult time. Within my profession I was fighting a battle with mainstream women, and on the panel I was fighting with women of colour. I was pleasing no one, and felt totally isolated. But I did what I felt was right.

Although it was very painful, I learned a lot from being on the Panel on Violence Against Women. It taught me to see change as a process where some must be very radical and others have to remain in the middle. I believe the women's movement has achieved so much because some very strong women took on the role of pulling people's chains. Radical women must push the issues so that women in the middle can bring them forward and create movement within the institutions.

Although I saw myself as quite radical when I was younger, I recognize that I'm not a radical any more. I've reached a comfort level with operating in the mainstream and I don't want to jeopardize the access that guarantees. For instance, as vice-president of the Liberal party of Canada I can pick up the phone and give the Minister of Justice a hard time about legal issues that matter to women. I wouldn't be able to do that if I were identified as a radical. I've also learned to choose my battles. I've watched too many women try to fight all the battles at once and end up burning out.

My relationship with my husband, who's an accountant by training, has been a growth process. He's five and a half years older than I am, so when we were first married, he was kind of a god. But as I grew and developed, the power relationship changed. I think he's very strong to have been so supportive in helping me grow. In some ways, my political involvement has been harder on him than on me. Some people think that having a radical wife means that I'm the man in the family. That isn't true; our relationship is equitable.

In 1993 and again in 1997, I ran as a Liberal candidate in the federal elections and lost. Politics is now my life, which is interesting since it's what I wanted to do in the first place. Law was an intermittent step to satisfy my father, who felt I should have a profession. The problem is that politics is a very expensive hobby. I am still paying for my candidacy, not for my election expenses — people were very generous about those — but for the income I lost by being away from my office for a year. Even though I recognize that it would be very difficult for my family financially if I got elected, every part of me wants to be a Member of Parliament. As a lawyer you can make individual change and possibly change for some people. But as a politician, if you're in the right place at the right time, you can make change for thousands, which is inspiring.

PART 3

RELIGION, EDUCATION, COMMUNITY SERVICE, AND HEALTH

"My commitment to righting social wrongs came out of a long tradition of prairie populism and social activism, which were the heritage of the United Church. Within that institution, I've always pushed the envelope on issues of social justice. I suppose, as a woman and the mother of four children, I established a rhythm of being both inside and outside the institution simultaneously. I'm both happily married and a feminist. I wasn't willing to push ordination unless I was asked. And although I'm not personally angry, I think anger can fuel social change."

LOIS WILSON

The Very Reverend Lois M. Wilson was born in Winnipeg, Manitoba, in 1927. She was ordained as a minister in the United Church of Canada in 1965 and distinguished her ministry with its strong community focus. In 1980 she became the first woman moderator of the United Church, and two years later became the first Canadian president of the World Council of Churches. She has received many public awards, including the Order of Canada, the U.N. (Canada) Pearson Peace Prize '84 and the Canada 125 Medal, which, in celebration of Canada's 125th birthday, honoured individuals who contributed to the country's well-being. She is currently chancellor of Lakehead University in Thunder Bay and in 1998 was appointed to the Senate.

I took theology in university, not because I wanted to be a minister, but because I was interested in the spiritual life and I thought studying theology might improve my understanding of spirituality. I certainly didn't have any career objectives — in those days, just after the war, not many women thought about pursuing an occupation. We were actively encouraged to stay home and have babies. When a girl I went to high school with entered medical school, I was genuinely puzzled. My consciousness was so low I couldn't imagine why being a physician would interest her. Whenever I considered my options, which wasn't often, I thought about becoming a teacher, a social worker, or possibly a phys. ed. teacher, since I loved sports. Mostly, I thought about getting married, but it was clear that getting married ruled out anything except being a wife and mother.

While I was at university, I became very involved with the Student Christian Movement and served as president of their United College chapter for three years. I was attracted by the biblical, international, and social justice thrust of the organization and the fact that they treated women as equals of men. Surprisingly, it never occurred to me that their concept of female equality was unusual.

I didn't decide that I wanted to enter the ministry until my last year of university. At that point it dawned on me that I'd have to do something and, as graduation got closer, I grew comfortable with the idea of becoming a minister. I had some practice at it. In the summers, as a student, I was sent by the United Church to provide services in rural areas. I travelled by bike and preached in school houses and at kids' camps, and I discovered that I liked it.

In 1950, when I got married, I was academically prepared for ordination, but I hadn't asked to be ordained. I have a memory of my husband, Roy, and I returning from our honeymoon and attending the ordination of my classmates. Roy, who was a year ahead of me in university and was already ordained as a minister, commented, "You look as if you'd rather be ordained than marry me."

"Actually, I'd like to have both — like you," I replied. There's no doubt in my mind that being the wife of a minister was the life I chose, and I chose Roy because he offered integrity and respect, among other things. Even though I wasn't employed, I had too much energy to stay at home, so I immediately became involved with community work. I was soon so busy that I had trouble juggling it all with the four children who arrived between 1952 and 1960. I took them along with me to most things — people say they remember the youngest coming to meetings in a laundry basket while he was still a babe in arms. My mother was my role model for that. She was a woman who offered open hospitality in her home and when she went out to things, she frequently took us with her.

I suppose I'm like my mother in many ways. She was very determined and focused and, as a result, I'm sure she alienated many people. I'm sure I do, too. But my mother was a real individual and someone who wasn't afraid to be herself. Once, she cut the legs off a chair because it was too high for her. She believed that life should suit you and if it doesn't you should fix things so it will. I think I absorbed quite a bit of that.

Roy and I stayed in Winnipeg until 1960, when we moved to the First United Church congregation in Thunder Bay, Ontario. I loved Thunder Bay. I knew the city well because I'd lived there from the age of two until I was twelve, while my father served as minister of a congregation in Port Arthur. I was the fifth and youngest child, which I think is a great position in the family because by then the parents are usually tired of raising children so you have an awful lot of freedom.

Not long after we arrived in Thunder Bay, the congregation took me on as a pastoral assistant. We invented the term since there was no such category in the United Church. I think I was paid — not a salary, but at least a recognition of my work and enough to cover my expenses. I never had the attitude that ordination was my right. I felt that if the church wished to call me and ordain me, that was up to them. But if they didn't, I could live my life without it. I always thought there was a great opportunity to do the work of a ministry, employed or not.

First Church United was a very busy congregation and my husband had such a heavy pastoral load that he really needed some help. The congregation searched across Canada, unsuccessfully, trying to find someone and finally, after I'd been a pastoral assistant for three years, they asked if I could do it. At that point our youngest child was only three so I hedged and said I didn't think I was ready. They searched again but still couldn't find anyone, so they came back the following year, when I gave a qualified yes.

Since I wanted to be free when the kids were on holidays, I agreed to work part-time only. That was a tricky point because the church had male ministers only and the job description included the phrase "give yourself *wholly* to the ministry." My point was that I'd give myself wholly when I was working, but that didn't include nights and holidays. I think they agreed because they knew me and trusted me. And so, in 1965, on my fifteenth wedding anniversary, I became an ordained minister.

In retrospect, the years I spent being a pastoral assistant were the best possible preparation for the ministry. I had a chance to mature and the opportunity to do things that ordained ministers don't have time for and, frankly, that never would have occurred to me if I'd gone straight into a parish. For instance, I spent most of my time in ministry in the community, not in the congregation — basically doing social activism work, mobilizing people to look at and take action on things that dehumanize people.

In those years, and later, too, I set a pattern. I developed my own particular style of ministry, which involved, I think, using my own gifts in a unique way. Before I was ordained, I had been what the church called laity, somebody who comes into the church and helps the minister. I thought it should be the other way around — the church should put more emphasis on supporting the laity in their secular jobs. As soon as I became a minister, I began to make a list of everybody in the congregation and the kind of work they did — looking after kids at home, working at the paper mill, being a police officer on the beat, and so on. Then I started visiting them on the job, to find out what the tensions were, what support the community could offer, and what implications Christian faith had for their life in society. People were slightly puzzled by that. They wondered why I wasn't back at the church building, but to me this was a very natural outgrowth of my understanding of the Christian faith.

Nature has always been important to me as a source of spirituality. When I was growing up, canoe trips were our family holidays. We had a twenty-foot freighter canoe that transported nine people, including two cousins, three tents, and all our supplies. To paddle along Lake Superior during the day and pitch our tents in some wilderness paradise in the evening was magnificent. After Roy and I were married, we took our own children canoeing on Lake of the Woods. That appreciation of nature was a gift from my parents, which we passed on to our kids and eventually to our twelve grandchildren.

In the 1960s, before I was ordained, I started taking high school girls from our congregation on wilderness canoe trips. I wanted to share some of that joy with them and to build a leisure activity into their lives that was based on Christian education. I had one stipulation: that we do an hour of Bible study every day. We canoed on the border lakes, between Canada and the U.S., and through Quetico Provincial Park for a week to ten days. My trips weren't physical tests like the Outward Bound program — I wanted the girls to enjoy themselves, to develop their self-esteem, and to get a sense of the spirituality in nature. I loved it myself, so I assumed everybody else must love it, too.

A girl who came with me on one of those trips introduced me to Betty Friedan's *The Feminine Mystique*, which was published in 1965. She was very excited about the book and told me to read it because she thought it resonated with what I was saying. My eldest daughter remembers me gasping with the shock of recognition as I read it. I suppose the book reflected some of the things I saw in Thunder Bay — not just in myself but also in the people I interacted with: all the women wheeling baby carriages and being told this was their destiny, while many were taking Valium precisely because they sensed it wasn't. But in those days nobody had a clear idea of how to get beyond those stereotypes. I guess the book also echoed my own feelings about ordination, which I had always wanted but wasn't totally sure would happen.

We were in Thunder Bay until 1969, when we moved to Hamilton, and then to Kingston and Toronto. In my church you don't use the word *transfer*. You receive an invitation, which you either accept or reject. I was happy with that — it was time to move. We worked from the premise that you should leave before the congregation tired of you and while there was still creativity left on both sides.

Professionally, Hamilton established a pattern for me. The congregation waited a year before hiring me. During that time I was happy to scout the neighbourhood, join volunteer organizations, and get a sense of the city and who I'd be able to work with. But as I worked in the community, my work took a significant new direction. I became connected with the Canadian Council of Churches and, eventually, the World Council of Churches, which led me into ecumenical affairs. That involvement introduced me to human rights issues, which really captured my interest. In 1974 I took a year off from the church to work for the newly formed Ontario Human Rights Commission. That was a wonderful experience because it gave me access to places that ministers usually aren't able go, such as factories that wouldn't hire Blacks or women. As I got to know the community, I also became aware of the devious excuses that Canadians have for sexism and racism. I wouldn't have believed that such things existed if I hadn't seen them for myself. That experience sharpened my understanding of Canadian society and the subtlety of our prejudices and discriminatory practices.

During the 1970s I spent three months at an ecumenical centre affiliated with the Mar Thoma Syrian Church of Malabar, near Bangalore, India. That experience was one of my most interesting and broadening, because as a Christian in a sea of Hindus with a smattering of Muslims I was out of sync. But that sense of discomfort made me question my assumptions as a Christian and ever since, I've put interfaith and ecumenical work ahead of working with my denomination, whenever possible. During this time, my feminism was gradually developing. For some time, I was a very mild feminist. Then, in 1976 — more than ten years after I read Betty Friedan — I was preaching at quite a prestigious church. Afterwards, one of my friends, who's a strong feminist, came up to me and said, "Lois, that was quite a good sermon, but your language was terrible. You preach as though you were a man." That was a turning point for me. I began to wonder what it meant to be a woman and a minister and to think about how I could bring my full experiences as a woman into my work. Feminism was just beginning in my church then and I used to go to meetings of some of the feminist groups, some of which I thought were pretty radical. I remember one woman saying, "If you're not comfortable here, come back when you are." And that's what I did.

In 1976, I was the first woman to be elected president of the Canadian Council of Churches. Since that was a national post and it was ecumenical, I became known in church circles. As a result, two ministers in Toronto mentioned that they wanted to nominate me as moderator of the United Church. The moderator, who is elected for a limited term, is the titular head of the church. In authority and status the position is the equivalent of an archbishop, and it had always been filled by men, mostly tall ones. Since I'm short, even for a woman, my initial reaction was, "You can't be serious." Quite simply, I'd never imagined myself in that role.

I had an additional reason for not allowing my name to go forward. Another woman had been nominated and I refused to run against her. My growing understanding of feminism had convinced me that women should support one another. I wouldn't back every woman — my support would depend on her values — but I recognized the need to bring the community of women forward. My work with the Canadian Council of Churches had made me particularly conscious that I was always one of the few women in any gathering. Since my university days, theology continued to be a male bastion. I can't say being the only woman was a problem, but I noticed the absence of women and would have loved female company.

In 1980, the next time the moderator's post became open, I was nominated from across the country. When the letters started coming in, my husband said, "You'll have to take this seriously." In fact, I took it so seriously that I went up to Jonquière, Quebec, to study French, and became passably bilingual. I felt that if I held a national position I should be able to appear on French-language television.

I think I was elected because of my international experience and my contribution to social justice. But at that point, there's no doubt that being a woman was an advantage. I loved every minute of my two years in office. People paid more attention to me because of my position and I had a built-in platform, which I used to raise issues such as poverty, racism, and sexism. I had access to every level of Canadian society and I was invited to all sorts of public events. Being the first woman in the position increased my public profile and I milked that for all it was worth to give a voice to issues affecting women. Being moderator expanded my understanding of ministry while giving me an opportunity to exercise this understanding in ways I'd never thought possible.

When my term was up, I wrote a book, *Like a Mighty River*. I submitted that book to the board instead of filing a report, as was traditionally done. I felt that it was important to define what was happening to me spiritually as I met with people around the globe — to show how I was opening up to other people and traditions. My term concluded, but the position continued. I hadn't realized it's a job for life. That's my place in society. I was elected one of six presidents of the World Council of Churches — three women and three men, affirmative action at its best! — and that opened up a whole new world for me. When I look back on the 1980s, I can see that I travelled from transit lounge to transit lounge around the world and I can count on the fingers of one hand those countries whose churches I have never visited.

Every two to three years the United Church awards a McGeachy scholarship for study intended to take the church in a new and worthwhile direction. In 1989 I was the recipient. I used the year to write *Telling Her Story: Feminist Theology Out of Women's Struggles*, and later wrote two books of Bible stories for children informed by feminist theology. The Bible stories grew out of an experience I had in Russia while attending an Orthodox church service. Although I don't speak Russian, a grandmother in the congregation somehow communicated to me that we both had three-year-old granddaughters. She asked if I had taught my granddaughter the Nicene Creed. I didn't like to say I thought that was inappropriate for a three-year-old, but the question she raised for me was important: How do you see your vocation as a grandmother *vis-à-vis* passing on your faith to the children? When I came home I asked one of my daughters, who has five children, what she was doing about this. She told me she had a book of Bible stories and suggested that I read them to the kids. When I looked at the book I was shocked! Nothing had changed in sixty years. These were the same stories I had read as a child. It was as though there had been no changes or advances in biblical scholarship during my lifetime. Since I was I well into feminism at that point, I found this very unsettling. When I complained to my daughter, she said, "You're a theologian. Why don't you do something about it?"

Basically, feminist theology is trying to determine how theology can be consonant with women. The issues centre on authority and tradition. Doctrine and scripture have been written by males, chosen by males, and interpreted by males for two thousand years. What effect has this had on women? It's made some very angry and disenchanted with the church. Yet women were not critical of the male traditions from the word go. For me, it was a slow but steady learning process. As Simone de Beauvoir said, "One is not born a woman, one becomes one." We were all raised in this society, in the same chauvinistic atmosphere. We went to the same schools as men.

Becoming a feminist involved a process of undoing, a process of deconstructing and then reconstructing the learned theology, and that's precisely what I did with the Bible stories I wrote.

I think a number of men who proclaim themselves to be feminists really mean that they support equal pay for equal work or something like that. But feminism is much more profound. It's a whole change of being and a change in our perspective and understanding of community and relationship to the created order. True equality involves both male and female bringing their distinctive corporate experience to the human community. In that sense, feminism is transformational. Eventually it can lead to a new community of women and men where there is mutuality, interdependence, and solidarity. That may never happen fully, but it's what feminism is about.

I think my canoe trips prepared me for coming to terms with the transformational aspects of feminism. Instinctively, I was always healed by the sound of wind in the trees, of water lapping on the shore. It helped me in my reflection of who I am. "Who do you think you are, Lois? Who do you think you are in human history? No one." Which balances off with, "But you're everything — you're a human being." Understanding that paradox is very important.

My husband retired in 1991 and I didn't see any point in continuing to work if he was retired. He says my retirement is a distinction without a difference since I'm still away more than I'm home. Fortunately, I've been blessed with tremendous physical energy. I think I recognized that I needed to find ways to channel it or I'd drive everybody stark raving mad. Maybe I do that anyway. Physical activity energizes me and I've got to be careful because I can't understand why other people don't love it as much as I do.

I don't really have time for regrets. When we were living in Hamilton, around 1974, I was asked by one of the political parties to run federally and I gave some thought to going into politics. They were looking for a woman, I had a high profile, and I think I had a very good chance of winning. I was very excited about campaigning because it provided an opportunity for interchange with people about things that matter to them, like housing and employment. As an elected representative I would have had a mandate to do something about their concerns. But when I thought about public life, I found it was a little scary. The divorce rate among MPs is rather high and my husband was not in favour of it at all since we were busy building a new church for the congregation — the old one, a historically significant building where Egerton Ryerson had preached, had burnt to the ground shortly after our arrival. If I'd become a partisan politician, my position would have created even more flak for him. When I also realized that if I won, I'd have to spend most of my time in Ottawa, I decided not to accept. But the decision was a difficult one, because in many ways going into politics appealed to all my instincts. Instead, I went to India.

I'm sure I made the right choice. But because I want to try everything that comes my way, I still wonder. My approach has always been if a door opens, go through it, and that was one door I didn't go through. Still, you make your choices and you live with them. I've had a great life and so many opportunities have come my way. We've been — I don't think the word lucky is strong enough. And I don't like to use the word *blessed* because it sounds sanctimonious. Maybe something in between — gifted, or full of grace. We've had a life of unexpected gifts.

"I became a feminist philanthropist because it was unfair that men and male institutions were getting all the money."

NANCY RUTH

Nancy Ruth Jackman was born to a prominent Toronto family on January 6, 1942, the youngest child in a family of three older brothers. In 1979, after receiving a substantial inheritance, she gradually began funding social change for women, and in 1990 ran unsuccessfully as a Progressive Conservative candidate in the Ontario election. She has received many awards for her work on behalf of women, including three honorary doctorates, the YWCA Woman of Distinction Award, and the Order of Canada.

In 1968, when I was twenty-six, I attended a World Student Christian Federation Conference in Finland, where, at a session organized by American women, the subject of feminism was introduced. The pennies started to drop. When I was thirteen, my mother and I began to share a bathroom. From time to time, I'd notice bruises on her body. When I asked about them she told me she'd bumped into furniture — an explanation I doubted since they always appeared after I'd heard my parents fighting. Once I understood that my father was punching her up, I decided to spend my life making sure no other woman would have to tolerate abuse.

I'd always been keen on social justice issues, so moving in that direction wasn't an enormous leap. If my mom wasn't in when I arrived home from school, I'd visit Thelma, the laundress, who worked in our basement. She'd be cooking starch in a big pot, with only a stool to sit on, and I complained about that. Trying to get

Thelma a chair is my first memory of taking action around social justice. Since my family were Methodists on both sides, concern about those who weren't as privileged as us was always part of the conversation. My father trained us all to be leaders, to do public service for Canada, to serve the world and our Lord. The principle was that we owed that to society because we were privileged.

My father and I disagreed mightily about many things, and I may have been aware from an early age that I didn't conform to his desires. Both his sisters were very beautiful and his dream for me was that I'd be thin and beautiful, too. I was always a chubby kid, so when he finally got a daughter he must have been a tich disappointed. Even so, I have many good memories of him and he often did things to encourage me.

My professional life really began in 1975 when, after being refused once, I joined the United Church Order of Ministry. By that time, I'd had a long history of involvement with the church. When I was twenty I spent a summer at a World Council of Churches work camp in Greece. In 1964, I went to another church-run work camp in Indonesia. My parents were worried because the Vietnam War was raging, but going to that part of the world seemed like a positive option to me, since secretarial school was the alternative. After my acceptance into the Order of Ministry, I worked in England for a year, doing organizational development in churches. Then, in 1978, I moved back to Toronto and opened a small consulting business with a friend, maintaining my connection with the church by working as an educational and organizational consultant. Suddenly, in 1979, out of the blue, I received a letter thanking me for my service to the United Church. I was so stunned I sat on it for a week. When I finally phoned the church office to ask what the letter meant, they told me I was being removed from the Order of Ministry.

The church had been twenty years of my life, and being dismissed struck me like a physical blow. I hired a lawyer, who advised me that "natural justice" hadn't been done because I hadn't received a hearing. I decided to sue the church, won, and was reinstated — an experience that taught me the law could be used to achieve fairness.

In 1979, when my father died, my life took another major turn. Like all his children, I accessed a substantial sum. I cashed in my chips, was "liquid," and decided to quit the church — who would want to work for $15,000 a year and endure the church's resentment of competent women if she didn't have to?

When my father died, my mother, my brothers, and I were appointed to the board of the Jackman Foundation. We all began to participate in deciding where money would go, and in 1979 I gave $5000 to the National Action Committee on the Status of Women (NAC) Educational Trust. NAC didn't often get cheques that substantial, so Kay Macpherson, the former president, called and invited me to a NAC Christmas party. Although I'd supported NAC in the past, that was my first meeting with Toronto feminists. Towards the end of January 1981, Kay Macpherson called again and invited me to a meeting to discuss women's inclusion in the proposed Constitution of Canada. Not only were the government's proposed sex equality guarantees inadequate, but Prime Minister Trudeau and Lloyd Axworthy were actively trying to silence women by cancelling Doris Anderson's conference on the *Charter of Rights and Freedoms*, organized by the Canadian Advisory Council on the Status of Women. Since my experience with the church had taught me that if your rights weren't enshrined in law you had nothing, I was primed for the issue.

If I hadn't been kicked out of the ministry, I don't think I would have become involved with the law. In those days I wasn't aware that my grandfather Newton Rowell, whom I knew as a distinguished legislator and litigator, had been the lawyer for the five women who fought the Persons Case, which made women persons legally in 1929. It's terrible how insignificant anything to do with women was in my upbringing.

In 1981, I had lots of free time since I didn't have to work, so I became involved in lobbying to get women's rights enshrined in the Constitution. I started speaking across the country and became a "full-time" feminist. In some sense, speaking publicly was a coming of age. It was manageable, I was good at it, and I liked working with other women. I no longer had to put up with bullshit about whether I'd be obedient to the church. But I think I'd been radicalized long before I became actively involved with women's rights. The furor around the Constitution gave me an outlet for the frustration I'd experienced with the church.

As I said, around the time I became involved with Toronto feminism, I joined the board of the Jackman Foundation. That experience sowed the seeds of my feminist philanthropy. As we awarded our grants, I began to notice that most of the funding — about ninety percent — was going to groups that benefited men and boys or male-controlled institutions. I'd suggest giving money to organizations like the Elizabeth Fry Society and my brothers would vote it down. Eventually, we were fighting so much that we decided to divide up the money, with each of us getting a percentage. I soon recognized that this arrangement would only allow me to give annual income. I'd never be able to take a million dollars and fund something big or long-term, which I was beginning to see was necessary to make meaningful change. I made up my mind to get my full share of the capital and kept raising the issue. Finally, my mother got tired of the responsibility and said she wanted her cut, too. When my brother Hal finally accepted that she wanted out, he made us an offer. Mother and I got $5 million each and left.

My money went into my own foundation. I'd been involved in founding the Women's Legal Education and Action Fund (LEAF), which was established to ensure that the precedent-setting cases using the *Charter of Rights and Freedoms* would actually benefit women. My first major gift was to set up the LEAF Foundation, which would create an endowment to assure the organization's permanence. My next major philanthropic gesture was setting up the Canadian Women's Foundation (CWF). My mother gave $500,000 to get it going and I gave half a million as a matching pledge. The catalyst for CWF was the death of Margaret Horan, my mother's downstairs' maid. I had Margaret's power of attorney, and when I discovered she had left $40,000 — a phenomenal sum of money for someone in domestic service — to the Scarborough Foreign Mission, I was upset. All her money was going to men! She might have left it to an organization like INTERCEDE, which works on behalf of female domestic workers like her.

People had been talking about setting up a women's foundation for years, so my idea wasn't new. I understood from my connections that most foundations were beginning to get applications from women's shelters and so on, which the foundations didn't know how to assess. I saw that an organization like CWF could be more than an estate beneficiary for people like Margaret Horan. It could also advise other foundations that wanted to contribute to women.

When I started, I didn't know I was involved with feminist philanthropy — which is what it's called now. I simply knew the distribution of money from the Jackman Foundation was unfair. My brothers gave most of it to their sex for things that helped to maintain the status quo and continued the oppression of women. I also saw this pattern on the public records of other foundations. When LEAF started its endowment campaign, I commissioned some research, which showed that private donations from foundations in Canada gave less than two percent to girls and women. Although it's gone up a bit, it's still only around five percent. Charities, like the rest of society, are hugely discriminatory.

In recent years, my professional interests have focused on politics. Since many of the men in my family, beginning with my grandfather, had run for political office, some successfully, doing so wasn't an unusual thing. When David Crombie, my MP, resigned, I sought the nomination in my home riding of Rosedale. If I had started earlier, I think I would have won. Even so, running for election was great fun and that's where I wet my feet. I ran in the 1990 provincial election in St. Andrew-St. Patrick and came very close to defeating the NDP candidate in an NDP sweep. I ran again in a by-election in 1993, which the press hoped I'd win, but I lost for a variety of reasons, most of which weren't very pleasant, and the experience made me very cynical.

During that election, my sexual preference became an issue. Svend Robinson, the NDP Member of Parliament from the Vancouver area, told me that in 1993 I was the first "out" lesbian to run in Canada. The media had known I was a lesbian for years, but for whatever reason they chose not to write about it until then. During the campaign someone asked why homosexuals should trust me on the issue of same-sex benefits and I said because of my human rights background and because I was a lesbian. *NOW*, a Toronto weekly newspaper, picked the story up, and from there it hit the *Globe and Mail* and went across the country. I guess it was news because at the time my brother Hal was the lieutenant-governor of Ontario. But I dislike being known as a lesbian first and foremost. It's not why I've done what I've done. My sense of social justice as a child had nothing to do with my sexual preference.

In 1993, during the by-election, my mother fell and then started to go downhill. I made a decision to be with her until she died. My brothers weren't helping in the ways I needed them to help, and I wasn't prepared to let her die alone. This meant I couldn't campaign for the 1994 nomination. My mother was a very formal woman, but I was quite close to her at the end. My brothers see her as cold, but I see the "coldness" as resolve. In 1944, when I was two, my father asked for a divorce. Even though he'd taken up with another woman, Mother said no. When I was in my thirties, she told me she refused so his money would be conserved for her children. The fortune would have been diluted if he had left and had another family. Still, none of my brothers or their children would ever admit that my mother contributed to conserving their capital and trust funds.

Now I can see that, on some level, I'm trying to redeem my mother's life. I've hired someone to write her biography and I realize that in some ways I'm more like her than like my father, since the objective of my life's work has never been to make money. Mother's tradition of public service was far more radical than Father's. I manage assets and dabble here and there in projects, but my gut is for social justice, not money.

My mother died at 4.10 p.m. When I arrived home from the hospital, my partner, Sirje, was visiting with some friends. After a glass or two of wine I found myself saying, "Thank goodness, I don't have to be a Jackman any more." So I dropped the "Jackman" from my name and left the two names my parents had given me, Nancy Ruth.

For the past year and a half, I've fought to come back from depression and cynicism after losing the by-election, my mother's death, and the experience of menopause. My psychic struggle is around good and evil and why evil keeps on winning. My current project is setting up a women's museum, an idea that came from my mother's wedding dress. Although it's a beautiful 1920s dress, nobody in the family wanted it so I decided to give it to the fashion design program at Seneca College. That experience got me thinking about a women's museum. I started talking to people, and the plan evolved into creating something that would push other museums to conserve women's history. We're doing it on the Internet, which is a bit sedentary for someone who's used to getting on and off airplanes and doing rubber chicken lunches, but since I don't have anything to say to the public right now, I think I'm better off staying at home until the next challenge materializes.

"In the late 1980s, homemakers had very low status. We were seen as not contributing to the community. We were thought to have no ambitions, to be people who couldn't get a job doing anything else. We were there by default."

CAROL LEES

In 1996, Statistics Canada entered a new era when, for the first time, the census forms asked Canadians how much time they spent on unpaid work. This change was largely due to the efforts of Carol Lees, a homemaker in Saskatoon who refused to answer the 1991 census question that required her to say she didn't work. Threatened with a jail term for her act of civil disobedience, she went on to found the Canadian Alliance for Home Managers and to lobby nationally for changes to the census. A member of the Unitarian Church, she has been honoured regionally, nationally, and internationally by that body for her efforts on behalf of unpaid workers.

In the mid-1980s, before I became committed to valuing unpaid work in the home, my kids gave me an apron that says "All Work and No Pay Makes a Housewife." The more deeply I got involved in the issue of unpaid work, the more clearly that message spoke to me. Over time, two things became evident: that only activity done for pay was classified as work and that the major source of devaluing unpaid work was government policy, which defined work exclusively as paid activity.

Early in 1991, as the census was approaching, I started to think seriously about this issue. One question on the census form asked, "In the proceeding week how many hours did you work?" There was a bracketed clarification excluding housework or home maintenance and, if I remember correctly, volunteer work in the community. I had spent the winter building a support group in which we determined that we would never say we didn't work, so I wasn't about to define myself on a government form as not working. Although I recognized that it was too late for Statistics Canada to make the necessary amendments, I determined I wouldn't complete my forms unless that question was changed. Basically, I had decided to take a political stand.

I wrote to the minister responsible at the time, outlining my position, and sent copies to women's organizations across the country, along with a letter asking them to join me in a boycott of the census if homemaking wasn't recognized as work. When census day came, I was lucky enough to receive the long form, which contained the relevant question. My refusal to complete the forms caused some consternation in my household. Not only was my husband working for the federal government at the time, but he'd served in the military and he wasn't comfortable with defying the government. Local census officials, who were hopeful we could work things out, visited several times to discuss the matter, but I was adamant. Eventually, I received a letter from Statistics Canada saying that if I did not complete my forms I would be prosecuted and was liable on conviction to a fine of $500 and/or a jail term. The letter is not a nice one to receive — it makes you weak in the knees — but I wrote back and explained, once again, why I refused to identify myself as not working. I also informed them that if I was convicted I would not be able to pay the fine because I wasn't a paid worker. As a result, I'd be forced to accept the jail term.

I knew I was backing them into a corner — there was no way they could win. If they prosecuted me and I refused to pay and they sent me to jail, they'd look like fools for jailing a mother of three because she refused to say she didn't work. They had gone so far as to threaten me, and to tell you the truth, part of me was hoping they would prosecute, as it would have made a wonderful spectacle. I was determined that the government wouldn't get away with sweeping the issue under the table. I was outraged that someone or something was trying to deny the reality of my working life. My days as a home-maker were always busy. I was often up at 5:30 or 6:00 and wouldn't get to bed until 10:30 or 11:00. I was always the last one in bed and the first one up. It was a long day.

I was definitely an unlikely radical. I grew up in Powell River, an extremely conservative pulp and paper town on the B.C. coast. My family, who belonged to the Baptist Church, was very religious. When I was seventeen I left home to go to university in Vancouver. Ultimately, I earned an English degree, a psychology degree, and a master's in applied psychology. I lived in the east for a while but by 1997, when my third child was born, we were living in Edmonton. At that point, I was enrolled in a doctoral program. I knew that if I completed my Ph.D., I'd want to invest a lot of time and energy in developing that career. I also knew that my family would suffer and that I wouldn't feel I was doing a satisfactory job of either my paid work or my family work. I decided it was more important to do my best job with my family.

I don't know how to explain that decision, and in some ways, when I look back on it, it surprises me. I didn't see myself as a maternal person. Even when the children were young I found it difficult to be a mother. I'm not a woman who gets goo-goo over babies. In fact, of all the occupations I've had — from teacher to educational consultant — I found being a full-time mother the hardest. Still, I don't remember the decision as being a terribly difficult one to make. I had never been driven to accumulate material wealth or to have a lot of things. And I evidently didn't — at that point, anyway — feel any need for power and prestige and the status that comes with paid work. I had a good education and a good brain and was confident that if I ever needed to return to the paid workforce I could, as many women have done over the years.

In 1978, when my son was six months old and my daughters were five and two, we moved to Saskatoon. My husband's parents were living here and having some family around helped with the social isolation of working at home. But I didn't have siblings or my own parents to visit, trade child care, or share concerns with, and I missed those opportunities for informal contact. Fortunately, there were a number of other women in the neighbourhood at home with young children and we used to get together once a week for coffee. That much-maligned institution of having coffee with your neighbours saved my sanity. Now I would identify it as networking and professional development, which is what meeting with your co-workers and discussing work-related problems is called in the paid workplace.

In the late 1980s, after I had been home full-time for about ten years, I was offered a part-time, paid job. Like many women, I succumbed to social pressures to be out in the world, participating and earning income. I started with one or two days a week, but that grew and it didn't take me long to see that my family's quality of life was suffering in many different ways. Our diet deteriorated because I no longer had time to cook, bake, garden, and preserve. Garry and I didn't spend as much time together and the kids had their worst year ever at school because we couldn't keep track of what they were doing and supervise their activities, as well. After a year and a half, I decided to return home. When I made that choice I was aware that I was one of the privileged few who were able to be at home full-time and that concerned me. I knew many women would have preferred to be at home, not necessarily full-time, but couldn't afford that option. I felt that was wrong and I recognized that I had been waiting many years for someone to take on this issue and make a change. I realized nobody was going to do it for me.

I also realized I was no longer willing to return to the home under the conditions I had left it. I had begun to see how devalued I was by society and I was no longer willing to be treated that way or to feel that other people saw me as lazy and unproductive. In the fall of 1990, I organized a free, one-day workshop with child care at the YMCA called "Connections." It was designed to bring together people in the community who worked at home. The upshot of that day was that we identified two major problems of being a homemaker: isolation and devaluation. When we looked at the Royal Commission on the Status of Women, which reported in 1970, it was clear that although the report had recommended that homemaking be recognized as work and more highly valued, nothing had been accomplished. No one, other than groups characterized as right-wing, had been focusing on those issues. REAL Women had become the voice on behalf of that constituency, but the way they addressed those issues made many women uneasy. However, I have made a point of communicating with REAL Women over the years, because I feel they have a legitimate voice and speak for a group of Canadian women who have a right to be heard.

We formed a support group, which in 1991 expanded to include a second small group of people who wanted to focus on advocacy. The Canadian Alliance for Home Managers was formed and we started to network with other like-minded organizations. After receiving the letter from Statistics Canada saying they would prosecute me if I didn't complete my forms, I hadn't heard anything further from them, and finally I decided to call. I got passed along until eventually I reached someone who told me that they had decided not to prosecute. In a sense their decision was irrelevant because the wheels were already in motion for a national campaign to boycott the census.

The first national conference on housework and family care was held in Saskatoon in March 1993. We invited representatives from feminist, mainstream, and right-wing organizations. Since I was determined that all voices would be heard, we also invited Statistics Canada. About 120 people attended the conference. The highlight was the presentation by a representative from Statistics Canada, who, unfortunately, spoke to us condescendingly. I can't remember the details of what he said, but it was along the lines of, "We are the experts and we know what work is and you don't." The reaction from the mostly female audience was so strong that he had to stop about ten minutes into his presentation to ask for comments. Women lined up at the mike and tore a strip out of him. I don't think he realized that many of the women in the audience were highly educated, and even those who were not well educated were eloquent about how offensive they found his attitude. His presentation mobilized the conference. Afterwards, delegate after delegate approached me to say, "Carol, now I know what you're dealing with."

Later that year, I heard about an international conference on measuring and valuing unpaid work that Statistics Canada was sponsoring. Since they knew about my campaign, I was quite surprised that I hadn't been informed, so I phoned the gentleman who had spoken at our conference and said I would like to attend. His response was, essentially, that the conference was a gathering of experts and I wouldn't fit in. I wrote letters to Status of Women Canada, the minister responsible for Statistics Canada, and everyone else I could think of, insisting that unpaid workers were the experts on this subject and that the conference organizers were doing the equivalent of organizing an agricultural conference to set policy for the country and inviting weekend gardeners, rather than farmers, to attend. Finally, ten women's organizations were selected to send representatives and I was able to attend the conference.

By this time we had a network in place and had formed a formal coalition to target the census as an instrument of social change. The census was critical, because it was the government document that defined what work is and who is a worker. This definition forms the basis of what is given value and included in the national accounting system that drives public policy. If you're not present there, you're not present in policy decisions and not present in policy development at the other end. By June 1994, we had a commitment from the National Action Committee on the Status of Women to support a national boycott of the 1996 census if unpaid work was not included, and shortly thereafter we were successful in getting the question changed. The decision was made by Cabinet, not Statistics Canada, which resisted right to the end. I don't remember exactly how I was informed. I do remember that I was in hospital, having just been diagnosed with diabetes, which I'm pretty sure was brought on by stress and the long hours I was devoting to the issue, since there is no history of diabetes in my family and I didn't have any of the risk factors.

Throughout this process, I received encouragement and support from friends and from Status of Women Canada. My religious community provided both moral and practical support. My daughters always supported me enthusiastically, but for much of the campaign my husband did not. We've talked a fair bit about it and I know my activism was difficult for him. I was not as available for the household chores and he lost some of my time and attention. In addition, he was uncomfortable with me being rather radical in some actions. I think he also resented men being treated as oppressors. The basic thinking around this issue, which has been developing since the most recent wave of feminism got underway, is that women pay political, economic, and social costs because of their family work and men reap the benefits. That's the reality. You don't have to be resentful or angry about it — it's just a fact.

I was quite surprised at how the elder female members of my family reacted. I thought the older women who had raised children would be one hundred percent behind me, but that wasn't the case. My mother used to ask when I was going to quit this women's stuff and get back to looking after my family. I had an aunt who wondered if it wouldn't be more worthwhile for me to return to teaching and remedial reading work, which she felt was a more serious issue than valuing unpaid work. Surprisingly, the relative who was most strongly supportive had taught school all her life and never had children.

Recently, I had to retire from social activism for health reasons. I now have two part-time, paid jobs because we need to help our kids, who are attending university, finish their education. I have taken part-time work that is low stress and low-paying but physically active in order to manage my diabetes. I am working one day a week at a nature shop and I do part-time work for a home support service. So I'm still doing family care, but for pay.

I don't have any regrets. I made some wonderful friends, had some very interesting experiences, and learned a lot. I don't even regret the diabetes. I would do it all again and pay that price because I believe getting the unpaid work of homemakers recognized was such an important thing to do.

"One of the interesting things about the women's movement is how things that were literally unthinkable twenty-five years ago became commonly accepted within such a relatively short period of time. I find that process completely fascinating."

MEGAN ELLIS

Megan Ellis has been involved in various aspects of violence against women since 1976, when she started to work with Rape Relief in Vancouver. With her law partner, Theresa Stowe, she is currently working to establish precedents in the area of remedies for survivors of sexual abuse.

I can still remember, almost word for word, the first telephone call I received dealing with incest. It was around 1977 and I was working at Rape Relief in Vancouver. A woman who sounded as though she was in her forties or fifties told me that when she was sixteen, her father had raped her while her mother was in the hospital. I was completely aghast! Nobody had ever talked about this and I'd never read anything on the subject. It was unthinkable! But during that year, the voices of survivors of sexual abuse began to be heard. By the early 1980s the sexual abuse of children had emerged as a very big issue. The Women's Research Centre asked me to participate in a research project on child sexual abuse that ultimately became a book called *Recollecting Our Lives*. The work on that project is directly linked to my practice as a lawyer today.

Although I'd announced my intention to become a lawyer at a very young age, there were many things I wanted to do in my twenties rather than law school. When I was fifteen or sixteen, I remember a male friend saying to me, "You can't be a lawyer — you're a girl." I didn't buy that for a minute — and I'm not sure why — those attitudes were still very prevalent when I was growing up. There were boys' things and there were girls' things — for instance, my brothers slept without pillows and took out the garbage, while I did the laundry. When I was about twelve, I wanted the reasoning behind this, and it became clear that the explanation for why males and females are treated differently, like the explanation for God, was lacking. In one of the volumes of her autobiography, Simone de Beauvoir talks about growing up as a middle-class child with the sense that everything in the world is right, that the good things can be enjoyed with a clear conscience, and then later discovering this wasn't so. That was very much my pattern. I had a fairly idyllic upbringing in suburban Vancouver as the eldest of four kids. My mother was a stay-at-home mom and my father was a provincial court judge. I was vaguely aware that terrible things like Biafra were happening in the world but didn't feel they were attributable to us in any way.

As a teenager, I didn't have any friends who leaned towards feminism, as least not active feminism, but I read all the newspaper stories about the feminists in New York and thought their activities sounded terribly imaginative and colourful. I wanted to do interesting things like them, though I was a bit too young. But feminism did more than capture my imagination. It went some way towards addressing a problem that was becoming slowly apparent to me — the gap between the liberal values of equality I was raised with and how people, especially women, were actually treated.

I went to work at Rape Relief in 1976 when, tired of university, I decided to do something other than being a student. Since I've always had a practical bent, the idea of working with a service organization, especially one that interfaced with the legal system, appealed to me. I saw it as a tremendous opportunity because it combined a way into the women's movement with a chance to do something concrete. Also, while I was at university, I'd done some counselling on the student night-line, so the work was a good fit.

In those days, Rape Relief was very much at the forefront of the women's movement, not only in B.C. but across the country. It was a gateway into the women's movement, a lively, creative, and highly critical network of ideas, discussion, and conferences. We were always having interesting, passionate debates and I went to meetings with representatives from other women's groups continuously — I'd start at breakfast and carry on until ten or eleven at night. I was in my early twenties and had lots of energy, but the older women I worked with were equally tireless — I suppose because we were energized by our creativity. We had achieved the satisfaction of building something, we'd flexed our muscles and governments, newspapers, and goodness knows who else had reacted. Our potential seemed unlimited.

To some extent, that sense of possibility stemmed from there being an NDP government in B.C. during the crucial time when many organizations were emerging. This government funded social programs and provided operating grants, with salaries, to many organizations, and these funds allowed us to be full-time activists. Although we constantly debated how to balance service and activism, we were fully engaged in both. We were truly committed to providing non-bureaucratic, direct support to the women who called us for help. As well, we, ourselves, were learning about the extent of violence against women. Today, our level of ignorance is unimaginable, but in those days the sole image of rape was a strange man jumping out from the bushes and attacking you. Yet it wasn't that unusual for women to be raped by men known to them. Although women shared this experience among themselves, the knowledge wasn't mainstream and date rape was generally treated with great cynicism.

In 1977 or 1978 I worked with the woman complainant in the *Pappajohn* case, which became quite a *cause célèbre*. George Pappajohn was a wealthy businessman whose real estate agent was found on the doorstep of a neighbouring house, naked with her hands tied behind her back. In those days, it was highly unusual for a woman who was raped by a man she knew to succeed in having charges laid, and this was the victim's first hurdle. When Pappajohn was finally charged, he argued that he honestly believed she had consented to sex. Some people at the time were critical of the treatment rape victims received in the courts and a number of very high-profile women, called together by city councillor Darlene Marzari, decided to attend the trial to witness the process for themselves, as well as to express concern about how the courts were treating rape. Pappajohn was convicted, but he took his appeal all the way to the Supreme Court of Canada. Although he failed to get the conviction overturned, the court accepted that it wasn't rape if the man sincerely believed the woman was consenting. As you might imagine, women were horrified by this ruling.

It's hard to believe that we were also just starting to identify and develop alternative ways to deal with sexual assault both *vis-à-vis* institutions and *vis-à-vis* ourselves, by having, for example, women doctors do post–sexual assault examinations at hospitals. This was a completely novel idea at the time. When I first started working with Rape Relief, a woman who was raped anywhere in the Lower Mainland would be carted off to the Vancouver General Hospital to be examined by a forensic specialist, who was reputed to be extremely cold, while male police officers waited outside the cubicle. It was about the furthest thing from women-centred medicine imaginable.

Because we didn't have tons of statistical data in those days to support what we were hearing, our reports were dismissed as anecdotal, a technique that is consistently used to dismiss the reality of women's experience. Then Lorenne Clark and Debra Lewis published their book *Rape: The Price of Coercive Sexuality*, which gave us tons of ammunition by providing extensive data about what was happening to women who reported sexual assaults to the police and attempted to use the criminal justice system to deal with their violation. We applied the book to great effect, collectively, across the country to lobby government to get the *Criminal Code* changed, and during that time public support for changes to the laws governing rape grew rapidly.

In 1983, a new law was enacted, which did away with "rape" as a legal term and defined the offence as various degrees of sexual assault. Significantly, it stated that a spouse could be charged with sexual assault and clearly identified the offence as violent rather than sexual in nature, something a man did to assert his power over another person. This was seen as an end to the widespread myth that rape was motivated by men's overwhelming sexual urges. Although the law was a major step forward, those of us who worked in the field were quite aware that changing the legislation was just the beginning and the real challenge would come with how the law was implemented.

In 1984, I finally enrolled in law school. By then I had done lots of short-term things but really needed to get a game plan together for the longer term. Besides, I was twenty-nine, which I viewed as getting on in years. While I was at law school I worked on a project for the Women's Research Centre interviewing adult survivors of sexual abuse and mothers of children who had been sexually abused, and it became evident to me that these were missing voices in the criminal justice system. Gradually, I began to develop the idea that suing perpetrators might be an interesting way of making the legal system face up to the experience of being sexually violated. I connected with a group of legal academics and activists to talk about bringing claims for damages for survivors of sexual abuse.

I qualified as a lawyer in 1988, and in 1989 took the plunge and set up a practice with other women. One of them, Theresa Stowe, now my law partner, was also a feminist who was interested in doing civil sexual assault cases. I don't think I would have been able to do these cases if I'd taken a job with an existing firm.

Initially, I did only family law, including many cases for battered women that were funded by legal aid. After I'd been in practice for about a year, a friend who worked at Vancouver Status of Women got a call from a brave young woman named Anne Beaudry, who wanted to sue her stepfather for sexually abusing her. I took the case, and in 1991 she was awarded a total of about $185,000, which I think was then the highest judgment an incest survivor had ever received by quite a large margin. There had been only four or five earlier decisions in B.C. and the awards had been in the $30,000 to $45,000 range. The judge in our case was the first in Canada to accept the notion that our client, who was under twenty-one at the time, had suffered a wage loss as a result of the injuries inflicted on her between the ages of seven and fourteen, and that her ability to earn in the future would continue to be affected. On the downside, the stepfather declared bankruptcy to avoid paying the judgment. In April 1997 the legislation was amended to close that loophole.

Then Theresa and I argued the first successful case in Canada to get around the *Limitation Act*, which had been a major barrier preventing survivors of sexual abuse from seeking claims. In B.C. — it differs from province to province — you have two years from the time of an injury to make a claim. The problem with sexual abuse is that it's often a long time before survivors even realize that they have injuries resulting from the abuse. Also, they're so traumatized that it can take years before they can deal with the situation. Within a matter of days after we won our case, the B.C. government announced that it intended to amend the legislation to eliminate the limitation period for sexual abuse.

Since then, child sexual abuse litigation has become the majority of our work. It's very challenging, in part because these cases don't fit easily into the system, but I feel very fortunate to be working in this area, at this time, in a legal practice where almost every case raises new questions. Often, our clients are amazingly courageous. I'm grateful, as well, to be working in partnership with someone who shares that interest and who is willing to share the economic ups and downs that come with doing test cases. Many of our clients can't afford lawyers, so we've done lots of cases on an "if and when" basis.

I didn't get married in the traditional sense and did not have children. I suppose I'm not very good at moderation. To be a feminist is to be critical about how things work and to call everything into question. No stone is left unturned. If you're vigorous about it, which I have a tendency to be, everything gets put under the spotlight, including relationships. Since litigation tends to be all-consuming and doesn't leave much time for other interests, I sometimes think about doing something else, but I don't have any definite plans. I do feel incredibly fortunate to have come of age when I did. Younger women tell me they feel that they missed a wonderful time of excitement and, tragically, that's true.

"Initially, I wanted a job to get out of the house a little more, but I soon became so interested in what I was doing that I was neglecting my family. That feeling of being enlivened by work comes out of following your intuition. Pat Thom taught me that. She used to say, "Nobody's out there teaching you, there's no book that will tell you how to do this. You'll just have to figure out what you've learned from your own experience and go with it."

ANNE IRONSIDE

In January 1973, Anne Ironside started work as coordinator of the new University of British Columbia Women's Resources Centre, the first such establishment in Canada. Ten years later, when she became president of the Canadian Association for Adult Education, she was the first woman in the fifty-year history of the organization to hold that position. In 1984 she chaired the national Task Force on Skill Development Leave and, over the years, she has published numerous articles on education-related subjects. She and her husband have created a small educational retreat on Bowen Island, where they conduct workshops on spiritualism and work-related issues. She is also president of the Bowen Island Conservancy.

One day, in the fall of 1972, my mother noticed an ad in the paper: "Wanted: coordinator of the Women's Resources Centre." Because the position was part-time, I thought it would be the perfect way to combine family responsibilities with having a job. In those days, I was pretty much a housewife who wanted to get out of the house. I certainly didn't see myself as a feminist. I'd read about feminists doing dramatic things like burning their bras and my response was, "Oh dear, I wish they wouldn't do that."

The Women's Resources Centre was the brain child of Pat Thom, a married woman with grown children, who had been running the daytime program at the University of British Columbia's Centre for Continuing Education. That program, the only one of its kind in North America with the exception of one at UCLA, offered non-credit courses during the day for people interested in learning. Not surprisingly, most of their clients were women.

Like me, Pat didn't see herself as a great social reformer. She'd been a psychologist before she became involved in education and in that role had spent a fair bit of time working in psychiatric settings. Remarkably, many of the patients were women who seemed quite sensible to her. This observation caused her to think deeply about how the structures of society don't work for women. Gradually, she concluded that much could be done to improve women's lives through intelligent support and redirection. Through her involvement in the Royal Commission on the Status of Women and the formation of the first Status of Women group in Canada, she met a band of like-minded women who were influential in getting funding to start the Women's Resources Centre (WRC).

That fall, seventy-nine women and I applied for the job of coordinator. Surprisingly, I got hired. Years later, I asked Pat why she had hired me, since I wasn't a feminist. "I never worried about that," she replied. "Any woman with a brain in her head will see the truth of women's lives." Of course, she was right, and I've subsequently hired many women on that basis. With hindsight, I can also see that my middle-of-the-road approach to feminism was exactly what the centre required.

When I applied for the job I assumed that Pat would know how to go about turning her concept into reality. Naively, I thought we'd be able to pull some book off the shelf with a recipe that would tell us what to do. Of course it didn't work that way — we were breaking ground and there were no models to follow. All we had was a sense of the direction in which we wanted to move. We knew we wanted to establish a mentoring atmosphere, a place where women could find nurturing that would foster their existing strengths. Pat's non-credit programming at the university provided the only guide, so we decided to use those courses to test our ideas. Since in those days women were seen as passive and dependent, we felt our titles had to pass what we called the "Dinner Table Test" — women would generate support by being able to tell their families, "I'm taking a course in Women, Money and the Family," instead of admitting they were building self-confidence. We worked by trial and error, which is quite remarkable when you consider that twenty-three years later the centre is still running and I've travelled around the world talking about it.

In spite of many impediments, by the end of our first year we'd received one thousand calls. Currently, WRC staff see about fourteen thousand people a year and the centre is mainly run by volunteers. Working there was a real growth experience for me. My socialization had taught me that after you prepare to do a job, somebody tells you what to do and you do it. The WRC was the first time I'd experienced an extremely unshaped situation. It was also my introduction to the feminist community.

At first I found the influential feminists I met alarmingly self-confident — very attractively so, but certainly not like anyone I'd known. Meeting women who had such strength of purpose and determination blew me away — women like the soon-to-be-judge Nancy Morrison; Lisa Hobbs Birnie, a gutsy journalist who'd reported from the Vietnam/Cambodia war; and Rosemary Brown, a soon-to-be MLA. These were women who didn't take anything from anybody. Initially, I didn't see myself as one of them at all. I was, as I said, very much a housewife who wanted to get out of the house.

At that point I didn't realize I'd need to undergo a psychological transformation in order to learn to stand up for what I believed in. But knowing those women and finding I could hold my own with them was part of my process of growth. They forced me to think about who I was and where I stood on issues. I soon realized I wasn't comfortable with some of the positions more radical feminists were taking. We eventually broadened our base, but at the beginning many of the women who came to the centre were middle-class housewives like me. By and large they didn't want to run off and become radical feminists. Although I came to value the radical left for the role they played in gaining attention for women's issues, I didn't feel it would be helpful to tell our clients that they had to abandon men or take up arms in the class struggle. These were women who were experiencing pain in their lives and they wanted immediate help. Since I was still struggling to keep it all together myself, I knew what they were feeling: they wanted a life beyond their family, but they didn't want it at the expense of their family. The question was, how could they work that out?

I think my background played a big role in my discomfort with radicalism. I was born in 1936 in Kamloops, B.C., where my father was a doctor. Obviously, I grew up in a fairly privileged environment, and I now see that the sense of security it created enabled me to take risks. There were four of us — three girls and a boy — and we were raised to believe, like good members of the upper-middle class, that we could mould and shape society. I don't think I really sensed that boys did more moulding and shaping until I finished university. While we were in school, girls were expected to achieve as much as our male classmates. Then suddenly the ball game changed and the girls were career-counselled into marriage and children, while the boys went on to do great, wonderful things.

It was normal for young women of my social class to attend university. Education was perceived as valuable, to some extent, I suppose, because it helped us to marry well and raise educated children. I graduated in 1957 with a degree in bacteriology, then travelled in Europe for a couple of years. That was my first, big, self-reliance and self-directed learning project. I came back quite changed, particularly by travelling around North Africa and the then USSR. I'd seen many different approaches to life and no longer simply accepted things at face value. One good thing about the 1950s was that it was a very secure, safe time, which meant we didn't feel that our lives were threatened or that our future was in peril, unlike young people today.

When I came back I got married, of course. Then I had my two daughters and was an absolute misfit in suburbia. I really didn't handle being a young mother at home very well. When I read Betty Friedan's *The Feminine Mystique*, I realized that many other women were like me. Basically, I was suffering from what she termed "the problem with no name." Though I had a nice family and house, I had the feeling there must be more to life. Child rearing was emotionally satisfying, but it wasn't intellectually challenging.

I went back to university as a part-time student and took a degree in social work because I didn't want to do science any more. Making the shift from bacteriology to doing social work took me a long time. In bacteriology you're taught, here are the facts, write them down, spew them back, and you'll do well. In social work it's not that way at all. The human condition isn't as predictable as the biological sciences.

It also took me quite a while to find my feet in the WRC. While I was figuring out how to make the resource centre work I was simultaneously developing as a professional. Given my background as a nice, well-brought-up girl who basically hoped that everybody would like me, learning to handle contentious situations wasn't easy. Whenever I went out socially with my husband, who's a surgeon, and people heard that I worked and I worked for women, I'd find myself under siege and I'd have to defend myself. It seemed that I was never free of confrontation. I was speaking up on the job and speaking up off the job. However, that certainly helped me to clarify my values.

Despite these problems, working at the WRC was my first experience with work that utterly absorbs and transforms. I hadn't known that work could do that for people and the realization was wonderful. In 1978, I had another opportunity to move forward when Walter Hardwick, who had been director of the Centre for Continuing Education at UBC, the umbrella under which the WRC operated, was appointed Deputy Minister of Education. I started writing him letters asking what he was doing for women and he replied by offering me a month's salary to write about what I discovered through my association with the WRC. I produced a forty-page proposal outlining the benefits of women's centres and explaining how to set them up. As a result of that document and a companion one written by two women in the community college system, the Ministry of Education allocated funding to set up women's centres at community colleges throughout the province. That was my first brush with small-p politics, which is where my career took me after that.

I soon discovered it's one thing to have a policy and quite another to implement it. The money for the centres went into the base budgets of all the community colleges, but in those days all the colleges were run by men — there wasn't a single woman head. When this extra few hundred thousand dollars suddenly materialized, they weren't dying to spend it on women. The resistance from the male administrators meant that women would be hired to run the programs and then the funding would start to slip away. We quickly recognized that we had to teach women how to push, shove, and lobby to keep things going.

That kind of small-p politicking made me interested in going onto the board of the Canadian Association for Adult Education (CAAE), a national organization that had been lobbying government on behalf of adult learners since 1935. That experience was significant because like many women of my age and class I'd never really understood how politics affects the intimate details of your life. Through my association with feminists such as Pauline Jewett, a federal MP, and Gene Errington, a long-time activist and civil servant, as well as my work at the WRC, I began to realize that life *is* politics — that women face many external as well as internal barriers. And working with the CAAE taught me how to lobby in a much more sophisticated way than I had previously understood.

In 1983, after four years of involvement with the organization, I decided to run for president. I think I won because I was a woman from the West. In those days people tended to think that everything innovative started in central Canada and the work we had done not only with the WRC but in getting the access centres established across the province was worth acknowledging. I became the organization's first woman president, a position I held for four years. It was a pretty big deal — until then, the CAAE had been very much an old-boys' club. I suppose I was able to break the mould because successful men and women encouraged me to believe I was capable.

I stayed actively involved with the organization for ten years and during that time I developed — because men taught me — a lot of sophistication about how to get your say in things. It also broadened my ideas of how to implement change for women. In my view, adult education is *the* route to change that lasts for women. Picketing restaurants may be interesting and fun, but in the long run education will make the difference.

As much as I enjoyed my work, keeping everything together was very difficult with two kids and a surgeon husband. I don't think I ever came to terms with the fact that the pace would continue for as long as I had a job. I kept going by telling myself that October is a busy month and although I was working hard, things would soon calm down. The problem was, it never calmed down. Life in our house was always a little frantic. There were days when my husband would agree to babysit because I had an important meeting and then he'd get called into the hospital on an emergency. He'd have to take the kids with him and park them on the ward. The nurses would have to look after them, which wasn't great.

My mom was a wonderful help — I don't know how young women manage without extended family. The worst days were when a daughter woke up in the middle of the night with an earache and I had important meetings scheduled for the next day. That sense of panic — what will I do? — is the worst pressure. Today, while both daughters say it was swell having me as a mother, one notes that it would have been nice if I'd been around more. Although my girls, who are now in their thirties, have become successful adults, if I were doing it over again I'd certainly do it differently. I would come to grips with needing more household help and less haphazard child-care arrangements, and I'd be realistic about carving out hunks of time to spend with my family. In fact, my new view is that unless the structure of work changes, expecting women to have high-powered careers and a close-knit family is a virtual impossibility.

I think my marriage stayed together because my husband and I had a lot of help in learning how to negotiate the changes as well as understanding what we wanted from each other and ourselves. During our various transitions we had a lot of human relations training and did counselling around specific issues when we felt it was necessary. I can also say that my husband was always very supportive and never threatened by my success. He knew I'd lose my mind if I didn't pursue my opportunities, although I think it was a strain on him because he grew up expecting a wife to stay home and take care of him and the family. I know I have much to be thankful for in him.

Looking back, I can see that I was trying to become a second-class man and encouraging other women to do the same. I wasn't acknowledging that our biology, our sensibilities, and our life rhythms are different. Women had to repress a lot of ourselves, particularly the more exuberant parts of our personalities, to be taken seriously in the male world. For instance, *Dress for Success*, which urged women to dress like ersatz men, was a gospel for how to succeed in business. But unlike men, as Carol Gilligan has noted, women see the world in the context of relationships. We're simply not as turned on about things like who reports to whom. Now that women are more accepted in the workplace, I think it's time for us to bring our spiritual and emotional intelligence forward to bear on our concerns. If I had the opportunity to do things over again, I'd be much less timid about expressing my needs. I also wouldn't assume that family relationships would be all right if I didn't attend to them, because that simply isn't the case.

It took me a long time — in fact, I still work at it — to reach a place where I'm comfortable with winning some battles and losing some battles and feeling that's okay. Before, I was overly invested in whatever I chose to take up. It *had* to succeed. Approaching my sixtieth birthday, I'm a little more detached. All you can do is give things your best shot.

The German philosopher Hegel thought that the truth about human nature is that most people are deeply passive and don't know what they really want to do. He believed that being in a relationship with work that we care about is what develops us, and that was exactly my experience with the Women's Resources Centre. It was a wonderful job that took me in many unexpected directions. Although I had no idea what I was getting into when I answered that ad in 1972, I wouldn't trade the life I've had for anyone else's.

"Doing *A Friend Indeed* put me in touch with a community of women who, in many ways, didn't accept the status quo. They certainly didn't accept the picture of themselves drawn in the medical textbooks. There's a certain kind of knowledge, knowledge with an emotional connection, that comes from other women and that you can't get anywhere else. Now I feel there is something missing in life if you are not in the company of women."

JANINE O'LEARY COBB

In 1984, Janine O'Leary Cobb founded A Friend Indeed, *North America's first newsletter on menopause. Through that publication and her subsequent role as a spokesperson on the subject, she has played a major role in bringing information about this much-neglected transition in women's lives to the forefront of public consciousness.*

I started to go through menopause while I was teaching humanities and sociology at Montreal's Vanier College. Although I didn't realize it at the time, menopause has a gradual progression. I was experiencing what today we call "perimenopause." Like many women, I was aware of getting older and losing the attractiveness I'd always counted on, which for me was very difficult. In some ways, it still is, because our society has such contempt for older women.

At age forty-nine, I became aware of symptoms that were quite incapacitating. I was chronically exhausted but couldn't get enough sleep. I could have slept sixteen hours a day — I suppose as a way of blanking out how I felt during the day. I wanted to cry, but couldn't. Looking back, I realize I was clinically depressed and probably should have been on antidepressants. I should have done a lot of things, like getting regular exercise, but that knowledge was not available at the time. In those days the medical system was no help because doctors knew as little as everyone else. The problem was, as physicians, they wouldn't admit to their lack of knowledge and dismissed my concerns as unimportant. Like many other women, I got very little support from doctors for a long, long time.

My symptoms made me interested in what happens to the body at this time of transition. My feelings were very mixed. On the one hand, I was glad to be losing the nuisance aspect of menstruation, but on the other hand, I regretted losing the faithful guide to my moods that my period represented, of having a regular sense of where I was and what was happening with my body that the menstrual cycle gives you. And although I wasn't grieving for loss of the ability to have babies — as a mother of five, I'd certainly fulfilled my maternal instincts — there is a big difference between being able to choose whether to get pregnant and being unable to conceive.

I hadn't expected to be affected by menopause. I'd had five normal pregnancies and I'd read that the more pregnancies you had, the less likely it was that problems would occur. I'd also read that women who work outside the home experience fewer difficulties than women who stay at home, so as a professional I felt I was safe on both counts. I was wrong.

My mother had a hysterectomy when she was thirty-nine, a year after my youngest brother was born. She knew nothing about birth control and she hadn't wanted to have five children — I think she wanted to have three — but she would never do anything about it. I have a different approach to life. My solution to uncomfortable feelings or problems is to take action. My husband teases me because whenever one of the kids left home, I'd clean out their room — that was my way of dealing with the pain of seeing another child go. I took a similar proactive approach to menopause and dealt with it head-on by finding out as much as I could.

Unfortunately, at the time, there was very little information on the subject. There wasn't much available in bookstores and there was very little in the medical library except for the prescription of hormones. In fact, the basic message from the medical profession was that the well-adjusted woman had no problem with menopause. At many moments in my life I have encountered a situation that needed fixing and have thought, Somebody should do something about this. But that somebody was never me. Possibly, part of being fifty and going through menopause is the "now or never" syndrome, that feeling that if you don't do something you have always wanted to do, time will pass you by. That feeling played a major role in my decision to launch *A Friend Indeed*.

By the spring of 1984, I knew a little about the subject — basically through sheer perseverance. Searching through medical textbooks and other source material, I was collecting information I thought other women might find useful, and I decided to write a newsletter. I certainly didn't think of it as something I'd do professionally — it was more of a hobby. My idea was that I'd sit down three or four times a year and share what I had learned. I assumed I could keep on teaching and do the newsletter on the side, probably because I enjoyed teaching and it had never occurred to me to stop.

In those days, I was naive enough to think that learning about menopause was just a matter of getting fairly technical information from medical texts and knowledgeable people, rewriting it into understandable language, and distributing it to women. I knew I was good at synthesizing information because my honours thesis had involved taking information from various sources and making it into a coherent whole. It was also something I enjoyed doing. But I certainly never imagined for a moment that doing the newsletter would keep me busy for more than a decade.

I typed my first edition on the family computer, photocopied it, and sent it out to forty or fifty women who might be interested — women I had worked with in my twenties who were now living across the country, wives of my husband's colleagues, teachers I worked with — anybody I could think of who would be around the right age and might be open to the idea. The response from most of the women was very positive, but the most constructive response of all came from Ruth, a woman I'd worked with years earlier in Toronto. She was now working at a radio station, CFRB. The broadcaster, Betty Kennedy, was on holiday and Helen Gougeon had taken over her show for a couple of weeks. Ruth showed Helen the newsletter and she loved it. She phoned me from the station and interviewed me on the air. Not long after, a reporter from the *Regina Leader-Post* called and wrote a story on me, and then Canadian Press did a story that appeared in numerous papers across the country. One Friday afternoon, the mailman turned up with two sacks of mail. "Mrs. Cobb, whatever have you been doing?" he asked.

Jack and I were going up to the cottage that weekend, so we took the mail with us. On Saturday morning we started opening the letters, Jack at one end of the table and me at the other. At one point I looked up and tears were streaming down his face. When I asked him what was wrong, he said, "I can't believe these women are telling you what they are." Like most men, he finds it hard to understand how much women share with one another.

The women were obviously in great pain and looking for help. It was Jack who said, "You've got to keep doing the newsletter. These women don't have anybody but you." I, on the other hand, was thinking, What have I got myself into? Summer was drawing to a close and there was no way I could get out of teaching that fall, so I taught and published the newsletter, which was a great strain. Everybody in the family worked for me. We had to stamp and mail the newsletter, and for the longest time, I sent it out first class. The next semester I took a part-time leave. After a couple of years, I realized I would never be able to return to teaching. The newsletter had taken over my life.

Soon, more journalists were calling me up and interviewing me, which was interesting in itself. When I started *A Friend Indeed*, most of the journalists I talked to were women in their mid- to late thirties. They didn't want to know about thickened waistlines or greying hair or losing interest in sex or any of those symptoms associated with middle age. They wanted menopause to conform to their vision, so they wrote chipper articles about how life is what you make it. You could guess how old the reporter was just from reading the article. Fortunately, this is changing because the journalists are getting older and becoming more realistic about menopause.

Shortly, I was being asked to speak at various events. At Jack's suggestion, I did a trip out west promoting the newsletter. Since his background was in advertising, he coached me on how to get publicity through radio stations. Nowadays, it's very hard to get any air time or print space for menopause because everyone thinks it has been "done." But in those days the topic was novel. Of course, it was also novel to have a woman who would participate in an open-line radio show and answer questions about such a "delicate" subject.

I loved doing those open-line shows. They provided a tremendous opportunity to connect with a wide variety of women and to discover the problems they were having. They were the source of many story ideas for the newsletter. Through travelling, I also met some very interesting people. The first time I travelled west, a subscriber wrote and invited me to stay with her in Regina. My first thought was, I can't do that! Then I moved on to, Well what's the worst that can happen? It's just for one night. I deliberately pushed myself because it's so easy to say no, and of course, when I stood back and looked at it, I saw that refusing to try new things is a symptom of old age. So I accepted the invitation and had a wonderful time.

Once I started doing the newsletter, my interest was maintained because so much controversy surrounded menopause. Should you take hormones? Do bone density tests actually tell you if you are at risk for osteoporosis? Are women really at such high risk for heart disease? A was saying this and B was saying that. Trying to make sense of conflicting opinions was a great challenge that engaged me. If the material had been cut and dried or if it had involved reportage rather than investigation, I probably would have become bored within the first few years. Even now, menopause continues to be fascinating because the subject is still surrounded by controversy. Since being in control is enormously important to me, my objective has been to provide knowledge that women can use to make their own decisions.

Generally speaking, women who are moving into menopause now have been educated to the controversies involving the medical profession. They know that their husbands are allowed into the delivery room, not because obstetricians decided that was a good thing to do but because women ahead of them pushed for it. There hasn't been one single step forward in women's health that women themselves haven't impelled, and that has usually involved an awful lot of hard work. When I started the newsletter, I had no idea I'd be taking on the medical establishment, and for the longest time they were not aware of what I was doing. Once it became clear that I had a following, they treated me as a doctor-basher, which is a way the medical profession has of dismissing those who disagree with them. Many women tell me that they took the newsletter to their doctor, who looked to see if I had an MD, and when it became clear that I lacked that qualification, disregarded the material. Now I'm treated with a certain amount of respect. Recently, for instance, I was asked to write an article for the *Journal of the Society of Obstetricians and Gynecologists of Canada.*

With promotion and word of mouth, which has always been our best advertising, the newsletter grew steadily from 1984 until about 1995. Now the competition is growing. There are two other menopause newsletters, one from Minneapolis and one from San Francisco, and within the past few years four or five women's health newsletters have started. That means the potential market for a *A Friend Indeed* is being fragmented. For the past few months, I have been remembering that when I started I said I would work at it until I thought women had adequate information on menopause. Now I think that point may have been reached.

One of the great rewards of doing the newsletter is that it has been a means of reaching out to people who I could not have reached in any other way. Sisterhood is an overused word, but I think that's what I found. Mid-life women are the most remarkable people in the world. They have an honesty and a selflessness that are wonderful — I think because they have been through a lot in coming to terms with who they are — but they are still very supportive of one another and they don't buy into the hierarchy that characterizes male society. I have met so many unbelievable women I never would have met if I had not done the newsletter.

I think, like a lot of trailblazers, I didn't know what I was getting into. If somebody had said to me, "You are going to be a trailblazer and people will accuse you of being this and that," I don't think I would have believed them. I'm almost ashamed to admit it, but I don't think I had the confidence to decide to start a business of my own. I think I had to go at it by the back door. But I'm certainly glad I was allowed that opportunity. Doing *A Friend Indeed* has enriched my life immeasurably, and I have gotten far more out of it than I've given.

"I'm always surprised when people say I have done so much for women's health. I think it was Conan Doyle who put the words in Sherlock Holmes' mouth, 'It doesn't matter what you have done, it is what people think you have done.' I think that sums up my life."

MARION POWELL

In 1966, Dr. Marion Powell made history when, as an associate medical health officer in Scarborough, Ontario, she helped to launch the first municipally funded family planning clinic in Canada. Born in Toronto in 1923, she married her husband, Don, in 1948, two years after graduating from medical school. In 1991, she received the Order of Canada for her pioneering work in health care. Dr. Powell died of a heart attack four days before Christmas of 1997, and six weeks after the death of her beloved husband.

The birth control pill was released in the early 1960s, about the time I went into public health. I'd recently returned to Canada after spending eight and a half years in Japan with my husband, who was a minister with the Presbyterian Church. Don was very ill with hepatitis, and during that difficult time I began to build my practice. From my perspective, there were two basic problems with being a physician in private practice: I never liked to bill people and I always took my patients to bed with me in the sense that I worried about their problems until I fell asleep. I went into public health because I thought I could work 9:00 to 5:00, on a salary.

In those days we held well-baby clinics in church basements, which were attended by 100 to 150 mothers and babies. At these clinics women would say things like, "I've got a ten-month-old baby at home and I'm pregnant again." One woman told me she was so afraid to have intercourse that she wouldn't let her husband sleep in the same bed with her. Although the pill was available, since doctors weren't taught anything about birth control they were reluctant to prescribe it. I'd been very influenced by a remarkable woman, Marion Hilliard, one of the senior obstetricians and gynecologists at Women's College Hospital. Among other things, she taught me how to fit a diaphragm. I didn't know that if you wanted a diaphragm in the 1950s, you could order it from Eaton's catalogue. It came in one size and cost $5. The problem was there was nobody to show the woman how to use it.

When Don was ordained, in 1948, we were appointed to Timmins in northern Ontario, where I set up practice in the manse. At that time there was a lack in sex and family planning education, and as a result there were many very large families in Northern Ontario. I have vivid memories of delivering the baby that resulted from a woman's twenty-sixth pregnancy. There were no birth control services for young women. If they got pregnant they had to come to Toronto, where they would have the baby and give it up for adoption. Growing up, I'd been greatly influenced by my mother's stories about the experiences of her friends, their unplanned pregnancies, and, in some cases, illegal abortions. I guess because I was planning to go into medicine she shared her concerns about how these women were going to cope with a baby when the family couldn't afford the children they already had. Mother herself had a pregnancy at forty-four and wasn't even aware she was pregnant until she was about five months along.

As a physician, I'd seen the horrendous effects of back-street abortionists on the ward, and I was also aware of how women who had abortions were treated. When I was a junior intern, a woman who had taken medication to induce an abortion came in when her kidneys stopped working. As soon as the doctors treated her — by hooking her up to an experimental artificial kidney — the police arrived. At Toronto General Hospital, they had a modesty curtain, which left a woman exposed from the waist down. Once, I was standing at a woman's head and she asked how many people were looking at her private parts. It was incredible. I don't know why it bothered me more than it bothered other people, but it did.

I didn't set out to be famous. I didn't see myself as a pioneer or an activist. I just couldn't stand the fact that nobody would provide birth control services for women. So in 1966 I decided I'd have to do it myself.

Fortunately, I was working in Scarborough, a suburb of Toronto, which had a very supportive Board of Health. Matt Diamond, Ontario's Minister of Health, went on the record saying he saw absolutely no problem with public health workers providing birth control services, even though that was technically illegal at the time. The chief of police said he didn't see a problem, as long as we didn't serve single women. So we went ahead and set up the first public-supported family planning clinic in Canada. I vividly remember the first single woman who came in and said, "I'm a teacher and I can't go to my family doctor and ask for the pill." Soon we were regularly supplying birth control for single women and it was no longer a question of whether the woman was married or not — it was a question of how young is too young? My own kids were growing up at that time and my daughters went to a Toronto girls' school. They knew girls whose periods were late and they would send them out to Scarborough to get pregnancy tests.

Not long after the clinic opened, I was asked to speak to a group of boys at a technical high school in the area about birth control. After my talk I passed around condoms, and after one boy's parents complained, I was called before the Board of Education and accused of peddling pornography. We knew the complainant had a strong church connection, so Don offered to speak with him. One Sunday afternoon he paid him a visit and the two of them ended up down on their knees praying together. That diffused the complaint, but I tell the story to make the point of how supportive my husband always has been.

In the 1960s, before the law was changed, I referred women to Sir Stanley Bond, a physician in London, England, for abortions, which cost $500 plus airfare. Just after the law was changed, I sent a woman to Mount Sinai Hospital in Toronto. She was admitted for three or four days and saw two psychiatrists who diagnosed her as depressed so she could have the abortion. Around the same time, I saw one of her classmates, whom I sent to England. She landed in London on Saturday, had her abortion, and was back in class on Monday. The two women compared notes and both agreed that the costly international trip was preferable to having to pretend you were crazy in order to have the procedure at home.

Once the law was changed, I became quite involved with setting up abortion services at Scarborough Centenary Hospital. By that time, I had become fairly well known and I was asked if I would take an academic position at the School of Hygiene at the University of Toronto, which felt it would like to set up what it called a population unit. I had never seen myself as an academic — I think I have a much more practical, person-in-the-street approach to things — but I was persuaded.

In 1973, along with a psychologist, a social worker, and a minister, I began writing a column for the *Toronto Star*, in which we answered kids' questions abut sex. Not surprisingly, it created quite a bit of controversy. I came from a strong evangelical background and people who knew my family would say things like, "I'm so glad your mother is dead so she didn't have to see what you have become." One of the ways I coped was by withdrawing. I never read anything written about me and I haven't seen myself on television or listened to myself on radio to this day. I suppose I was pretending that if I didn't tell anybody I was on television, then I really wasn't there. A psychologist could probably analyze it and conclude that I am really not terribly comfortable with what I am doing, but I think my intention was to protect my family, especially my children. I thought that if I didn't tell them I wrote in the *Star* they wouldn't know I was doing it. Recently, though, one of my daughters said they used to think it was great to have a mother who told kids where they could get birth control.

My husband's connection with the Presbyterian Church was another matter, because I was conscious of protecting Don. Unfortunately, I had a love/hate relationship with the church. I think they had a hard time accepting what I did. However, I always felt that if Don had objected to what I was doing, I wouldn't have done it. Don was probably smarter than I was. I think he knew if he objected I might have taken off, because these issues meant so much to me.

I suppose my desire to achieve and my commitment to reproductive choice are rooted in my childhood, although some of those connections are a bit murky. My father did his undergraduate degree in political science before 1910, which was fairly unusual, and then went into theology. After he graduated, he decided he was not cut out to be a minister, so he became a high school teacher in Toronto. I guess he was frustrated because he had an MA in political science and taught in a commercial high school. I think we were super-achievers because both Mother and he were thwarted academics. Mother, like a lot of women her age, went into teaching and was frustrated at her inability to have a career after marriage. She was a very well-organized, very capable woman, who a generation or two later might have had a very different life.

I grew up feeling there was nothing I couldn't do. Gender had nothing to do with achievement. I was in that category of kids who came home with a mark of ninety-five and their parents wanted to know what happened to the other five marks. Nobody ever said I couldn't be the first female editor of the Jarvis Collegiate magazine. I didn't even realize I was the first female to hold that post until many years later when I saw a list of all the editors. And when I went into medicine it never occurred to me that being a woman doctor was unusual.

I decided on medicine when I was very, very young, and I don't quite know why. My birth coincided with my parents' fourth wedding anniversary and I was my mother's third full-term pregnancy. I was also the first child to survive to adulthood. When I was five, my elder brother, who was seven, died of measles, in a bad epidemic. Perhaps my mother's yearning for more than homemaking played a part in my decision as well. I do remember that all my play involved being a doctor. I never mothered dolls — I doctored them.

My strong evangelical background undoubtedly played a role in my decision to enter medicine. I was raised on stories of great medical missionaries — the kind of people who set up medical schools in India were held up to me as the ideal. I had the idea, I guess, that I would be a medical missionary, so it was natural that I looked towards theological school for a husband. Don and I met as undergraduates and we married shortly after he was ordained as a Presbyterian minister. I thought I would go wherever he went. I would provide care for the bodies and he would look after the souls.

The Presbyterian Church had a different idea. After our stay in Timmins, we were appointed to Japan, where there was no medical work for me associated with the church. At one point we wrote home, saying we would like to be posted to a place where I could do something and we were reprimanded and told to behave ourselves. When I was invited to join the staff of the Southern Presbyterian Church from the southern United States, which ran a small out-patient clinic in a badly bombed area of Osaka, I accepted. Eventually the church built a hospital, where I set up the Department of Obstetrics and Gynecology.

In 1948, Japan was the first country to permit legal abortions, so when we arrived in 1952 and saw the difference between what went on there and what went on in Canada, it helped to clarify my position on the issue. In Japan, I hadn't seen any consequences from a well-performed procedure, but in Canada I saw the horrendous consequences of illegal abortions.

In 1975 my career took another turn when I was appointed by the federal Department of Justice to a committee, chaired by the sociologist Robin Badgely, to look at access to abortion in Canada. We travelled across the country, visiting hospitals and meeting with community groups because the medical profession thought abortion was too hot a issue on which to hold public hearings. It was a great learning experience. I had never been trained to write reports. I had no idea how to set up a questionnaire. I had no idea how to do statistics. And I had to learn it all on the spot. On top of that, it was tough, personally. I'd never been on the receiving end of so much anger before. I got crank calls in the middle of the night and had to get an unlisted number. That was my first experience of being singled out in a very disturbing way. But I had this ability to cocoon myself and pretend the rancour didn't exist. For instance, one morning in Calgary, I turned on *Canada AM* and the local news showed a clip of picketers. I remember being very surprised to discover that I was the person they were protesting. The police came to the hotel to make sure that I reached the hospital safely, and they posted security outside my door.

From that perspective, being a member of the Badgely Commission was a horrendous experience. But at the same time it was a watershed in my professional life because suddenly I realized there was more to life than answering letters in the *Star*. I knew I wasn't taken very seriously at the university — partly because I was a woman, partly because birth control wasn't seen as academic. But after being on the commission I decided that I had to start taking myself seriously. I took a course in epidemiology at the Center for Disease Control in Atlanta, and at the age of fifty-five wrote my Royal College exams. I was probably the oldest person ever to get a Royal College degree. At that point, I went into a tenure stream, and being subjected to that type of scrutiny was tough. I finally got promoted to full professor the year I retired. It was humiliating to be told that if I had been a man I would have been promoted earlier. To some extent, ageism and sexism both got me at once, although I didn't realize that until later. However, I do take some responsibility for my failure to advance rapidly in academia. Tenure and promotion had not been high on my priority list and neither had public honours. I don't think I had ever seen myself as doing anything very special.

I've never really considered myself an academic. I don't think my life would have been nearly as interesting if I had gone straight into an academic career, if I had been confined to epidemiology studies, or if I had confined myself to clinical research. It think it's the combination of those things that has made life interesting and fun.

I always kept a foot in the clinical field in birth control, so when I retired Women's College Hospital asked me to run its birth control clinic. In 1985 I wrote the Ontario government's report on access to abortion. In the meantime, Dr. Henry Morgentaler was setting up his clinics and had been arrested. He took his case to the Supreme Court of Canada and the abortion law was struck down. Reading through the case and seeing how often I was quoted made me aware of the impact I'd had on public policy, and I did feel a sense of pride.

The media have always been tremendously kind to me, probably because I look like somebody's mother or grandmother and I'm very soft-spoken. I don't have the image of an angry feminist. I don't think I have to apologize for the fact that I am who I am. Maybe I was a coward, but I always felt that by providing birth control pills and by making sure that women had access to abortion, I could achieve more for them than if I spent my time marching up and down on Parliament Hill with a placard promoting abortion on demand. Deep down I don't think I'm the red-hot radical people portray me to be. I always have that dreaded feeling that somebody will discover I'm a fraud.

I really don't know why I did what I did. I think it was a question of responding to the issues that meant a lot to me. I remember my father saying he didn't think I should go into medicine because I would become too involved with my patients. I guess that is what happened. I never did get rid of the patients. No matter what I did, I always took them to bed with me. Maybe it was empathy. I really can't say.

"It took me a while to gain the courage to speak out about the reality of breast cancer. But once I saw that the silence of women with breast cancer and our invisibility was a political issue, I felt compelled to write my story in a political way and to publish it — not in a lifestyle column or a women's magazine, but on the op-ed page of the Montreal *Gazette*. Coming out as an activist was exhilarating. I was no longer just a woman fighting cancer, but a citizen ready to participate in a larger societal battle with the disease."

SHARON BATT

Sharon Batt is the author of Patient No More: The Politics of Breast Cancer. *She is a founder of the advocacy group Breast Cancer Action Montreal and, in 1993, chaired the committee that brought women with breast cancer to the National Forum on Breast Cancer in Montreal. She has worked with women from across Canada to build the Canadian Breast Cancer Network, a national organization for women with breast cancer.*

When the doctor told me I had breast cancer, I didn't believe him. At forty-three, I felt and looked vibrantly healthy. The horror of the word *cancer* was at odds with my impression of physical well-being, and this sense of dissonance was eerie. For a week I held on to the slender chance that the diagnosis might be a mistake, but when the lab confirmed that the tumour was malignant, my mind had to accept reality.

After two stressful weeks of tests, the surgeon said the disease might have spread to my bones — fortunately, a false alarm. But another test showed that the cancer had spread to one of my lymph nodes, which dramatically reduced my long-term odds for survival. My surgeon tried to cheer me up with the thought that I "might very well live to be fifty-eight," but his words had the opposite of their intended effect, especially when he added that I shouldn't postpone anything I really wanted to do with my life. Once again, I was overcome by disbelief. Like many women, I followed health in the popular media and believed their message that the war against cancer was being won.

Since I'm a journalist by profession, I know how to do research, so I decided to learn everything I could about cancer. The first few books I read rang thin and false — like those bright Cancer Society slogans "Early Detection Is Your Best Protection" and "Cancer Can Be Cured." Then, one day, searching through the McGill University library, I found a battered, old copy of *Breast Cancer: A Personal History and Investigative Report* by Rose Kushner, which was published in 1977. This was the book I'd been looking for.

Rose Kushner was a journalist with a background in psychology. When she was diagnosed with breast cancer in the mid-1970s, she quickly identified the dearth of material for women suffering from the disease and she decided to do her own research. I was horrified by her discoveries, but fascinated, too. She recognized a big discrepancy between the common beliefs about breast cancer and the actual experience of living with the disease.

The standard line about breast cancer is that it's a curable disease if it's detected early. But that wasn't what my doctors were telling me. The treatments would merely improve my chances, and even if they worked, they could have serious side-effects. I didn't feel I had enough information about any of those options I was offered, but a sense of urgency prevailed. I felt I *had* to make decisions. Equally unsettling, nobody was available to listen to my concerns and help me sort through them. The scenario was very much, "This is what's recommended and that's that."

Rose Kushner had criticized the medical community for paying so little attention to the pain and anguish women endure from the time they find a symptom to the time of treatment. I was living through this and I knew the experience was emotionally devastating. When I was diagnosed I had no significant other, but my mother, my two sisters, my brothers, and a circle of close friends were very supportive. On the medical side, things were very different. I phoned several hospitals, but I couldn't locate a support group for women with breast cancer. Finally, I found a female family physician who played a counselling role.

Some women decide they can't work during their treatment. I had the opposite reaction. When I was diagnosed, I was employed as the editor of a consumer protection magazine published by the Quebec government. I found the routine of a job enormously useful in helping me to stay sane during chemotherapy, since my work required a lot of concentration and I hardly had time to think about cancer during the eight hours I spent at the office. After work, I lived with the disease, sifting through my emotions and reading. From the beginning I kept notes, which I hoped would result in a book.

The enormity of writing a book was intimidating — not only because it was something I'd never done, but also because I wondered if I would have time to finish such a long-term project. As well, I wasn't accustomed to writing from my heart or my gut. Like many journalists, I didn't expose my personality in my writing but hid behind my research and the objective style that journalism generally encourages.

My career as a journalist is directly linked with the women's movement. In the early 1970s I was working on a Ph.D. in psychology at the University of British Columbia and having trouble finding my niche. When the fellow student I was involved with got an academic position in Edmonton, I moved there with him. Gradually, I became disillusioned with academia and my doctorate fell by the wayside as I became involved in other things. In 1973 I saw an ad in the classified section of the University of Alberta newspaper. A woman named Susan McMaster was starting a magazine for women and looking for volunteers. I attended the first meeting, where I met some extraordinary women. Four months afterwards, we published the first issue of *Branching Out*, a Canadian counterpart to the feminist magazine *Ms.*, which had been launched the year before in the U.S.

When I was in graduate school, the women's movement was just beginning to permeate the universities, mainly with consciousness-raising groups. I was asked to join one and declined because I was frightened by the prospect — to some extent because I was shy and didn't want to expose myself to being criticized for not measuring up. But even then I remember being tremendously excited by the feminist ideas I came across in books such as Betty Friedan's *The Feminine Mystique* and Simone de Beauvoir's *The Second Sex*.

Starting *Branching Out* was a heady experience. We were publishing many exciting writers and developing cutting-edge ideas. Before long, this work became the centre of my life. It was everything my office job wasn't — challenging, meaningful, a project owned and run by women. When Sue McMaster left Edmonton a year and a half after *Branching Out* was launched, I became the editor. There was no income attached to the position, but I decided to leave my paid job even though it meant I'd be financially dependent on my partner.

Jobs were plentiful then, so I didn't worry about not being employed for a while. However, the job market began to dry up, and by 1980 when my partner left town with one of his students, I came back to reality with a thud. I had no savings and had been out of the paid workforce for six years. Fortunately, I was now known in both the women's movement and the publishing community, so I was able to find a job.

By the time I was diagnosed with breast cancer in 1988, I'd been living in Montreal for seven years, three years of which I'd been an editor at *Protect Yourself* magazine. Within months of my diagnosis, probably because of my background in psychology, I became interested in the idea of the cancer personality — the theory that certain types of people get cancer — and made a proposal to the CBC radio program *Ideas* for a two-hour radio documentary to examine the debate surrounding the subject. The *Ideas* program was my first attempt to find the voice of the person living with cancer. Through that process I abandoned the detached "researcher" voice I had used for most of my career and found my own voice as a journalist.

In June 1989, while the *Ideas* program was in development, I wrote an op-ed piece for the Montreal *Gazette*. By then, I'd been undergoing traumatizing treatments for eight months. I was feeling ill and was frightened I'd die. I was very conscious of the fact that all my specialists were male and I hated having so many men examining my breasts. Obviously something was wrong when a woman's disease — especially one centred in a female sex organ — was so male dominated. However, I told myself I shouldn't quibble. Even though they were inarticulate when dealing with emotions, my doctors were technically competent, which the treatments required, and they were not, personally, bad people.

I was equally frustrated that I didn't know any women with breast cancer with whom I could share my experience. I was aware that dozens of women in Montreal were diagnosed with breast cancer every week. Why were we all sitting at home suffering in isolation? Then I had the insight that our very silence, our invisibility, was a political issue.

By fluke, two eye-opening events happened in the same week. The 5th Annual AIDS Conference in Montreal — probably the most raucous AIDS conference ever — dominated the news. I also watched an American network television special on breast cancer called *Destined to Live*. I hated the show, which was all upbeat, "put-it-behind-you" bravado. I don't blame the women who participated — much of the problem was the packaging, and besides, this was how most women talked about breast cancer then, at least in public. But the contrast with the AIDS patients was striking. The men were impatient activists; the women were passive optimists.

Once I had this insight, I felt a burning desire to write an article that shattered the comfortable mythology about breast cancer. At the same time I feared the consequences. I was calling for women to speak out, to question, to become visible, and to criticize the lack of progress in fighting the disease — to go against the grain of acceptable "feminine" behaviour. In this first step, I was alone. Going public with my diagnosis could close doors — to jobs, friendships, even medical care. People with cancer are silent for good reason. My doctors, too, would surely read the piece. How would they and the powerful medical community react?

When I saw my article in print, I had another surprise. I'd wanted to dramatize the reality of breast cancer, so I'd enclosed a photo my friend Kersti Biro had taken of me when I was undergoing chemotherapy. I was hairless, and the effect of seeing myself so exposed and vulnerable in print shocked even me. But there was a subtle impression of strength, too. I had dared to expose myself as a fragile human being in need of others.

I asked Kersti to take photos of me with no hair because I wanted my own record of this critical moment in my life. My changed appearance had some pleasant surprises. When I saw the contours of my bald head in the mirror, I was amazed by the clean strong lines — I'd expected my skull to be bumpy and uneven. In some ways baldness was an apt metaphor for the cancer experience. Stripping away the clutter of your life may reveal strengths you didn't know you had.

By this time I was reading the stories in the media in a totally different way and was infuriated because they all seemed so false. I was sick of reading upbeat profiles of women who looked beautiful while beating the disease, and seeing nothing about all the women who were dying — 5400 a year in Canada and 45,000 in the U.S. The media perpetrated the myth that medical treatments transform women with breast cancer into perfect people. In fact, even those of us who survive are forever changed: we never again have the same easy confidence in our health. Struggling with issues of appearance helped me to come to terms with the reality of the diagnosis: I, too, was mortal. I actually might die in my forties of breast cancer. It was frightening to let go of my belief that I was destined to live to a hale and hearty eighty-five, but this awareness brought me to a new level of maturity.

As I worked away on the outline for my proposed book, it became increasingly clear to me that women's views had been left out of the debate on how to deal with the disease. I felt that if women became more involved in research, treatment, and support we could bring the spending and the messages about breast cancer into line with our needs and experiences. But to bring about this kind of change, women needed to organize. At the time, there weren't many other breast cancer activists in Canada, although a few groups had sprung up in the U.S. I wanted to act, but I was exhausted. I'd gone through surgery, chemotherapy, and radiation and was really worn out. I knew from my time at *Branching Out* that I could organize, but I also knew that political action is all-consuming. And I no longer had a partner with a job. In 1991, *Protect Yourself* closed, and I didn't even have a job myself.

Even so, that spring I decided to act. I was one of thousands of women of the baby boom generation who were getting breast cancer. We had been active in the women's movement, the peace movement, and the racial equality movement. Ours was not a silent generation and I wouldn't be pushing against the tide if I tried to start a group.

In the fall of 1991, four women started meeting in one another's homes about once a month. Basically we were strangers — our only obvious common denominator was that we all had breast cancer. We shared some understandings right from the start: that it was crucial for women to have a voice in all aspects of treatment of the disease, that an emphasis on prevention was important, and that there was a need to develop a community and educate people about what we felt was being left out of the picture.

Our first public meeting, which launched Breast Cancer Action Montreal (BCAM), was held in a church hall. About sixty women attended and the media gave us national coverage. The intensity was incredible. It was as if people had been waiting for this, and I found it invigorating to be part of a collective entity at last. Since that first public meeting, the group has been busy. We've done lots of educational work, such as creating a newsletter, holding panel discussions, and bringing in exciting speakers such as Dr. Susan Love, the well-known surgeon and author. Meanwhile, I continued to work on my book and my understanding of the politics of breast cancer became more sophisticated. Gradually, I identified the split in values that I believe underlies much of the movement for change: women with breast cancer tend to embrace prevention as a goal, while the medical community remains fixated on treatment.

I began to see that the struggle in breast cancer was to gain credibility for the women's point of view. When we started the group, I was worried that we'd be either laughed at or attacked. Instead, I was surprised to discover that we had the respect, if not the outright support, of a surprising number of people in the medical community. That made me realize that you can't view the medical community as a monolith. Even my oncologist began to make conversation about my activism with comments like, "We need people to push the system." We began to relate on a more human, less doctor-patient, level.

The parliamentary hearings on breast cancer, which were held in 1991 and 1992, had a tremendous impact on legitimizing our approach. Among other things, they produced a powerful report entitled *Breast Cancer: Unanswered Questions*, which cut through the optimistic platitudes and documented how little was really known about the disease. The turning point, at least in terms of mobilizing women throughout the country, was the National Breast Cancer

Forum, held in Montreal in 1993. The media gave us incredible coverage and that visibility allowed us to put our case before the public. I don't think anyone really expected that the presence of women with breast cancer would have such an impact, and when I look back I'm amazed at what we accomplished. We completely changed the perception that policy was beyond the understanding of patients.

My own feminism has definitely shaped my work. I've drawn from my experience in the women's movement in the 1970s, both in my ideas and in my community organizing. The issue I feel most passionately about is the imperative for women to speak out about our needs and beliefs, and this has guided my approach to breast cancer activism. No doubt my early shyness has influenced me. My childhood and early adulthood were filled with moments in which I didn't say how I felt. As a result, others spoke for me, but they gave voice to their thoughts, not mine. That left me feeling frustrated, angry with myself, and impotent.

The breast cancer movement still faces many obstacles. Even so, I believe the movement will continue to grow, because for the next twenty or thirty years women who have been active in feminist work will be a large part of the population diagnosed with the disease.

Many things are starting to turn around because women have been pushing the system. But lobbying by women, not new scientific evidence, is what has cracked the wall of orthodoxy. We have made the private grief of breast cancer a public issue. We are demanding the right to map our own futures within the very real constraints imposed by a life-threatening disease. Although I would never choose to get breast cancer, the experience pushed me to grow both personally and politically. I attribute this in equal parts to my twenty years of experience in the women's movement, to the support of other women with cancer, and to my luck of the draw in the tumour lottery. If I had indeed had only four years to make my contribution, as my surgeon initially warned I might, I would not have been able to accomplish very much.

"I've known for more than twenty years that medical care has much more to do with illness than with health and that we've been feeding the medical model of health at the expense of other factors that contribute to health. Unfortunately, until recently, those of us who felt that way were lonely voices crying in the wilderness of health care."

RITA STERN

Rita Stern has spent most of her career working for the federal government as an advocate for citizen participation in developing health programs and policies. Her primary interest is women's health and she has worked tirelessly to legitimize the idea that social factors such as poverty, education, and gender play at least as significant a role in improving health as our health care systems. She currently sits on the boards of the British Columbia Centre of Excellence for Women's Health and the College of Midwives of British Columbia. In 1996 she was awarded the Canadian Public Health Association Janssen-Ortho Inc. Award, which is presented to an individual who has significantly advanced the cause and state of the art of public health.

I became seriously interested in women's health in 1975 when I was hired as national coordinator of the federal government's Non Medical Use of Drugs program. In the 1970s, thousands of women across North America were meeting in small consciousness-raising groups to examine their lives within the context of feminism. Their ultimate goal was, of course, political and social change, and the women's health movement, which focused on giving women more power in decision making around health care issues, emerged as part of that process.

In those days, a few people, such as Ruth Cooperstock, a cutting-edge medical sociologist from Toronto, were beginning to notice the gender disparity in prescriptions for tranquillizers. Women were receiving twice as many minor tranquillizers as men and the implications of this inequity were troubling. Fortunately, I was working with a group of women within Health and Welfare Canada who, like me, had been influenced by feminism. We knew that with Ruth's help, many women would be willing to talk about their experiences with tranquillizer abuse and that gave us the confidence to start raising the issue within the bureaucracy.

The late 1970s and early 1980s were the heyday of the women's program at Secretary of State, and since Monique Bégin was Minister of Health and Welfare, we felt tacit approval for our interest, even though we had little support within the government as a whole. But listening to women talk about why they took tranquillizers launched me in a new direction. It helped me to envision a wider picture of health than the one portrayed by the medical model. I could see the links between why women felt they weren't coping with the world and the social reality of their lives: their lack of employment; their unhappy, sometimes violent, marriages; their sense of inadequacy as parents; and their low self-esteem.

In those days the idea that social factors were linked to health was a radical concept. By documenting women's desire to take drugs to lessen the pain of their experience, we were entering new territory. We were just beginning to see that health promotion shouldn't be viewed solely within the narrow framework of factors such as smoking, exercise, and nutrition. Health was part of a larger framework that included social inequities, such as housing, violence, and wage disparity.

Underlying these new perceptions was women's growing disillusionment with the medical model. The burgeoning women's health movement embraced self-help, reproductive politics, and efforts to regain control over birthing, among other things. Women were rebelling against their perceived powerlessness, and this gelled with the picture of women's lives we gleaned from studying tranquillizer abuse. Women were receiving a negative message from doctors: Don't tell us about your problems, because we can only give you fifteen minutes. Take this little pill, instead. It will make your pain go away.

In 1981 we produced *It's Just Your Nerves*, the country's first resource kit on women and drugs. It contained lots of hard information on mood-altering substances, some solid research papers, and, perhaps most important, many candid first-person accounts that told the story of how and why these substances became part of women's lives. It also challenged assumptions about doctor-patient interaction and created quite a furor, even within the bureaucracy. Many people found the idea of the federal government legitimizing a feminist analysis of why some women were prescribed mood-altering drugs to be unthinkable.

Health and Welfare Canada still worked under the framework of the medical model — "doctor knows best" — and the general reaction was, "What do you mean, women shouldn't be given drugs? If that's what the doctor prescribed, it's fine." The assistant deputy minister was — of course — a man, and since he didn't see this as a battle he wanted to fight with the medical profession, he gave us a very hard time and did his best to marginalize the resource kit. Senior bureaucrats weren't the only ones who reacted negatively. We also offended middle-level bureaucrats, addiction counsellors, AA, and self-help voluntary groups. Instead of telling women they were addicted because they weren't coping well, *It's Just Your Nerves* dared to expose the societal sources of women's anger and the sexist stereotypes that underlay their treatment — not a message many people wanted to hear.

Naturally, we had no intention of accepting this backlash without a fight. Fortunately, as I mentioned, Monique Bégin was our minister. She was scheduled to visit a women's group in Toronto and she wanted somebody from the department to accompany her. I was chosen and I used our time together on the plane to brief her on what was happening to the resource package. I'll never forget her response. "Rita, leave it to me," she said. "I'll display the resource kit in my office so the men will be able to see that I support it." Once the senior bureaucrats realized the minister was on side, we could move things forward.

It's Just Your Nerves had an incredible impact. Women across the country used it, mainly in small groups, to explore some of the issues surrounding alcohol and tranquillizer abuse, as well as their treatment by doctors. I can't take credit for the project. There were many women from inside government as well as in community groups who worked with women with addiction problems, and they made an enormous contribution. It was a totally involving and remarkably satisfying process. I know it sounds corny, but when I meet someone who is still working in the addiction field and we recall working on *It's Just Your Nerves*, a warm feeling rushes over me.

When I reflect on my career, I can see that I've always been an activist for women's health who worked from within an institutional base. In the late 1970s the relationship between federal bureaucrats and the women's movement was perceived as a legitimate partnership for progressive action. This provided women like me with an opportunity to challenge established practice. Even though many men — and some women — ridiculed our ideas, there was a willingness to at least debate the issues. During that period, a great deal of indirect government support fostered the women's movement in this country. We were very conscious of that, but we assumed it would always be there, which I can now see was very naive.

I suppose my view of women's health was always feminist-oriented, in as much as I've been a feminist virtually all my adult life. I was born in 1946 in Bucharest, Romania, and I grew up in Montreal's Esplanade, the area Mordecai Richler made famous. Since there were lots of people like me, children whose parents had survived the Holocaust, my childhood gave me a sense of being part of a community. There are many theories about children of Holocaust survivors, but I think my childhood allowed me to experience the comfort of community as well as the inner strength of survivors and immigrants — people who are outsiders looking in. It also fostered my commitment to social justice.

I attended Sir George Williams University during the 1960s and studied psychology and sociology because that gave me a way of seeing the world that made sense. It provided me with various frameworks — ways of seeing, listening, talking — that gave voice to my inner feelings and observations. It also enabled me to grow intellectually in an environment where it was safe to debate ideas and think differently from the status quo. At that point Sir George was a hotbed of radicalism, and although I was a leftist, some of my ideas didn't quite fit with the left, which didn't validate women's experience or support the idea that women were oppressed. I could see the gender hierarchy being formed. We were all bright, articulate women, but we were always assigned second place — accepted but simultaneously marginalized. Many of us were seen as sex objects because that was how people viewed women's participation in politics: providers of sex as opposed to policy developers and leaders. Gradually, I began to locate my own thinking in the new framework of feminism, because that was how I experienced the world.

After I graduated, I joined the Canadian University Students Overseas (CUSO) because I wanted to go to West Africa. I also got married to Bernie Lucht, who's now the executive producer of the CBC radio program *Ideas*. We'd been going out for about a year and a half and we decided to get married because CUSO wouldn't let unmarried couples travel together. My mother is forever thankful for that policy, because otherwise I would never have been a bride.

In 1969, Bernie and I went to Nigeria. He taught history and I taught English literature and English as a second language in an all-boys secondary school. We were in a place in northwestern Nigeria that isn't even on the map and was pretty rustic. Although there were many interesting aspects to my experience, I wasn't totally happy there because there were few women I could really relate to. The Third World women's movement was in its infancy and I, personally, was a bit of an affront to the Muslim image of womanhood. My students wanted to know why I wasn't at home taking care of my family instead of teaching. Since I wasn't shy about expressing my opinion that women are equal to men, which isn't an idea the Muslim culture supports, I had difficulties from the time we arrived.

When I came back to Canada in 1971, I didn't know what to do. Now, I recognize a pattern: when I'm feeling uncertain, I go back to school. I decided to do a master's degree in social work, and enrolled at the University of Toronto since it was the only school with a social-activist slant. I'd been influenced by Saul Alinsky's ideas about community organizing and mobilization and I was interested in more than studying the theory of social change that the other schools offered. I wanted to become involved with the practice of social change. I had a great time because at that point U of T was another hotbed of activism. Meanwhile, the writing was on the wall concerning my marriage. Although Bernie and I had similar ideas about life, we have very different personalities. We separated in 1975 and have remained good friends.

When we split up, I went to work for the federal government, where I began to get interested in the idea of the social model of health. After we launched the resource kit, I felt I needed another break. As I said, whenever I need a rest I go back to school. This time I decided to move west and get my master's of science in health services planning at the University of British Columbia. After a year, I realized I wanted to be in sociology, not health, and was accepted into the Ph.D. program in sociology. It was a serendipitous move, since that's where I found legitimization for my ideas about the social context of women's health. A few academics were starting to talk about "qualitative health outcomes," which looked at how issues such as employment, finances, violence, and harassment affected health.

After getting a handle on this intellectually, I soon found myself longing to be back in an institution, because I recognized I'd need an institutional base to launch these ideas as policy. Conveniently, I was asked to take a summer job managing Health and Welfare's regional office for health promotion in Vancouver. Almost immediately I ended up in a permanent job and, much to my amazement, in 1985 was invited to come back to Ottawa, where I was able to work with the World Health Organization (WHO). The director general of WHO didn't feel that the Western medical model was appropriate for developing countries. Gradually, health was no longer seen as the absence of disease but as a resource for everyday living. Once WHO legitimized that idea, Canada was viewed as a leader in the thinking about the social model of health. In 1986 we produced the Achieving Health for All Framework, under then Minister of Health Jake Epp. It was the first document in the world to legitimize the social model of health, and I felt for a brief moment a great sense of triumph to be part of a group that helped to form the issues and thinking behind that document.

At that point we still didn't have a scientific explanation for how the interactions actually line up between income, employment, and health. We had data from the sociology of health and illness, the academic literature on disability and coping, and the feminist literature on gender and health, but we did not have all the causal explanations.

Then, a group that is now called the Canadian Institute for Advanced Research started to study what they labelled the social determinants of health. When their head, Dr. Fraser Mustard, looked at children's health, he found that things like early childhood nutrition and good parenting had bigger payoffs in health outcomes than the availability of health services. Because of their stature, their scientific credentials, and the way in which they could mobilize research and resources all over Canada, his group was able to legitimize the concept within the bureaucracy.

Today, at the age of forty-nine, I feel very certain about a lot of things — for instance, how institutions work or don't work, how power corrupts or how it can assist you to achieve positive results. But I don't find myself all that certain about the future. Maybe you reach a critical mass and then you have to take one step back. I've always led my life like that. The more certain I've felt, whether through the legitimization of my ideas or through the kind of work I happen to be doing, the more I feel the need to take one step back. I'm becoming more comfortable with that. I used to think I was just muddling through, but now I realize it's a way of sorting out my life.

I've never wanted to remarry and I've never wanted to have children. I've had — let's see, how do I put this? — interesting affairs, some more interesting than others. I think the positive side of marriage is about a sense of place, and that wouldn't have come easily to me since I'm a bit of a wanderer. Obviously, without marriage and children, I've been able to devote a great deal of energy to my work without feeling conflicted, and that has been positive. Fortunately, there's good evidence that friends benefit your health, and I've been lucky that way. Without the women's movement, I would have been a lot lonelier. My friends — primarily women, but some men, too — have supported me in expressing my ideas and comforted me when I felt I was muddling through. I've valued that support because I'm a bit of a worrier. If I had it to do over again, that's the only thing I'd do differently — not worry so much about whether or not it was worth it.

PART 4

SCIENCE, TRADES, AND TECHNOLOGY

"I suppose I felt I could accomplish things because of the tradition of strong women in the family. Also, having four younger brothers gave me the sense that women were capable."

ANNE UNDERHILL

Anne Underhill is one of the first Canadian women to pursue a career in astrophysics. She earned her MA from the University of British Columbia in 1944 and completed her Ph.D. at the University of Chicago in 1948. The author of more than two hundred research papers in astrophysics, she has been a visiting lecturer at Harvard and held a major research post at NASA, where she helped to develop satellites that observe astronomical objects. She officially retired in 1975, but she continues her research as an honorary professor at UBC.

In 1949, after a year of post-doctoral studies in Copenhagen, I accepted a position at the Dominion Astrophysical Observatory in Victoria. I was one of five Ph.D.s and the first woman on the professional staff. My colleagues were Scottish and rather conservative, and they weren't happy about having a woman on staff. That set the tone for the rest of my tenure. Although we never quite buried the axe, we managed to function.

For the longest time, my only responsibility was the annual count to ensure that we had enough photographic plates. After I had been on staff for about five years, we hired some young men. They weren't that well qualified — one didn't even have a Ph.D. — but the men took to them and started giving them more responsibility than I had. This favouritism bothered me because I knew I could wipe the floor with them, but it wasn't worth raising as an issue.

As an astronomer at the Dominion Astrophysical Observatory (DAO) I was doing research on the physical properties of the massive stars and publishing my research as technical papers. I used the model-atmosphere technique, which, thanks to powerful computers, has been greatly developed since 1970. I did most of my work in "hand-computing" techniques, which meant my predicted spectra were relatively crude, although my observed spectra were as good as any until very large telescopes came into service. I think it's true to say that I was the first Canadian astronomer to develop the study of the spectra and physics of stellar atmosphere to a relatively high level of sophistication.

One day, without my stirring the pot at all, I received an unexpected letter from a professor at the University of Utrecht in Holland. They had just formed a second chair in astrophysics and they wanted me for the position. I wasn't particularly keen. I was a western Canadian, born and raised in Vancouver, the product of families who had much to do with the development of British Columbia, and I didn't want to leave the province. I went to see the director of DAO and showed him the letter. He didn't say a word. Not one word. I still don't understand it. Then he gave me back the letter. I picked up my things, walked up the hill, opened the dome, and worked that Sunday night observing. During the night I thought about the letter and the director's reaction, and began to wonder why I shouldn't go to Holland. I knew many of the people there and I knew the University of Utrecht had an excellent reputation. It's hard to believe that no one tried to dissuade me from leaving, but nobody ever said, "You're one of Canada's best astronomers. You wouldn't think of going, would you?" So I left. The decision wasn't an easy one and I don't suppose I would have made it if I hadn't been treated so badly.

On the one hand, I was no stranger to difficulty. My mother, who was seriously ill from about the time I was fifteen, died just before I turned seventeen. Since I was the only girl, I inherited the job of running the household for my father and four brothers, which meant I couldn't get a summer job to earn money for my university education and had to concentrate on winning scholarships, instead.

When my father's sister, Aunt Wilemena, heard I was going to university, she sent a cheque for fifty pounds, which was quite a sum of money in 1938. That paid for my books. I'd never met Aunt Wilemena, but I'd been told she made a point of helping all the Underhill girls with their education. She must have had a commitment to encouraging younger women to succeed. In any case, there were many strong, well-educated women on both sides of the family, and those role models supported me in continuing the tradition.

I got a BA in chemistry and physics, and then finished an MA in physics and math. Then war broke out and many young men, including my brothers, enlisted. When I was a graduate student, the physics department was asked to give some courses for air force men and although it was customary for students at my level to run the lab courses, there was concern about having a female graduate student instructing air force men. My father knew Colonel Shrum, who ran the physics department, so I went into Dr. Shrum's office and reassured him that having lived with four brothers, I could handle teaching undergraduate men. He didn't object.

It was still wartime when I got my MA and there were regulations that graduates in physics, maths, engineering, and so on couldn't leave Canada. We couldn't even enlist in the armed forces because the small fraction of people who were skilled in these subjects were needed for the war effort. That meant I couldn't go to the University of California at Berkeley for my Ph.D. in physics. That was where people on the west coast went, since in those days there were no Ph.D. programs at UBC. I received quite a substantial scholarship from the Canadian Federation of University Women and, in the meantime, one of my aunts suggested I look into working at the Dominion Astrophysical Observatory in Victoria, which had one of the best telescopes in the world at the time. I worked there for the summer as a combination secretary–technical officer, liked it, and decided to specialize in astrophysics — the study of stars and the physics of astronomical bodies, which was very undeveloped at the time.

My scholarship provided enough money to live on and I enrolled at the University of Toronto, the only place in Canada that really taught astronomy then. That was a bit of a bust because it turned out that U of T was very weak in astrophysics. I don't know if it was the institutional culture or my personality, but after a while I got quite frustrated. For instance, they had a telescope — not quite as good as the one in Victoria — but practically no staff knew how to use it, and although I wanted to learn, they refused to let me because I was a woman graduate student. I went to Dr. Frank Hogg, who was one of the senior people in the department, and explained my frustration. In the middle of my speech, I started to cry and couldn't stop. That's how upset I was. Dr. Hogg, bless his heart, decided that something had to be done and made arrangements for me to use the telescope twice a week. So the tears served me well, although I wouldn't have planned it that way.

After my year was over, I still couldn't leave Canada, so I went to work for the newly formed National Research Council in Montreal. Most of their work was connected with the atomic bomb, but I joined as a spectroscopist, measuring and analyzing the spectra of stars, and stayed for about a year and a half. By this time I knew that the University of Chicago was the place to learn about astrophysics, so I went there for my Ph.D., then did a year of post-doctoral studies in Copenhagen.

By the time the offer came from Utrecht, I'd been at DAO for twelve years. I left in 1962 and spent several good years in Holland, helping to modernize the department and lecturing at the graduate level. I liked my other colleagues in the faculty and I made some good friends, but I was the only woman in the department. During this time I published *The Early Type Stars*, a technical book interpreting the spectra of hot stars that was the first "modern" — that is, written after 1950 — technical book on the spectra of stars. My colleagues started giving me the message that I may have thought I was an important astrophysicist in Holland, but they were more important because of their international connections. Unfortunately, once you get a group of men together, they invariably start playing, "I'm the biggest bull in the field," and some turf battles came up. I didn't think we should be fighting over turf. I felt we should be working together to ensure that Utrecht was recognized as a centre of excellence in astrophysics. I wanted to build the team; they wanted to build themselves.

I was trying to solve that problem, when along came another completely unexpected letter, this time from NASA. The Goddard Space Flight Center in Maryland was expanding and wanted to set up a centre for optical astronomy. I had advised them from time to time about instruments to observe stars from space and they asked me to take the position of lab chief. It was 1970, the U.S. program in space astronomy was pretty important, and they offered me quite a significant position, so I left Utrecht.

At the Goddard Space Flight Center I had a group of about fifty people working with me. Our job was to develop the rockets and satellites that could observe astronomical objects from space. That was great fun and the U.S. Civil Service, for whom I worked, was an excellent employer. Goddard had some very good scientists and a broad outlook. They didn't care whether you were a man or a woman; they just wanted to know you could do the job.

I stayed for fifteen years and by that time I was sixty-five. Things were tightening up at NASA and Dad wanted me back, and since I preferred western Canada to Maryland, I returned to Vancouver. Although I'm officially retired, I have an honorary professorship at UBC and I still do some research.

Looking back over my lifetime, I suppose I would have had some interest in getting married, but my early family responsibilities got in the way. I didn't have a chance to find a husband because I was too busy looking after my father and my brothers. By the time I finished university, I'd been running a house for years and I wanted a career, not another household. Also, in my time, men didn't like girls who were clever. I suppose if you were willing to hide your light under a bushel, so to speak, you could manage, but I'm afraid I was a little tactless. I was never a woman who could kowtow to a man. If he was doing something valuable, then we'd recognize each other as equals, but darned if I was going to have somebody assuming he was more important than me just because he was male.

I'm sorry that I had to leave Canada to achieve a satisfying professional position, but I didn't get any offers in Canada that reflected my abilities. So when the offers came, first from Holland, then from the United States, I took them. I gave those positions what I thought was my best, and I guess that was good enough.

I have no real regrets. When you live a single life, you make some good friends, and even with siblings you have moments of considerable loneliness, but I think I managed things quite well. It is terribly frustrating to feel you are a capable woman who wants to do science at a professional level, then to discover you can't because you aren't a man. I did it anyway! Thankfully, the outlook on the propriety of women doing science and engineering has changed greatly since I started my career.

"I like challenges and I love to succeed, but I also know that failure isn't the worst thing that can happen. Experience teaches you how much you can put up with and how strong you can be. In the long run, adversity made me a stronger person."

SONJA HEIKKILA

As an engineering student in the late 1970s, Sonja Heikkila became accustomed to being the first or the only woman to study a certain subject or hold a certain job. Before achieving the distinction of being the first Canadian-born woman to receive Ryerson's Bachelor of Engineering Technology degree, she held a summer job as Bell Canada's first female "building equipment man." She was later the first woman to sit on the council of the Ontario Association of Certified Engineering Technicians and Technologists, and in 1993 became the first woman president of that organization. After being hired by Transport Canada to review aircraft modifications, she became the first woman to travel the world reviewing aircraft designs as a member of the headquarters team. She lives in Ottawa with her husband and two children.

In 1985, when I joined the Ontario Association of Certified Engineering Technicians and Technologists (OACETT), I never imagined that eight years later I'd be their first woman president. I'd just moved back to Toronto after spending three years working as a cold-weather tester in Kapuskasing, Ontario. I received a letter from the president of OACETT, who I later learned had written to all members with female-sounding names — including a man named Sandy who declined with humour — suggesting that the organization establish a women's issues committee. I'd been speaking to students about pursuing technical careers since I started university in 1976, so I was interested in the idea.

I attended the meeting with approximately twenty other women, all of whom had interesting backgrounds, and much to my surprise, I was chosen to chair the committee, possibly because of my past involvement with the group Women in Science and Engineering. Initially, the committee looked at equality issues such as how women technicians and technologists were treated at work and if male and female members of OACETT were earning the same salary. Surprisingly, these tasks provided real challenges, since the association wasn't even collecting registration data by gender — which explains why the president had to guess which members were female. In fact, some association chapters were so far behind the times they were still holding their meetings at strip clubs.

In any case, the president's idea was to have the chair of the Committee on Women's Issues sit as a full voting, ex officio member of council — a pretty terrifying experience for someone as young and relatively inexperienced as I was, particularly since I was the only woman except for the recording secretaries. Worse still, many of the men made a point of informing me that I wasn't welcome. Although I was intimidated, I forced myself to give a report at every meeting because I felt my peers were counting on me to help them improve our association's treatment of women. Some men were extremely rude and deliberately talked the entire time I spoke. After three or four meetings, my irritation won out over my fear and I decided I wouldn't tolerate their behaviour any longer. When I spoke and, for instance, Fred started talking, I would say nicely, "And even you, Fred, would be interested to know...." I continued, politely singling out the men who interrupted, and eventually they kept quiet. For years I was constantly on edge while I sat at that table, but I didn't leave — I suppose because I'd been invited and felt I had every right to be there. Truth be told, I also have a streak of real stubbornness and every time they told me I didn't belong, it increased my desire to stay.

Although I was the only woman on council for quite a long time, I certainly didn't think of myself as a trailblazer. That denial probably helped me to survive. When I looked around the room I saw a homogeneous gathering of men. The person looking through the window is the one who would have seen a large group of men and one woman.

I plodded along, learning many useful skills that have served me well, including how to handle a council as it grew to forty people and became more professional and more representative of the cultures that constitute the organization's membership. Slowly, things began to change. In 1991, the president decided that every committee should have at least one woman member. I also encouraged him to allow one woman member to attend each council meeting as an invited guest. It was the first time many women had the opportunity to actually see the council in action, and with the fear of the unknown behind them, they eventually felt confident enough to seek higher positions within the association.

While I was volunteering with the association, I was attending night-school courses at the University of Toronto to become licensed as a professional engineer. I also got married — in 1986 — and had two children, my daughter in 1988 and my son in 1989. During the ten years I was actively involved with OACETT, I missed only one council meeting — the week I gave birth to my son.

In 1992, after I'd been on council for seven years, I decided to run for president because I had a vision of where I wanted the organization to go. Of course, a group of men who were opposed to my bid attempted to stop me by threatening to challenge my eligibility because I was only a thesis away from being certified as a professional engineer. I consulted with our Discipline Committee and was told they had no case, so I ran for president — unopposed, I might add.

In June 1993, I gave my inaugural speech as president, with my daughter, who was then five years old, sitting in the front row of the audience. When I finished speaking, I looked down at her and she gave me the "thumbs up" sign. It made me realize how much my motivation stems from a desire to make the workplace better for her. I tell myself it's hard for me today, but if I survive it will be easier for her tomorrow.

Growing up, I wanted to be either an actress or an engineer, but my high-school guidance counsellor channeled my interests towards engineering. I became seriously interested in science in grade five when I had a teacher, Mr. Poirer, who showed us how much fun it could be. I zeroed in on mechanical engineering partly due to a family tragedy. When I was in grade twelve, my nineteen-year-old brother, who was four years older than me, was killed by a drunk driver. He was brilliant and I really admired him. By the time he died he'd finished his bachelor's degree in the philosophy of science and was working on his master's. He advised me to study mechanical engineering because he felt the need for cleaner, cheaper forms of transportation would be the wave of the future. In some ways, my career path was a legacy from him.

I also happened to like mechanical things. When I was in grade twelve, I toured the General Motors plant where they built earth movers, one of which was the biggest truck in the world. They called it "The Titan" and it could carry a 350-ton payload. When they put it on display, they welded four full-size cars and a Chevette in the payload bin to demonstrate its capacity. The cab was three storeys up and it took three ladders to reach it. While I was touring the plant, they started the truck's engine. I was captivated by the idea that this vehicle was bigger than my house and it was moving. I knew mechanical engineering was the career I wanted to pursue.

In 1976, I enrolled in engineering at the University of Western Ontario. When I started, in all four years, across all engineering programs, there were forty-seven women and hundreds of men. Whenever I run into one of my former female classmates, we discuss our high tolerance for what we now recognize as a hostile environment — things like pictures of naked women posted all over the place. That was quite acceptable and we didn't dare challenge it. Even so, certain things stick in my mind. For instance, in first year, like many students, I was finding my course in statics, the study of forces on stationary objects, very difficult. The concept of torque was particularly hard to grasp, so I asked the professor to explain it. He paused and said, "I can't think of anything in the kitchen to illustrate that." He was dead serious. Then a guy asked pretty much the same question and the professor answered, "Think of a door rotating on a hinge." I was so upset I screamed out, "There are hinges on a kitchen cupboard!" I didn't think I was much of a women's libber, but his behaviour made me furious.

I spent three years at Western and then decided to make a change.

My marks weren't that good and there were problems at home, so I switched to Ryerson Polytechnical Institute, now called Ryerson University, which was offering a four-year bachelor's degree in engineering technology. I was the first Canadian-born woman to go through the program, although a woman from Argentina graduated the year after I started. I'd finished three years in the engineering program at Western, but Ryerson gave me credit for only one year. Since I knew guys who had completed one year at U of T and received more credit, I went to the dean and asked if I was being discriminated against because I was female. "Of course not," he said. I knew there was nothing I could do. That was one of those tricky situations that crop up from time to time where you don't know for sure whether the differential treatment is based on valid reasons or qualifies as discrimination. In those situations, all you can do is roll with the punches.

In many ways Ryerson was worse than Western because I was the only woman. On the first day of classes, we filed into a room full of double desks. All the guys found partners, but no one sat beside me. This went on for weeks — the other students wouldn't even talk to me at lunch. One day I decided this couldn't continue, so I arrived late and sat beside a student who was already seated. He immediately got up and moved. I was devastated. This exile continued until we came back from the Christmas break. Then, when the instructor was dividing the class into groups, he asked, "Who wants to team up with Sonja?" and hands went up around the room. It was as if I had passed some mysterious test known only to them. To this day, I have no idea why that happened.

Once, after I'd been ill and missed a few days, my classmates admitted that it was nice not having me around because the instructor could relax and tell dirty jokes. After that I made a point of telling the teacher to tell dirty jokes if he wanted because I didn't want to put a damper on the class. Although most of the discrimination was subtle, I did have one instructor who made no bones about his hostility towards women. He referred to me as a "thing" and he used to say, "I have five children, three boys and two things." He was cruel, rude, and obnoxious. He called my assignments "garbage," spit at them, threw them off the table, and ridiculed me so much that he made my classmates uncomfortable. When the end of the year came, he glanced at a project I'd worked on all semester and said, "This is worth a C." I felt he was being completely unreasonable and said, "No, Sir, it's worth an A." That initiated a debate on the value of my project. I refused to give in and ended up with a B-plus. I was very proud of myself because I had stood up for myself and argued for what I believed was right.

After that exchange he asked me why I kept wasting my time trying to please him. I explained that I thought I was very good at engineering and I wanted to work at it until I got a better mark. He said he'd never give me a better mark, but after this discussion he became rather decent and started to treat me like a friend. The problem was, I never thought he was my friend; I thought he was despicable.

While I was at Ryerson, between 1979 and 1982, I worked during the summer. My first year, a posting went up at the school for a building equipment man/woman for Bell Canada. Although Bell had never had a woman do the job, the company was very proactive in hiring women. I headed off for interviews with five male colleagues and I'm proud to say I was offered the job. On the downside, some of the guys were very bitter and it created a huge rift.

The job was "get your hands dirty" work that involved looking after a twenty-three-storey office building, and it paid much more than any other summer job I'd ever had. The problem was, the men I had to work with weren't consulted about bringing a woman into the group and they had obviously decided to make my life miserable. I was assigned to a team of two, an older man who was counting the days until retirement and a younger, brawny fellow who was simple and kind but who played along with the others because he thought he should be one of the guys. My first day, they provided me with the company outfit: overalls and a tool belt, steel-toed work boots, and safety glasses. Although I was a size nine at the time, they gave me overalls in a men's size fifty-two. They were so huge, the crotch reached my knees. The tool belt, which weighed about twenty pounds, was a lifesaver because I wore it tight about my waist and it had so much heft that it held the overalls up so the crotch ended up at thigh level.

The building cafeteria, like many others of its size, had an enormous soup vat, designed to produce soup for hundreds of people. At the end of every day, any leftover soup was drained into a huge hole called a soup sump and the vat was cleaned using its own built-in washing device. Once a month, this big pool of old soup was cleaned out. By that time, the soup at the bottom had been there for thirty days, cooling daily and being reheated by the next day's leftover soup. It was disgusting. Although most of the soup could be pumped out, when you reached the bottom, somebody had to jump in and suck up the residue with a wet-vac. Naturally, that somebody was me. At one point I bent over in my huge overalls, and my prescription glasses and the notebook we all had to carry fell out of my chest pocket and into this disgusting concoction. The guys thought it was hilarious when I had to rummage around in this foul-smelling mess to retrieve my stuff.

That's just one example of the kind of thing that went on day after day. They gave me the heaviest and the dirtiest work. Jobs that I suspected normally took two men, they made me do myself. If I had difficulty, they'd say gleefully, "You see. She can't do the work."

At one point I asked to be put on the night shift to broaden my experience because some of the equipment, such as the backup power equipment, which was very noisy, could only be run at night when there were no employees in the building. The second level manager, a delightful man and a true gentleman, was hesitant since there weren't many people around at night, but he finally agreed. On my first night, I was working in a large supply room on the twenty-third floor when one of my co-workers called me over. When I reached him, he grabbed me and started to sexually assault me. I kicked and fought — there was no point in screaming since the closest person was twenty-three storeys away — and finally escaped. Afterwards he treated me as if I had done something wrong. He kept on telling me he forgave me and that it was okay — as though by fighting his advances, I had somehow failed to measure up to his expectations!

I didn't ask for any more night shifts and chose not to say anything until I left at the end of the summer. I knew if the story came out it would affect my chances of working there again. When I went for an exit interview, I told my second level supervisor about the episode. He was upset that I hadn't reported it to him at the time and after I left, my co-worker was moved to an equipment building with no people. Eventually he was let go.

The next summer, when I returned, Bell offered me the opportunity to be a foreman over the group of men I had worked with the previous summer. I decided not to accept because I felt it would be more hassle than it was worth. If those men didn't respect me as a colleague, how could I possibly expect them to respect me as their supervisor? I worked at Bell for three summers in all, and although I thought the company was excellent and very committed to supporting women, many of the guys I worked with were another story.

After I finished at Ryerson in 1982, the economy was in a recession and I had a great deal of trouble finding a job. I have no doubt that some of my difficulty had to do with being female. I remember one company posting an interview sign-up sheet for the students. Everyone in the graduating class — including a guy who was failing — was interviewed except for me. They gave no explanation for the variance. One headhunter I interviewed with was very explicit. He said, "Women, Blacks, and Indians don't deserve a job. Go home, have babies, do whatever it is you do. I'm in control of who gets a job here and you're not getting one." I was astounded. "You can't say things like that to me — it's against the law!" I protested. His response was, "Baby, the job market is tough. I can do anything I want." After that, every interview I had was good because it couldn't have been as bad as that one.

One of my more memorable interviews that year was with a recruiter for a meat-packing company. The interview was held in a hotel room and when I arrived, the recruiter, who was sitting at a desk with his leg slung over the arm of the chair, didn't even bother to get up. Instead, he immediately launched into a graphic description of a slaughterhouse. "Have you ever watched a cow die?" he asked. "Do you know what we do? We shoot a bolt through their brain and while they're still warm we put them on a hook and bleed them. Could you watch that?" The entire interview continued along that line. I hedged most of my answers. "I'm not sure, but if that's what the job entailed I'd have to get used to it." Or, "I'd like an opportunity to tour the plant to see if I could handle that." He was very vivid and throughout the interview his leg remained slung over the arm of the chair. Finally, he said, "Well, I'm done with you." I stood up and thanked him for giving me the time. When I put my hand out to shake his, he ignored it.

That afternoon, when I was back in class with my fellow students, I asked them what they said when the recruiter mentioned the bolt in the cow's head. They were uniformly surprised. Their interviews had been entirely conventional — the sharing of information about the mechanical systems in the plant and so on — and there was absolutely no mention of bolts through cows' heads.

I didn't get an engineering job until December 1982, seven months after finishing school. At that point I moved to Kapuskasing, Ontario, to work at a company that, basically, tested cars in cold-weather conditions. I spent three years there driving and riding in everything from two-seater sports cars to Rolls-Royces, which I thoroughly enjoyed. The major downside of the job and of living so far away from my family and friends was the loneliness. I was the only woman on the technical staff and my boss told me not to tell anyone what I did. He was afraid I might seem like a women's libber and that would give the company a bad image. Worse still, I was twenty-three and single — according to the townsfolk, the oldest single childless woman in town. Everyone referred to me as "the spinster." This issue was complicated by the fact that my cheques were pretty hefty because the job involved lots of overtime. The tellers in the bank had never seen a woman earn so much money, and they eventually confessed that they thought I was a hooker or a stripper. I was so upset I blew my cover and told them I was a technologist at an engineering company. They had no idea what that involved and when I explained what I did, they couldn't believe that a woman could do that sort of work.

Looking back, I probably survived those three years in Kapuskasing because of my gutsiness, some of which I can attribute to my family situation. My father was a very demanding man. When I scored ninety-nine percent in math he wanted to know why I hadn't got one hundred percent. That made me an overachiever. When I was fifteen, my mother became seriously ill, and as the eldest girl I became responsible for the housework and helping my father to run his business, while continuing to attend high school. I grew up quickly that year and don't remember the fun things of being a kid.

There was one good outcome of being in Kapuskasing: I met my husband, Art, a local fellow who was one of the company's test drivers. He's shy, exactly the opposite of me, and a very hard worker.

He's a Class A mechanic, not a highly educated person, but he's exceptionally intelligent and extremely supportive. I couldn't have even dreamed of doing the things I've done without him. I was flying off to France when my tots were one and two, and he looked after things at home. For the last three days of our honeymoon, we were at the annual general meeting of OACETT, which was in Ottawa. I was the only woman in the meetings and he was the only man in the "spouse's program." Since he wouldn't go to the Mary Kay demonstrations, he toured the capital alone.

In 1985 I went to work as an airworthiness engineering assistant for the aviation branch of Transport Canada. When I was transferred to headquarters in 1990, I became the first woman to travel the world reviewing aircraft designs as part of the approval team. It was so much fun travelling around the world, talking about new aircraft designs. Compared with what I experienced in the private sector, government is a pretty good place to work, although I always found if difficult to be the only woman.

My first big problem in the government came in 1987 when I got pregnant. My boss had no experience with a pregnant engineer —the only workers who got pregnant before me were secretaries — and he didn't know what to do with me. When I told him the news, he stood up and bellowed, "This will ruin everything." Then he told the woman who handled the travel and training to cancel all my trips because he didn't want to be responsible for the loss of my baby.

I had no idea he would react this way. In fact, I had expected to receive congratulations. I was appalled and made a mental note not to share this kind of information with him again. When I got pregnant the second time, I didn't officially tell him until I was seven months along and had been showing for months! I very clearly got the message that I was on my own, so while I was at the office I tried to downplay the pregnancy as much as possible. I never complained if I was feeling ill, and carried on as if nothing had changed.

In the early 1990s, after I had moved to Ottawa, my career took another major change in direction. One day the director general addressed all the staff and announced that if people were interested in moving up within the organization they ought to move out and get some different experience — another degree, an assignment in another department, whatever. I immediately made an appointment to see him and I was so nervous my knees knocked as I walked into his office. "Sir," I said. "You told us if we wanted to move up, we had to move out. I'm here to ask you where out is because I am moving up."

"So tell me about yourself," was his response. My twenty-minute appointment turned into an hour and a half, during which he told me about and recommended me for the Career Assignment Program, which is designed to prepare people with certain skills to take on executive roles in the government. You have to undergo a two-and-a-half-day assessment and if you pass you're considered for the program. I did exceptionally well and I've been in the program since 1993. I hope I'll be successful in obtaining an executive position in the future that will allow me to use the skills I've acquired and give something back to the system.

Over the years, I've had some interesting times talking to high-school girls about pursuing engineering and technology as a career. When they ask if it will be hard, I can't lie, but in spite of the difficulties I've experienced, I encourage them, because I think it's tragic to waste the talent and skills that so many women possess. Also, I believe that the more women there are in these fields, the better it will be for everyone. I sincerely hope that by the time my daughter goes looking for a job, nobody talks about shooting a bolt through a cow's head.

When I was a kid, I used to watch the reruns of the television show *My Three Sons*. Fred MacMurray played Stephen Douglas, the father, who was an aerospace engineer. His desk was decorated with models of the great planes he'd worked on. For the longest time I used to dream about being his wife. Then one day it struck me that I didn't want to be his wife — I wanted to be him.

Of course, I can now see how much better it would have been if I'd had female role models to look up to, but he was my first hero. The day I completed work on my first aircraft-type approval, the company that designed the plane presented each person on the team with a model of the aircraft we had approved. I put it on my desk. I can't explain the satisfaction I felt when I thought, Now I *am* Stephen Douglas. That was my dream come true.

"As a pilot I have viewed all of Canada from the air and it is spec-
tacularly beautiful. I have seen the changing seasons and the
northern landscape from a unique perspective. About a month ago
I was flying to Yellowknife. We were above the clouds and the sky
was illuminated by the aurora borealis. How many people get a
chance to see that?"

ROSELLA BJORNSON

*Captain Rosella Bjornson was inducted into Canada's Aviation
Hall of Fame in 1997 with the following citation: "As a young
child she had a dream to be an airline pilot and, by working stead-
fastly toward that goal, became the first female in Canada to
achieve that level. Along the way she encouraged young people,
especially females, to set and work toward their goals and continues to be an outstanding role model." She was the first woman to
be hired as a first officer flying a jet for a scheduled airline in
North America and the first woman captain with a major airline
in Canada. She is the recipient of numerous awards, including the
Amelia Earhart Award and the 1991 National Transport Week
Award of Achievement.*

The day I received my air transport rating, Doug Rose,
the chief pilot of Transair, offered me a tour of northern Manitoba in the jump seat of the airline's Boeing 737. I asked so
many questions about the aircraft that he gave me the manuals to
take home to study and advised me to put in an application with
Transair. Almost a year later, Transair took delivery of two new F28
aircraft and was hiring pilots. Since I had filed my application and
had the required qualifications, they hired me. It was a tremendous

thrill, a dream come true, because so many people had told me that an airline would never hire a woman pilot.

Transair was a regional airline that served northern Manitoba and northwestern Ontario. I was hired April 16, 1973, to fly a Foker 28, a sixty-five-passenger twin engine jet as a first officer, or co-pilot, as many people say. First, like all pilots hired by airlines, who must be trained on the aircraft they will be operating, I had to pass the three-month training course. This includes a ground school, which involves learning all the systems of the aircraft such as hydraulics, electrical, pneumatics, and so on, as well as flight training, which is usually done in a simulator. Since Transair did not have a simulator for the F28, I did my flight training in the aircraft. Captain Rose was willing to give me a chance and I was not going to let him down. His attitude was, "I don't care if pilots are male or female, as long as they can do the job." The training was difficult since the largest aircraft I had flown to that point was a Piper Apache, but I loved what I was doing and passed with flying colours.

Strangely, my interest in flying developed from my agricultural background. I grew up on a farm northwest of Lethbridge, Alberta. After the Second World War, many pilots didn't have flying jobs so they took aircraft out to the small towns and encouraged farmers to learn to fly. My dad trained on a Tiger Moth and in 1947 bought an Aeronca Champ with three other farmers. As a child, flying with my dad was the highlight of my life. I have vivid memories of sitting on his knee and playing with the controls, making the aircraft go up and down. It was so exciting! My father was an excellent pilot and I showed a real interest in flying from the beginning, so whenever he'd go flying I'd beg to go along with him. Since my younger sisters were not very interested, in many ways I became the son he never had.

My desire to be a professional pilot started around the time I was in grade seven. When the guidance counsellor asked me what I wanted to be, I replied, "A pilot." I remember one teacher saying, "But you can't be a pilot. There are no women pilots." I never let that discourage me. I was sure they were wrong because my parents had told me I could be anything I wanted to be. I convinced my dad to let me take flying lessons in return for all the work I was doing around the farm. On my seventeenth birthday, my mom and dad surprised me by taking me to the Lethbridge Flying Club for my first flying lesson. The instructor must have been impressed because when we landed he asked me if I had flown before. During the summer between grades eleven and twelve, I managed to complete the flying time and ground school requirements for the private pilot's licence.

From a very young age I felt confident that I could handle an aircraft, and my father trusted me in the air. Although I was only seventeen, when I got my private pilot's licence, he'd give me the keys to the airplane, with the suggestion that I take it out for a couple of circuits. His confidence in me and the growth of my flying skills did wonders for my self-development. Before obtaining my private licence I had been relatively shy. But with that credential, I was my own self. I was an individual and nobody could take that away from me.

The year I was in grade twelve, I saw a pamphlet from Air Canada outlining the necessary qualifications for pilots. Since they gave preference to pilots who had completed a university degree, an air transport rating, and had fifteen hundred hours of flying time, I decided my goal was to have all those qualifications by the time I was twenty-four years old. After graduating from grade twelve, I enrolled at the University of Calgary to take a bachelor of science, majoring in geography. After moving to Calgary, I soon made my way out to the airport, where I introduced myself to Gina Jordan, a female instructor I had heard about. Since there were so few women in aviation, I felt I had to get to know her. Gina became my instructor for the commercial licence and my instructor's rating. She was a tremendous influence on my life at that time because she validated my goals and became my mentor.

In the spring of 1970, I started my first job as a flight instructor at the Winnipeg Flying Club. I loved instructing — taking people who have never flown an aircraft before and teaching them how to climb and descend, how to take off and land, was a real challenge. There is so much more to flying than driving a car. A pilot must learn meteorology, navigation, theory of flight, airmanship, and radio communication, among other things. While I was instructing, I was also logging flying time and studying to upgrade my qualifications. In 1972, I completed the multi-engine instrument rating and upgraded to a Class II instructor's rating so I could teach instrument flying.

When I had two thousand hours of flying time, I wrote the exams for the air transport rating. They were difficult, but I had reached my goal. Now I was ready to apply to the airlines.

I was very fortunate to be in Winnipeg then because through my work at the Flying Club I became acquainted with most of the pilots who worked for Transair, including the chief pilot, Captain Rose. I think my timing was good. By then there was a certain acceptance of the idea of a woman pilot. When I finished the training on the F28 and was ready for my first line flight, my parents were in the back of the aircraft with my first passengers. During my early days as a pilot, I felt that people were watching me to see how I performed. I did begin to feel the pressure, because I knew that if I dropped the ball, I'd ruin things for other women. Transair promoted the fact that they were the only airline to have a woman pilot, since it was free publicity for the airline. I was hired over the telephone and when I walked into the Winnipeg Flying Club the next day the TV reporters were there to interview me.

I flew for Transair for five wonderful years until Pacific Western Airlines bought out Transair and we were amalgamated with PWA in 1979. Although I had met my husband, Bill Pratt, in 1971, we did not get married until 1977, after I felt I was established in my career. At the time, he was a corporate pilot flying a Lear Jet around North America, so often he would be going south and I would be headed to Churchill or some other northern destination. We led an interesting life!

In 1979 I became pregnant with our first child. There was quite a to-do about my pregnancy. At the time, a pregnant woman was considered medically unfit to be a commercial pilot, so I couldn't fly. When I applied for a medical leave of absence, they told me I wasn't sick — I was only pregnant. Since the company had no provision for maternity leave, I took an unpaid leave of absence for eighteen months. When I returned to work in 1980, I was assigned to Edmonton as a first officer on the Boeing 737 with Pacific Western Airlines. My husband was now unemployed, as the company he was with had just sold their aircraft. He applied to PWA and was hired as a second officer on the Hercules, so we planned our move to Edmonton. I was looking forward to getting back to work, but I was not prepared for the problems that I had checking out on the Boeing 737. Their director of training was not sure about a woman pilot, so he did the training himself. It was a very difficult course and at the time I was concerned that I wouldn't pass. In addition, I was homesick, missed my baby, and found that by being away from flying for that length of time, I had to relearn my instrument flying skills. I also found the simulator a challenge because I had always done my F28 training in the aircraft.

When I did my final check ride with the Transport Canada inspector, I wasn't sure I was going to pass, but he was impressed and told me I had done a good ride. After my licence was signed, the director of training took me aside and said, "I hope you realize what's going to happen when you get on the line. The other pilots won't accept you." I was absolutely shocked, because I had never had any trouble with the pilots at Transair and I certainly didn't anticipate difficulties with their counterparts at PWA. I have a lot of respect for the men I work with, and I know from the way I am treated that they have respect for me.

In 1983 I discovered I was pregnant again. It was not an opportune time because my husband, who was quite junior at PWA, had just been laid off. I had to take another leave of absence without pay because they still didn't have maternity leave, and within several months I, too, was laid off. Thankfully, my husband was able to find a job as a corporate pilot. I chose to stay at home with my three-year-old son and we were blessed with a beautiful daughter in March 1984.

The next couple of years were a period of great changes. PWA did some creative financing and bought Canadian Pacific Airlines to create Canadian Airlines. When my husband and I were recalled to the airline, I was based in Toronto as first officer on the 737 and Bill was based in Vancouver as second officer on the DC10 flying overseas. We did not know where to move, so we left the children with the nanny in Edmonton and commuted. After six months I managed to do a base trade and came to Edmonton, but my husband was based in Vancouver for two and a half years.

In November 1990, I checked out as captain on the 737, the first woman with Canadian Airlines and the first with a major airline in Canada. I am happy to report that I am not alone — Canadian now has nine female pilots. Two others have checked out as captains; the others fly as first officers. Although having other women pilots is wonderful, I wish we had more, because I like the camaraderie. In fact, through my voluntary activities I make a point of encouraging other women to pursue a career in aviation. I'm quite active with the International Organization of Women Pilots and I've been involved with the Amelia Earhart Scholarships, which help younger women to pay for their flight training. I also go to schools and talk to the kids on career days. Even now, some boys are shocked to see a woman in a pilot's uniform and they'll say things like, "I didn't know women could fly airplanes." The young girls are impressed. Of course, I am very enthusiastic about my career and highly recommend it.

My husband has always been supportive of my career. We make family decisions together and always manage to find time for important family things. Our son is eighteen and just got his private pilot's licence. He intends to pursue a flying career. Our daughter, who is fourteen, will get her licence as well, but we are not sure what career path she will follow. We own a small aircraft, which we use for recreational flying, and have had a lot of fun going to fly-in breakfasts and visiting relatives throughout Alberta. I feel very fortunate to have been able to follow my dream.

One thing about flying, there is never a dull moment. Somebody once asked me if I was bored at 35,000 feet with the auto pilot on. I was shocked. "Do you realize what's going through my mind?" I replied. "I may not look like I'm doing anything, but I always have to be aware of the upper winds, the weather at my destination, air speed, altitude, air traffic control, and so on. I'm continuously analyzing the situation and am totally involved with my life at that moment. It's a wonderful feeling."

"Being a trailblazer is a heavy responsibility because you're alone and out on a limb in the crowd of 'others.' At the same time, you're representing all women."

MARCIA BRAUNDY

In 1980, Marcia Braundy became the first woman to work in the construction sector of the B.C. Carpenter's Union. She is a founder of the WITT (Women in Trades and Technology) National Network, which advocates for women in trades, technology, and blue collar jobs, and, among other achievements, has developed and taught trades courses for women. From 1986 to 1991 she was a member of the Federal Advisory Committee to the President of the Treasury Board on Employment Equity for Women in the Public Service. Currently, she is working on her doctorate in technology studies at the University of British Columbia.

In 1972, I helped to found the Slocan Valley Free School in the West Kootenays of British Columbia. We had thirty-five students and we needed a building to house the school, so we decided to construct a community centre ourselves. As a community organizer learning carpentry skills, I assigned the volunteers to the jobs decided upon at weekly meetings and worked alongside them. The construction site was a microcosm of gender relations at that moment in time. Women didn't own their own tools and men often took over to "show us how," frequently making us feel inadequate. Finally, we decided to hold women-only building days, which allowed us to experience the joy of making our own mistakes and the thrill of building something we could point to with pride. Ultimately, women, men, and children constructed a well-built and beautiful building with wonderful acoustics.

I worked as a volunteer carpenter for about three years. By that time I knew that people could make a good living as carpenters; since I loved the work and was good at it, I decided to give it a try. I was aware that as a woman I'd need more qualifications than a guy because people would assume that any male would already have basic carpentry skills, so I decided to take the province's six-month preapprenticeship training course.

Clearly, as someone who had just spent three years building a community centre, I was a good candidate. I guess the apprenticeship counsellor didn't see it that way. After a year of getting nowhere, I called the director of apprenticeship in British Columbia and said, "I have been discriminated against and I want into school right now." He recognized a problem when he saw one and offered me a course starting January 3 in Dawson Creek. Not only is Dawson Creek mile zero of the Alaska Highway, in the northernmost part of British Columbia, his offer came on December 29. When I left for school, thirty women of the Kootenays chipped in and bought me a sander to send me off.

I agreed to go because I really did want to become a carpenter, but the move to Dawson Creek initiated six of the most hideous months of my life. It was 1977 and my student colleagues were sixteen guys who seemed to feel that the best way for them to prove they were men was to denigrate the lone woman. They made my life hell by putting up lewd posters and writing dirty messages on the board. Some of their tricks were just plain disgusting, such as filling potty seats with excrement in the bathroom and labelling them with my name. Basically, I tried to pretend it wasn't happening. My thinking was bizarre, but I think I felt that if no one else saw it, then maybe it wasn't real. Finally, I couldn't handle it any more, so I told my instructor about the situation and showed him a "Fuck you, Ms!" message on the board. "I want you to know that this stuff has been here every day and I have been coming in at 7 a.m. to erase it," I said. "I want you to do something about it." The next day he erased the morning message but he didn't say a word to the class, I think because he wanted the guys to like him.

When it came time to create the class T-shirt, ours read "The NLC [Northern Lights College] Hammer Slam-hers." For a college event, every class was supposed to make a poster. Ours was a six-foot-long painting of a naked woman with the slogan "NLC Hammer Slam-hers bang um better." I found it so offensive — particularly so because they planned to put this up in the gym representing my class — that I picked up a can of paint and threw it over the poster. In response, they picked up a can of paint and threw it over me. The night of the event, our MLA was sitting on the podium with the principal of the college. I had succeeded in rendering our poster useless, but the guys from the auto body shop made a poster that said, "Auto Body Boys Beaver Patrol." *Beaver* is a crude expression for women's genitalia and it was one of the words the guys would scream at high-school girls who visited the school on "career days." The MLA turned to the principal and said, "Excuse me, but does that poster say what I think it does?" That sort of set the tone. By that point I had reached my limit. I was the first woman to go through the college's trades training and I constantly heard about women who started and didn't make it. No wonder they dropped out! Using my journal, where necessary, to document my experiences, I wrote a letter to the College Council. I told them that since they had made the decision to have me at the school, they had a responsibility to make sure that my learning experience was satisfactory and to take a stand on the degradation of women on the campus. Three days later the principal visited every trades training classroom and told the students and instructors that sexist language and harassment were totally inappropriate at an institution of higher learning. He went on to say that if it continued, the offenders would be thrown out of school and not allowed into any apprenticeship in British Columbia. I was surprised and pleased by the response and felt good that I had decided to take a stand.

Although I got the highest mark in the class on my final exam, I walked out of Northern Lights College a damaged woman. I was very hurt in deep places. If I had been less skilled to start with, perhaps they would have succeeded in beating me down. But I was as good as most of them, and better than many, and that knowledge buttressed my will to succeed. For my second year of upgrading, I went to Pacific Vocational Institute [now the British Columbia Institute of Technology

(BCIT)], where I had a fine experience. I was still the only woman in the class, but I was with a different group of guys. I also enjoyed my third year in Victoria, but my fourth year back at BCIT was problematic. When I walked into my classroom, three naked crotch-shot pictures of women, 3' x 5', were hanging on the back wall. I walked right over, took them down, and started rolling them up. One of the guys yelled, "Hey, you can't take those pictures down. They belong to us." Not knowing what the truth was, I laid them on his desk and said, "Fine, they're yours. Take them home! They don't belong in the classroom." The next morning, the pictures were back up, so I made a point of telling the instructor and he quietly took them down.

I got along with everybody in my fourth-year class except for two guys who were real jerks. Basically, everybody ignored them, and as a result, they weren't able to get the wolf-pack energy going. But on the last day of class, when I walked into the classroom, one of them marched to the back wall and put up an absolutely disgusting picture. "That's for the guys in the next class. We hope there aren't any women in it," he announced. Very quietly, during a break, I went to the back of the room, pulled down the picture, shredded it, and threw it in the garbage. I left the classroom briefly, and when I returned, my signed Fredrickson framing square had been twisted into a pretzel and the word "cunt" was written in big letters across my desk. I was just about to take my interprovincial exam, the only exam in my four years of study that really meant anything. If I flunked, I wouldn't become a carpenter. The timing was terrible! I took the twisted mess to my instructor and asked for a new square. He said, "They should pay for this," and I said that was up to him. He gave me a new square but didn't say a word to anybody in the class. As we walked to the building where we were taking the exam, one of the guys came up to me and said, "Don't worry about him. He's just an asshole." I looked him in the eye and told him, "Why didn't you say that when it was going on?" Then I walked away. I couldn't believe that these guys, who had been my friends, had allowed that to happen. I passed the exam with a seventy-two, but I know I would have done better if I hadn't been in such a state. At least I passed. At that point, I was thought to be the first woman to graduate from the four-year carpenter's apprenticeship. Later, I went through the records and discovered that in the mid-1970s one other woman had gone through an apprenticeship, but I have no idea what happened to her.

Becoming a carpenter certainly didn't occur to me as a girl, likely because it wasn't something girls of my era did. Even so, I knew I didn't want a traditional female life. I grew up in Pleasantville, New York, home of *Readers' Digest*, which, I think, was a big influence on me. I used to walk about two miles to school and every morning I'd see these green busloads of women driving to *Readers' Digest* to do key punching. I knew I never wanted to do work like that. I was the second girl of four children, born in 1946 into a Jewish family. When my brother was born, my mother got a gold watch for a job well done. This pretty well defined my relationship with my father, which was difficult for many years, although we've finally worked it out. He was quite proud of me when I got my interprovincial journey ticket, and now we can talk shop together.

My father was a mechanical engineer who became a construction contractor and ultimately built recreational facilities around the world. My mother's father was a housing developer who made and lost several fortunes. When I was growing up I wasn't welcomed onto the construction sites, but at the time I didn't think much about that, even though my mother did all the building projects around our home. When we built a playroom addition, my grandfather's worker, Gus, helped her with the heavier jobs, but she always worked alongside him and she built the framework, put up the panelling, and completed the interior finish herself. She also installed the recessed lighting around the fireplace in the living room and laid our backyard patio. She was a very smart and talented woman with an artistic bent, but she wasn't able to pursue her interests, and that made her very unhappy. Since she confided in me, I was aware of the choices she made in her life and I could see how those choices led to the rest of the things that happened to her. I was determined they wouldn't happen to me.

I was always a rebel. I didn't want to be good, like my older sister who was in a sorority and on the honour roll. Since this was the early 1960s, I wanted to be a beatnik and spent every weekend in Greenwich Village hanging out. That broadened my horizon beyond Pleasantville High School, as did attending Emerson College in Boston, a college quite famous for theatre arts. Actually, I majored in bridge, and when I got a C average, my dad pulled me out of school after first year, with the suggestion that I become a secretary, like his sister. That didn't appeal to me, so I suggested hairdressing school. In 1964, I enrolled at Charles of the Ritz School for Hairstyling in New York, where my teachers included Vidal Sassoon, because my father thought that if I was going to do something as unacceptable as hairdressing at least I should go to the best school. I didn't like permanents or colouring, but I was good with the scissors and have maintained that skill — people still come to me for haircuts. I worked as a hairdresser for a while and then, when I got tired of that, almost by accident got a job organizing and running drug education and educational reform conferences on college campuses. It was a far cry from hairdressing, as was the BA in environmental education I got in 1972. At that point, I moved to Canada, and when I reached the Slocan Valley, I felt as though I was home.

While I was still an apprentice, I went to work for a construction company doing renovations on Victorian buildings. I enjoyed that, but the guy I was working for didn't have work for me all the time, and since I was working non-union, I wasn't earning great money — $6 to $8 an hour, depending on the job. I thought that if I joined the union I'd get more work, so I started talking to their business agent, who kept telling me to wait until the work situation improved. Finally I said, "Len, I've been waiting for a year for the work picture to get better. I think it is as good as it's going to get." He told me he wouldn't be attending the meeting that month and suggested that I go in and talk to the executive myself. When I walked into the union meeting, the guys asked if they could help me with something. When I said I wanted to join, their mouths fell open. Clearly, in the entire year I had been talking to the business agent, he had not once mentioned me to the executive. They hemmed and hawed and said, "Put your application in and come back next month." When I returned, they congratulated me on being the first woman to join the carpenter's union in British Columbia. Later, I learned that the business agent had told them that they'd have a human rights case on their hands if they didn't allow me in.

Of course, by joining the union I increased my wages dramatically. I was making $16 to $17 an hour, which was a big difference. Since a woman was going out on a construction site as a unionized carpenter for the first time, the steward called all the guys together and told them to watch themselves. That set the tone; the union sent the message that they wanted me and the job was wonderful. On my last day, the guys threw a party and gave me a velvet-wrapped bottle of fifteen-year-old rye whiskey. I felt completely honoured.

Over the years, I've worked with a lot of guys, and I've always made a point of keeping sex off the job. It's a rule: I don't go to bed with construction workers. You build a quality of relationship among the crew and that becomes a collegial brother-sister type of relationship that sex would undermine. Choosing not to become sexually involved with my co-workers has limited my choice of men, because those are the men I come in contact with. So, in a sense, I've had to isolate myself sexually, which has contributed to my being single for a long time.

Another problem with working as a carpenter is that I inadvertently distanced myself from the women who had previously been my friends. My old support system — the thirty women who bought me a sander and threw a big going-away party for me when I left for school — was crucial to making it through my apprenticeship. But when I got back, I found the quality of that relationship had changed. By becoming a tradesperson, I had created a barrier between us. At that point, I also had to focus on making my living as a carpenter and I no longer had a lot of free time to devote to community activities, which contributed to a further decline in my connectedness.

To some extent, I compensated for the isolation by keeping very busy with work. I was one of the founding sisters and the first national coordinator of the WITT National Network. In 1983 and 1986 I taught the Women in Trades and Technology Exploratory Program at Selkirk College and at the College of New Caledonia in Prince George. I realized that many women were taking these programs, and there was no consistency in what they were taught. I convinced the Ministry of Advanced Education, Skills and Training to sponsor an articulation meeting and was eventually contracted to write the curriculum for British Columbia.

While I was writing the curriculum, my mother was dying of cancer. One day I got a phone call from someone in Ottawa who was looking for a woman with my background and experience. That's how I got onto the Federal Advisory Committee to the President of the Treasury Board on Employment Equity for Women in the Public Service and became involved with power politics on a national scale. I was interested because it got me closer to my mother, who was in upper New York State. She died later that year, which was very hard for me, and once again I threw myself into my work.

If I had it all to do over again, I'd change two things. I would like a love partner — a man, since I'm heterosexual. I'd also change the isolation that comes with being a trailblazer, because I very much value compatriots. Now, in order to do my work, I have to leave my community, which I love. The world of power politics on a national scale is foreign to many people in the Slocan Valley, who are focused on local issues. Although people admire trailblazers, they are a little afraid of them, because they usually challenge them to change.

"I like the idea of putting things together and making them work. Being a ship's engineer involves a lot of troubleshooting, which is fun because the solution to a problem doesn't jump out at you."

JOY THOMSON

Joy Thomson was born in Calgary in 1961. She was the first woman mariner on the west coast to achieve her first-class engineering certification and at the time of this interview was a chief engineer for the Victoria Line Ltd. She is currently an instructor for the Pacific Marine Training Campus in North Vancouver, where she instructs in the propulsion plant simulator and teaches engineering knowledge.

I grew up on the prairies and think of myself as a typical prairies person, so when a friend suggested I think about joining the Coast Guard I was surprised. I didn't know there was such a thing! After giving the idea some thought, I decided that life on the sea sounded interesting. I've always loved the water, but more important, I'd never lived anywhere except Calgary. I was twenty-two years old and I realized that if I didn't leave soon, I'd be there for ever. I felt there was more to life and I wanted to experience some of it.

I left for the Coast Guard College in Sydney, Nova Scotia, in August 1984. Prior to that, I hadn't done much travelling and I'd seen the ocean only twice. After graduating from high school, I worked with a petroleum consulting firm doing technical analysis — I was very good in maths and sciences. I'd always lived with my family, and was very attached to my friends. Going off to Sydney was pretty uncharacteristic, and nobody thought I'd last very long.

The nice thing about the college was that everybody had to live on campus. That meant that all the other students were as lonely as I was and it was easy to make friends. Even so, at times I came close to throwing in the towel. My engineering class had sixty students, eight of whom were women. By the end of first year, just four women were left. The instructors apparently assumed the women would fail or quit right after graduation, so they paid much more attention to the guys. The first time my class trained at sea, we docked in Shelburne, Nova Scotia, for a refit. When another female cadet and myself were introduced to a ship safety inspector, his response was immediate. "One of you took my son's spot at the college. They had a quota on the number of women they had to accept, so you're there and he's not." Then he rambled on for a long time about how even if we graduated we wouldn't last and we'd robbed his son of his lifelong livelihood so we could do our own little thing for a couple of years. There's no doubt that being a woman in this field exposes you to prejudice.

A hostile environment was another problem. When I first started, nude calendars were everywhere. Once I was on a ship with a female cadet who was explicit about her intolerance for pornography. As soon as she arrived, she announced that she wouldn't put up with it and immediately tore everything down. I think the way she did it turned the men against her. They put a calendar up that wasn't as bad — I guess you could say it was more tasteful — and she immediately stuck a calendar of a nude male beside it. Her message was, "You have your calendar, I'll have mine." Within half an hour, hers was totally defaced. Her behaviour created a war between her and the fellows that got so out of hand she considered bringing sexual harassment charges against them.

I can't say I've had a problem with pornography. Unless it was disgusting or pervasive, I've chosen not to push the issue. Lately, I've discovered that if people know I'm coming on ship, they remove anything that might be offensive before I arrive. That might have something to do with my seniority, but in general I think pornography is becoming less of an issue simply because there are more women on the ships — not so much in engineering, but in catering or up on deck.

Another problem is the prevailing attitude that a woman can't do the job as well as a man. That means you constantly have to prove yourself. The men want to know that you can lift heavy things and that you're not afraid to get dirty. Paternalism is the other side of that coin and it's almost harder to fight than hostility. Once, I was working with a couple of rather elderly fellows who took a fatherly interest in me. Whenever I went to lift something heavy, they'd jump in and do it for me with a "don't hurt yourself, dear" attitude. They think they're doing you a favour, but they're not, and I had to convince them that I was capable of doing the job without getting hurt.

I definitely enjoy the challenge of engineering. I like working with my hands and if something breaks, particularly when you're a thousand miles from any habitable place, you really have to think and be creative to get it fixed. The downside is that you're often locked in an engine room. You don't see daylight for the whole time you're down there and it's hot, noisy, and dirty.

I suppose I got my interest in technical stuff from my father and my uncle. They had a trucking company and did all their own maintenance and repairs. I'd hang around on weekends, and since there was a gas station on part of the property, when I was old enough I started pumping gas. I never got a sense it wasn't appropriate for a girl. The fact that my mother worked — as a bookkeeper — was probably an influence. I guess she would have preferred it if I'd been into dresses and frills and played with dolls, but I wasn't interested. When I was two I got a beautiful doll for Christmas and my brother got a truck and I cried all day because I wanted the truck. In junior high I wanted to take shop instead of home economics, but at that point it wasn't allowed.

I graduated as an engineer with a fourth-class combined ticket after three years at the Canadian Coast Guard College. Then I went to Laurentian region, which is based in Quebec City, and worked on the ice-breakers. I really enjoyed that, particularly my five trips to the Arctic, which I found very beautiful. I especially liked being on the twelve-to-four watch in the summer, when it's daylight for twenty-four hours. When I got off at four in the morning, I'd go to the aft end of the ship and look at the sunsets. During the four-hour period of sunset-sunrise, the entire sky is lit with incredible shades of orange and red.

When I joined the Coast Guard, I had no idea what I was getting into. I certainly never expected to visit Inuit communities or to experience the thrill of steaming past a herd of walruses or having a polar bear running along the ice beside the ship. I did have one problem on an ice-breaking trip in the Arctic. I was about twenty-eight and one older fellow — about sixty-four — was having some sexual problems. He was a nice guy, but I later learned from one of the crew that things weren't working as well as they used to. Since he and I got along really well, I guess he decided I'd help him out. One night, after he'd been drinking, he came into my cabin at three o'clock in the morning, wanting to get into bed with me. Luckily, the chief engineer's cabin was right beside mine, so I told him if he didn't leave I'd bang on the walls and wake him up. It took about forty-five minutes until he left. Afterwards, he told some of the fellows what had happened and they got down on me because they felt I should have boosted his spirits by obliging him. I explained that it doesn't work that way, but things were a little uneasy for about a week. I think he was embarrassed, so I had to pull away — from the other guys, as well — to let things settle. After we got through that, it was never mentioned again.

I spent three years in the Laurentian region and by that time I had written both my third-class and my second-class ticket. I was accelerating — most people don't do it that quickly, but I like to get to the top, to set a goal and go for it. Unfortunately, my rapid progress offended some of the fellows — not so much the guys who came from the college, but those who came up the hard way, the ones who entered the system as oilers. They do the dirty jobs and are the low men on the totem pole, and they resented graduates from the college because we automatically got the junior officers' positions, which made it difficult for them to get promoted. Being a woman to boot didn't help.

Once I got my second-class ticket and was in a position to become a senior engineer, my proficiency in French became a problem. Although we spoke French on the ship, I wasn't totally comfortable with the language — at least not to the point where I felt I could fulfil the requirements of a senior engineer's job, which required, for instance, the ability to negotiate pricing on materials over the phone. I was even more terrified of being in charge of the fire parties. In case of a fire on the ship, I would be responsible for handling it and all the radio communication in French. The idea of taking charge of an emergency over a radio in a language I wasn't totally familiar with really scared me.

I knew I wasn't ready for the responsibility of being a senior engineer, so at twenty-eight I decided it was time to move on. Also, my father had been diagnosed with cancer and I wanted to be closer to home. This was during the Meech Lake negotiations and my request for transfer was okayed by the Quebec region but squashed in Ottawa, apparently because somebody thought if English people were leaving the province, it would make Quebec look bad. That meant I had to leave the Coast Guard to get back to the West. I spent the winter in the Arctic working for a company responsible for the maintenance of the short-range radar system up there. Despite the dark, the Arctic has winter moments of incredible beauty, such as the northern lights, but after about eight months I was itching to get back to the sea.

Also, I hadn't finished what I had set out to do. When I graduated from the college, my goal was to get my first-class ticket within five years, and going shoreside had put a hold on that. I had an idea that I'd be the first woman to achieve that certification, but that wasn't why I was doing it. It was a personal goal. So I spent a year and a half working for B.C. Ferries and another two years working on the new fast passenger ferries, and after that I was offered a second engineer's position on the Victoria–Seattle ferry. A year later, one of our senior chief engineers had a stroke and I walked into the chief engineer's job.

When I received my first-class engineering ticket in March 1995, I became the only woman on the west coast to have that qualification, although there's a woman with a first-class ticket who works out of the Newfoundland region. I was proud of what I had achieved, but I was embarrassed by all the publicity. My motivation was personal and having my achievement "exploited" by the media made me feel uneasy. But now that I've realized how many women actually work at sea and how few of them are in engineering, I feel differently. I've concluded that if I can be a role model for even one woman, then it's worth the exposure.

Other than being tested more than a man would be, I don't think I've had any particular problems in the job. I'm not big on pushing issues, although if there's something I don't like, I'll try to get it changed. I just do it subtly and don't make an issue of it, unlike some women. Once I followed a woman who spent her entire watch ragging on the guys about this and that. When I arrived they were all pumped up because they expected me to do the same thing and I had to work at being accepted. Another time I followed a woman who'd been sleeping with a lot of guys. When another female cadet and I joined the ship, the men assumed we'd do that, too. The first night we docked, they insisted we accompany them to a bar. Within minutes, it was a big race to see who could hit on us first. They couldn't believe it when we said no.

Working that closely with men is a real balancing act because you need to feel part of the same team but at the same time you don't want the guys to take liberties. Right now, my guys will do anything I ask them to do. To some extent that has evolved because I'm willing to listen. I give them the opportunity for lots of input because I think that works better than firing orders at them. Basically, that reflects my personality, but I also recognize that I'm a woman and I'm their boss, and if I'm too overbearing they're likely to resent me. Many of the fellows I work with have been in the field much longer than I have and it would be stupid for me to tell them how to do their job, even though I have a higher certificate.

The work has certainly interfered with my personal life. I'm thirty-four and I'm not involved with anyone, but at this point that suits me. Much of my social life revolves around sports. Dragon boating and outrigger racing are my current passions. Basically, I love the water and I love my work and I earn pretty good money, especially for a woman. I guess my life has been pretty interesting so far. I definitely don't regret heading off into the unknown thirteen years ago.

"When I reflect on what have I done in my life, the first thing I think of is my experience at Stelco. The second is my son Joe's lunch program. It took me three years of working with the school to bring it off, but now hundreds of kids at his school eat a beautiful, home-cooked lunch."

DEBBIE FIELD

In 1980, Debbie Field made history as a member of the first group of women, with the exception of those recruited for the war effort, to work in a blue collar job at the Steel Company of Canada (Stelco). In 1991, she ran unsuccessfully for Toronto City Council and is currently the executive director of FoodShare, a non-profit organization devoted to providing nutritious, affordable food to low-income families.

In 1980, I was working as the equal opportunity coordinator for the Ontario Public Service Employees Union (OPSEU). The first women's caucus, in which I'd been involved, forced the union to create the position, then the president had the gall to appoint a man. Naturally, we rebelled, and I got the job even though I was ambivalent about taking it. I didn't think it was right that the equal opportunities coordinator earned $28,000, plus a car and various perks, when many of the secretaries made $8000 or less. I'd been earning $13,000 a year teaching at a community college and I argued — without success — that the union was sending the wrong message by making the position so highly paid.

Not only did I hate the job, I wasn't very good at it. As someone who was more comfortable with grass roots organizing, I couldn't imagine making change from the top down, and I wanted to do something that utilized my skills. In the late 1970s I'd helped to found a group called Organized Working Women, which looked at work-related issues affecting women, and by 1980 we'd begun to understand that one of the key problems was women's lack of access to non-traditional jobs. Gradually, we realized that the issue wasn't equal pay for equal work but equal pay for work of equal value — it wasn't that a female secretary earned less than a male secretary but that the male janitor was being paid more than the female secretary. We realized that cracking this barrier meant getting women into blue collar jobs. That understanding, combined with my job dissatisfaction, motivated me to look for industrial work.

I left OPSEU and moved to Hamilton. A week after my arrival, Cec Taylor, who was president of Local 1005, the union that represented the then thirteen thousand people who worked at Stelco, wrote an article in the *Hamilton Spectator* about his mother, who had been employed in a steel plant in England during the war. In the article he said the union would support women who were willing to try to get hired at Stelco.

Basically, women hadn't worked at Stelco since the war, except in one tin mill, where a small number of women, all in their sixties, were still employed. Following publication of the article, about ten women contacted Cec and he arranged for us to meet. We didn't have a plan — we decided that we'd go down to Stelco and apply. After filling out our applications, we noticed that our completed forms were placed in the bottom of two drawers. By observing, we discovered that men's applications were put in the top drawer.

Then Cec decided that we should start a campaign. I suppose this is where I made my real contribution, because I had organizing skills. I knew how to build a coalition and get publicity. I realized we needed the support of the community, so we wrote letters to all the local union offices, the churches, and so on. We also got people in Hamilton to write us letters of endorsement. The experience of grass roots organizing was wonderful: we had an issue that we believed in and a community that was ready for it. It didn't make sense to most people in Hamilton that the Steel Company of Canada, the city's main industrial employer, wouldn't hire women for its relatively high-paying jobs. People had fathers, brothers, uncles, and cousins who worked at Stelco. Many men who had no intention of working permanently in the plant paid their way through university by working there in the summers. Yet the girls in those families were deprived of access to those jobs, simply on the basis of their sex.

Within a week or so of filing our applications with Stelco, we also filed our case with the Human Rights Commission. Then we put a picket in front of the plant. The economy was very buoyant in those days and we knew that men were hired daily. Sometimes men with no work experience were hired, while women in our group who had work experience and even technical trade skills were overlooked. We applied to Stelco in November, and by April, the Human Rights Commission ruled in our favour. In addition to forcing Stelco to hire us, they awarded us damages, and I ended up with several thousand dollars in back pay.

I don't think any of us actually believed we'd ever work at Stelco. We thought we were trailblazing. We wanted to mount a human rights case that would open people's minds to the idea of women working in non-traditional jobs. I'm good with my hands in some ways, but unlike some women I'm not naturally inclined to factory work. Also, it wasn't my dream to break the barriers prohibiting women from industrial work. Trying to become an industrial worker was an assumed identity for me, based on intellectual rather than heartfelt reasons, although that wasn't true for some of the other women. I was more interested in barriers that restricted intellectual activity and related jobs.

On March 25, 1980, 180 women started work at Stelco. I got a job paying $7 an hour, plus benefits, which was quite substantial, since in those days traditional female jobs paid $3 or $4. The problem was, I didn't really want to work at Stelco and I suppose it showed. The men couldn't figure out why somebody who had been a community college teacher would work in the coke ovens, which resembled a living hell. They thought I was a spy for either the company or the union, or that I was writing a book.

In many ways, the women were doomed from the start. Instead of assigning groups of women to work together, which would have allowed us to create some support systems, the company divided us into twos and dispersed us throughout the plant. That had the effect of isolating us, and was partly our fault. We thought the idea was a good one because it would immediately democratize the plant by making everybody aware that women were coming in.

Another problem was the absence of washrooms. Stelco gave us a trailer that was a little bigger than a Johnny-on-the-spot, with a shower and lockers. It was a great distance from where we actually worked, and once we were on the job we had to share washrooms with men. The main washroom in the coke ovens, where I worked, had two urinals and two stalls. To address the arrival of women, they installed partitions around the urinals. One day, coming out of a stall, I ran right into an old man who didn't speak any English. As he was leaving a urinal he was closing his fly. I was traumatized and I'm sure it was equally awful for him. Temporary partitions also sent a very clear message that the women weren't likely to be staying very long.

I think I got put in the coke ovens because Stelco saw me as one of the ringleaders of the campaign. Many of the women hired at the same time did just fine. They worked in relatively clean mills, where various types of steel products are produced. We worked in unbelievably hot and dirty conditions. It wasn't that the job was physically demanding — it was just that the air was terrible and there was so much filth. I used to slather Nivea all over my face to protect it from the dirt. I wore a brown turtleneck and a separate hood, which I fastened with a safety pin under my chin, and then perched a helmet on top of my head. My work clothes were fireproof and I wore safety glasses and a ridiculous mask, which was supposed to filter the air but didn't really do its job. You can imagine how unattractive I looked.

Even so, for the first few weeks we were happy. The men were, too, and they'd give us victory signs when we came in. In the beginning they wanted the experiment to work because they were part of the community that believed in what we were doing, and had the company played ball with us — if, for instance they'd given us a women's coordinator or other kinds of support — it could have succeeded. But without that support it ended badly.

After I'd been there six months, I got transferred to another job in the coke ovens. This one involved physical strength — using a lever to open a lid. It usually took about 150 pounds of pressure, which I could handle, but if the lid was stuck with tar it took two hundred pounds and I found that difficult. I should point out that there was no test to ensure that the strongest women got this job. One of my co-workers was a very large, strong woman and she managed quite well, but during the summer Stelco hired some young women students who had difficulty, and that created antagonisms with the men. If hiring and affirmative action aren't done with training and assessment, it creates backlash.

The culture of the workplace was another problem. Horrible anti-woman graffiti that had been there for years — long before we came — was all over the washrooms. After I'd been at Stelco a few months, a guy who was bored wrote some graffiti about one of the attractive young women students. I got mad and made a very big mistake: I retaliated by writing graffiti about him. That initiated an escalating graffiti war. Instead of attacking the men who didn't want us, I now recognize that I should have developed a strategy to work with the older men who didn't like the graffiti. I was rabble-rousing and destroying a long-standing workplace culture, and I ended up polarizing everybody.

While this was going on, I was exhausted. I was working three shifts — in itself, very hard on your body — in a very dirty, physically dehabilitating place. I was constantly coughing up black stuff, which was pretty grim, and, as I said, there wasn't a lot of support. Attempts to create a women's caucus were unsuccessful because we were all on different shifts and spread out across the plant. My co-worker, who was decidedly anti-feminist, hated me for being such a rabble-rouser. She was a working-class woman who just wanted a good paycheque and hoped that I would shut up. Eventually, some of the men started bringing pin-ups to work to provoke me. One day I came into the lunchroom with my female co-worker and the men had completely covered the room with beaver shots — all the walls, the ceiling, and every table! The message was that this was their workplace. I was the one who would have to go.

While the graffiti wars were raging, I attended a meeting on sexual harassment, which in those days was a fairly new concept. When the expert presenter said that blue collar men were worse harassers than white collar men, I disagreed with him. I pointed out that I'd worked in both white collar and blue collar workplaces and the harassment just took a different form. On my first day as the equal opportunities coordinator at OPSEU — and you couldn't get a much more sisterhood-brotherhood workplace than that — one of my co-workers welcomed me by taping a Sunshine Girl on my door. On the other hand, in the coke ovens, where the guys were treated like dirt themselves, the meanness of the workplace brought out a meaner form of sexual harassment.

At the meeting, I spoke my mind and talked freely about my experience at Stelco. My main objective was to counter working-class male bashing. Unbeknown to me, a reporter from the *Hamilton Spectator* was in the audience. The next day, a big article appeared in the *Spectator* which noted, among other things: "Coke oven worker says sexual harassment is rampant." He'd twisted what I had said and hadn't provided any of the context. The men at work were heartbroken and embarrassed because their mothers and wives were outraged. When they confronted me it was very painful, and when they retaliated it was even worse. The graffiti wars became extremely dark and dirty. For about a month, I was constantly harassed. It was intolerable. Finally, I accepted that I had to quit.

Two months after I left Stelco a big strike hit the company, and after it was over none of the women was recalled. I was pretty shell-shocked by my experience there. However, during that time there were some positive events in my life, such as getting married to my husband, David.

I suppose I was able to trailblaze at Stelco because I was used to being an outsider. I also come from a long activist tradition. I'm the daughter of Jewish refugees who survived terrible experiences during the war. My parents immigrated to Peoria, Illinois, which is where I was born in 1952. When I was three, my father died. This left me with my mother, who barely spoke English, in Peoria, which is very isolated and anti-Semitic. Eventually we moved to New York, where we had some relatives, then to Israel, where we lived for three years before going back to New York.

In New York, my mother worked in Macy's and in Gimbel's basement as a salesperson and a bookkeeper. She was a very low-income mom, but in the tradition of the Jewish immigrant, our house was culturally rich. There was always money for food and education, but never money for anything else, like toys.

From 1966 to 1970 I went to the Bronx High School of Science, a public high school with an emphasis on science and mathematics. I had four years of wonderful student movement activity there. I was at the forefront of student strikes and got involved in my first feminist activism. We had a code that you couldn't wear pants to school, so I broke the rules and was suspended. The worst part of that experience was a disgusting male teacher who said, "Debbie, I can see some girls wearing pants, but with your legs, really."

Racism in the U.S. was getting me down, so I decided I had to get away. I needed to get away from my overbearing mother, too, and since I had no money I went to my guidance counsellor and asked, "What have you got in the way of Canada?" That's how I ended up at Trent University in Peterborough, Ontario, where I graduated with a BA in English and sociology in 1974. It was a wonderful experience — it's where I met David and many of the people who are still my very good friends.

When David and I came back to Toronto after I finished at Stelco, I went to work at an educational resource centre. I stayed for six years, and while there I had my two kids, Molly and Joe. Then I became executive assistant to Dale Martin, who was a Metro Toronto councillor. Being a mother trying to do something about my son's lunch is what brought me to FoodShare. Joe had always been a daycare kid, and when he went from daycare to grade one, all of a sudden, the kid who would eat everything — tofu, broccoli, whatever they served him — wanted me to pack a salami sandwich and a Coke every day. At that point, I was Dale's assistant and I was attending many meetings that revolved around trying to get better food for kids in schools. At the same time, I was a parent bugging the principal about getting a good lunch program at my son's school. Instituting the program took years of work, but it is currently operating in thirty-five schools in the City of Toronto and we've developed the backbone of a province-wide program. Now we cook a hot, delicious meal and kids pay, basically, what they can afford. After the recent welfare cuts in Ontario, one mother, who's on welfare, told me what a great relief it was to know that her kids got a nutritious lunch. That made me feel great. The program is growing slowly and I feel deeply connected to its momentum because it's so linked with my own life.

In 1991 I ran unsuccessfully for Toronto City Council. After the election, FoodShare was looking for an executive director. To make a long story short, I got the job. Most people think we're a food bank, but that's not true, except for our Hunger Hotline, which tells people where food banks are. All our programs involve grass roots ways of getting people nutritious, affordable food. We have a humongous buying club and we distribute fresh fruit and vegetables in low-income communities at cost. We're also involved in community kitchens and gardens and various programs that promote healthy eating and community control over food.

Today my life is very privileged, and I recognize how that privilege acts as a barrier to communicating with low-income women. But in many ways the image of my mother helps me. She raised two daughters on her own on a very low income and saved money so that we could go to university. As David always says, "Bubba made money out of pennies." She taught me what it's possible to do, and I think that helps me to communicate with the women FoodShare serves.

Being at FoodShare has really helped me to understand my mother's strengths. It has also changed the way I feel about food. Part of the early message I got from feminism is that women shouldn't cook; we should get a good job so we'd be able to eat out or buy prepared food. Today, I work with working-class and poor women who hate feminism because they link it with professionalism. In their eyes, professional women reject traditional women's values because they have enough money to do other things. I'm trying to heal this rift. I'm trying to figure out how I'm a feminist, a working woman, but also a woman who's interested in the healing power of garlic and who spends most of the weekend trying new recipes. I think we should be attempting to glorify and regain relationships with the things in traditional women's roles that as feminists we rejected. I'm hoping that low-income women can learn some of my mother's survival lessons and that that knowledge will help them through these terrible economic times.

One of the things I love about being at FoodShare is that I speak in my own voice on my own issues. My liberation isn't about cooking fast food. I cook from scratch, and when I meet women who are less privileged than me, I can speak to them from that honest voice about healthy eating that works for low-income families. Working at

FoodShare has done more than change how I feel about food — it's also healed my relationship with my mother. In many ways, I feel that this job is my greatest achievement to date. Other things were as right and as necessary, but they didn't come as directly from my heart.

> "I never felt that I was breaking ground. I was taking incremental little steps because I needed to get a job or look after my kids or fix a problem."

> **ALICE PAYNE**

Alice Payne graduated from the University of Alberta as a geologist in 1962. The first woman president of the Canadian Society of Petroleum Geologists, she is the winner of numerous awards for her work as a female pioneer, including the Canada 125 medal, which recognizes an individual's contribution to the social fabric. In 1997, she received the Order of Canada for, among other achievements, her long and distinguished career in geology, despite early limitation, and for encouraging young women to pursue non-traditional occupations.

I guess I was predestined to be a geologist. It came naturally to me because I'd grown up around mines, even though I didn't actually see a mine until I was in my late teens and my dad made the miners take me underground — against their better judgement, since superstition held that it was bad luck to allow women there. We lived in Edmonton and every summer we went to Yellowknife, where my aunt and uncle ran my dad's prospecting camp. I gravitated towards geology and, as a toddler, carted little wagonloads of rock around as part of my play.

My dad, who was quite a bit older than my mother, didn't get married until he was almost fifty because he couldn't afford a family until he found his gold mine. My mother was a nurse but, of course, she had to quit nursing when she got married. Then my dad dragged her up north to go prospecting, which I don't think she was wild about. I was born in Edmonton in March 1940.

I was supposed to be a boy and I was supposed to do geology, but when I turned out to be a girl, my father didn't let that interfere with his plans. As the eldest child, I assumed the role of a son. Dad bought me a horse and I rode horses and hung out with him as much as I could. During the year I had school, music, and homework, so summer holidays in Yellowknife were the longest period we had together. By the time I came along, my dad had struck it rich, and he rolled around Edmonton in great style, taking me everywhere with him before school interfered. Every morning we went to the "bucket shop," which is what he called James Richardson's, the brokerage firm, even though it made them mad to be called that because it implied they were not very honest. We watched the ticker-tape and dad talked to all his friends. When the price of gold went down, he became an oil man. He really had the most wonderful time. It never seemed that he got old and retired, and I suppose that image influenced how I imagined living my life.

As it turned out, I was the only one in the family who ever did geology. My brother is an entrepreneur and my sister, who is two years younger than me, is an artist. She had terrible allergies when she was little, so she couldn't go to Yellowknife and stay in a tent. In general terms, she wasn't too interested in all the rough stuff that really captured my fancy.

When I was in grade five I told the guidance counsellor I was going to be a geologist. He said, "You can't do that. It's not suitable for a girl. You should be a secretary, a librarian, or a chemist." I told him that I fully intended to be a geologist and to find a gold mine. "What are you going to do if that doesn't work out?" he asked. I suggested an RCMP officer, because I liked horses, or maybe a rancher. Finally, he gave up. He opened his office door and I walked out. I was really annoyed by his comments. I couldn't understand why he was giving me that advice. I went home and told my parents and my dad advised me to ignore him. "There are always guys like that in every camp," he said. That goes a long way towards explaining why I think it's so important for children to have exposure to dreams. If someone like that guidance counsellor comes along, you assume he's nuts and dismiss him.

I did well academically. For high school, my parents sent me to Havergal College in Toronto. As the daughter of a gold miner, I was perceived as very romantic, yet very odd. Other girls from gold-mining families attended Havergal, but their objective was to get as far away from mining camps as they could. Instead, my dream was to find a mine. But with hindsight, I can see that my years at Havergal were very positive in the sense that all my science teachers were women and they all had master's degrees or Ph.D.s. Also, not having boys around made it easy to concentrate on learning.

When I graduated, my dad took me to the geology department at the University of Alberta and introduced me to the professors. I was still a kid with braids, but I was all fired up to learn geology. I got through the academic part of university just fine, but I couldn't get the necessary practical experience. In those days you had to do field work, which women weren't allowed to do. I did have one professor, Professor Folinsbee, who was a big help. He hired me to work in the lab for $1.50 an hour. He also took me on the odd field trip to Yellowknife.

For the most part, though, my undergraduate time at university was very discouraging. Not only was field work my heart's desire, it was necessary to become a credible geologist. A structural geology course, which included a field trip, was part of my third-year curriculum. The dean of women called me in and told me I couldn't go because I needed a chaperone. "But I won't graduate if I don't go," I protested. "If you go, I will have you expelled," she replied. "It is entirely unsuitable for young women."

I had no intention of letting my career in geology go down the tubes at that point, so I enlisted a couple of my girlfriends as chaperones and we camped out in a tent in the campground in Cranbrook. All the male students stayed at the motel, which we periodically visited to have a bath. My dad advised that I not let this get me down, and he gave me a big bottle of champagne to take on the trip. Without his encouragement I think I would have given up. My mother thought my wanting to be a geologist was crazy, although she never actually said so. I know she would have preferred that I take nursing or something more suitable for a female. If I had been a normal sort of person, one who wasn't as determined as I am, I never would have had a career in geology.

After I got my B.Sc. from the University of Alberta, I got a job with the geological survey in Ottawa, where I worked in the lab, doing rapid-method rock analysis. I had studied rock analysis and I was good at it, but I didn't want to do it for a job, so I asked to be assigned to field work. Once again, field work was something they wouldn't allow a woman to do, and after eight months I quit. One thing I learned at the survey was that all the men running things were Ph.D.s. Getting a graduate degree seemed like a respectable thing to do, so I signed up to do a master's in age dating at the University of Alberta. By that time, I could work as a teaching assistant and I did all my field work by myself. My dad was in collusion. He sent me to the mine in Yellowknife to get outfitted and that's how I got started in field work.

One experience I had while working on my master's still makes me angry. Two professors on my thesis committee organized a field trip and when I applied to go, they told me I couldn't because there was no place for me to stay. My dad knew the vice-president of Eldorado Mines, so he phoned him up and explained the situation. "No problem," he said. "She can stay at our house or she can stay in the infirmary, or something." When I told my professors I'd found a place to stay, they said the plane was full. It's a small world, because it turned out the pilot was my mother's cousin, who had helped my dad stake his claims in Yellowknife in the 1930s. "We could transport the whole damn department in this plane," he said. When I reported that, I immediately received a visit from my professors, who advised me to drop the matter for the good of my future. Bang. These are the guys who would decide whether I passed or failed my thesis, so the matter wasn't trivial. I rolled over and everybody else went on the trip, but I was so mad that I took all the samples I was age dating for my thesis and pitched them in the North Saskatchewan River.

In 1965, I finished my master's degree and was back in the job market again. By this time I was married to my first husband, an entomologist who was working on his Ph.D. He was studying spiders and did a lot of field work, too. He had been in Antarctica and up to the Arctic collecting spiders. He really wanted to get a job doing taxonomy, the classification of spiders, which is sort of a dying trade, so there weren't any jobs in that area, which meant we trekked around the country a fair amount while he tried out different things. Life was always a bit of a scramble, particularly after our daughter and son were born in 1967 and 1969, respectively.

When my first child, Katherine, was a baby, I was working at the University of Alberta. I'd take her into work with me at night in her baby basket and put it in the corner of the lab. I would work for three or four hours and go home at midnight. I don't know how I did it. After my son was born, I had deals with friends. We used to trade kids. I would take my kids to their house for one day a week and they would bring their kids to my house for one day a week, and during our time off we could do whatever we wanted. I got to work in geology. Although I love my kids and wouldn't trade them for anything, by getting married and having children, I introduced one more complication in my life. My first husband was no support. He would work nights on his spider research and I had to read the stories, put the kids to bed, and do all the household work. If I wanted to go out in the field, I had to organize child care, which was difficult.

Finally, I decided to make a five-year plan that involved forgetting about field work until my kids were in school full-time. Basically, I wanted to have kids and work part-time, which in some ways suited me because I didn't want to have my kids farmed out. I wanted to do it all. It's a terrible thing, wanting to do it all, but I managed because I am a high energy person. I did convenient things in town, which meant I got the jobs that nobody else wanted. I also kept publishing, thanks to more help and encouragement from Professor Folinsbee.

In the late 1960s, women's rights suddenly erupted and all these young women who said, "forget sex roles," made it possible for older women like me to get out of our trap. By the time the 1970s rolled around, things were looking up. My kids were in school and I could get a full-time job. Moreover, the social climate had changed. Women could do whatever they damn well pleased. It was the beginning of the end of the "do what you are told" 1950s mentality. At the end of my five years, I had a track record of papers I had published and jobs I had done. I hadn't dropped out of everything and I was marketable.

In 1975 I got a job with an engineering firm called Dames and Moore, who hired me on an if-as-and-when basis. One of their projects involved looking for water in the east bank of Jordan. Nobody read the fine print that said, "No women allowed," so I got the job, and nobody noticed it wasn't suitable for a woman until I showed up. The man I was working with went to the Middle East instead of me! Later, I went on salary with Dames and Moore and I worked with my male partner on a long contract they had with Syncrude. That was the year I got divorced, which was very painful. I cried a lot and was glad I had my work. I finally accepted that I wasn't getting any help from my husband. When he wanted to do something, I was expected to help him along, but when my turn came, he was absent. I realized if you are going to have a life with someone, he has to support what you do.

The main problem with working for Dames and Moore was that they sent me to do contracts wherever they came up. They'd phone and say, "Can you be in Pinchi Lake at nine a.m. Monday morning?" I'd have to get organized, get someone to stay with my kids, and head off.

My last job with them involved sitting on a rig drilling for coal near Lethbridge in southern Alberta. One day, a well-known engineering professor, whom I remembered from university, arrived in a helicopter. He looked around and didn't say two words to me. I was earning $100 a day. I knew he was getting much more than that, and he didn't have to worry about babysitters or pay for them out of his salary. The inequity of it all overwhelmed me, and I decided I wasn't going to do that any more.

At that point we were living in Edmonton and my kids were eight and nine. I didn't want to leave home as much as working for Dames and Moore required. When the job on the rig ended, I took my two weeks' holiday, came to Calgary, and hustled a job at Gulf. It seemed like a much more civilized lifestyle. I could sit in a nice office all day, my kids could go to school, and I could go home at night, make cookies, help with homework, and be a mom.

Sometimes I felt sorry for my kids, but overall I think they had a pretty good mom. I kept a garden, made jelly, jams, cakes, and bread — all the domestic things. I kept the kids clean and tidy, but they would have preferred it if I'd been there just hanging around. I did that when they were little, but once they got into school I was out working. I signed them up for swimming at the YMCA after school and kept them busy and out of trouble, but they probably would have preferred to come home and watch TV and eat home-baked cookies.

I stayed at Gulf for fifteen years and I really had a good time. I got to be a supervisor and have people working with me. I like running things and I'm good at it. I got to do exploration and I was paid well. In the oil patch, being a woman was a new thing, but I didn't realize that when I started working there. I did find a mentor at Gulf, Irmgard Weihman. She had emigrated from Europe after the war with a Ph.D. in geology. Gulf hired her to work on fossils because she was an expert. She was a groundbreaker in her way, because if it hadn't been for Irmgard, Gulf wouldn't have hired me. They could see that a woman could do the job. The difference between me and Irmgard was that I liked running things and she didn't, although she was an expert in the technical stuff.

Once I got hired, I immediately went to work upgrading my skills, since I didn't want Gulf to find out how little I knew about the oil business. I took all the field trips in one summer and my boss called me in and told me I couldn't do that because people were supposed to go on only one a year. My response was that I couldn't wait that long. One course a year was fine if you were twenty-one, but I was forty and had to get my show on the road.

In Calgary, encouraged by Irmgard, I joined the Canadian Society of Petroleum Geologists (CSPG), which turned out to be the best experience of my professional life. It has been around since 1927, and when I joined in the early 1980s, it had about 4500 members from across the oil patch. Among other things, it provides an opportunity to get to know everyone in the business and to find out what's going on. Being involved enables you to develop a huge network. I could always count on the people at CSPG for help and advice when I needed it. Also, some of them had been consulting in the oil industry for a very long time and they started out in the hard-rock business. I thought, if they can do it, I can do it, too. So although they were not direct mentors to me, they provided examples that I could follow.

In 1992 I became the first woman president of the CSPG. It was a bit of a surprise. Nobody was quite sure if the organization was ready for a woman president, but the person who asked me to stand for election said, "Alice, I think you are the only woman who has ever done the work and has the credentials." As it turned out, my move to Calgary also worked out very well in terms of my personal life because I met my second husband and we married in 1987. Allin has a Ph.D. from MIT in geophysics and he moved west for a job at

Petro-Canada. It's a small world: he is the eldest son of Professor Folinsbee!

In 1994, I retired. I was fifty-five and had worked for Gulf for fifteen years, which adds up to seventy, the magic number representing the combination of age and years of service. When you reach that number, you can retire with a full pension. Basically, I wanted to be a vice-president and they weren't ready. One of my bosses told me I was too old, that they are looking for people who are thirty-five and grooming them. I didn't start working there until I was almost forty. I suddenly realized my goal was not in the cards. You are supposed to start work in your twenties and, if you have any spark of life or whatever, by the time you are thirty-five you are either a vice-president or you are not. All those years I had gone along thinking if I did well I would be vice-president. Then I realized it was not going to happen.

I'm enjoying retirement. We live outside of town, on eighty acres, and we have cows, horses, dogs, cats, and ducks, which are a lot of work. I still have an office at Gulf, where I work on my father's biography. He told such good stories. They sound like fiction but they aren't. Once I finish this book, I'll do geology again.

I'm in a good position now because I can do what I please. I feel very fortunate. My dad didn't find his gold mine until he was in his late forties. He didn't find his oil wells until he was almost sixty. After that, he did a whole bunch of other things. So I don't see life as being over. There is a lot more opportunity now than when I started out. Probably, the only thing I couldn't do is work in the Middle East.

I know I put a lot of people off because they can't stand pushy women, but I cannot let things go away. I am fifty-eight and I said to my husband, "No more soap boxes. I am going to say things once and give up." Everybody just laughed.

Now I make a point of helping younger women. I visit schools with a slide show, twenty minutes of what people actually do in geology. I wear all my diamonds and really do a number. When I was a kid, all I wanted was to go out prospecting and paddle a canoe. Now I don't want to hoist canoes around in the bushes — I want to encourage other people to do it. Working in the oil patch has spoiled me. If I go out on a field trip, I want to take a helicopter and an assistant who runs up and down the hill, collecting the samples and carrying the forty-pound backpack. Times change. Now, I figure if I go around giving talks that inspire a couple of kids to tell their guidance counsellor to go to hell, it's worth it.

Last spring I got a letter in a plain brown envelope that I almost threw away. I thought it was junk mail. I didn't notice "J.A. LaRoque, Secretary to the Governor-General" stamped in the corner. It was a letter asking if I'd like to be a member of the Order of Canada. I never expected to get an Order of Canada — I really didn't— but now that I have it, it's very important to me, a great honour.

I was just lucky. A lot of things have happened at the right time and the right place. None of this would have happened if I hadn't had my dad and Professor Folinsbee, if I hadn't had CSPG and all those other people saying, "You can do it, Alice."

PART 5

ARTS AND COMMUNICATIONS

> "When I was starting out as a journalist, many people took an interest in me and helped me, I think because I was so keen. Years later, when I was recruiting journalists myself, I looked for that quality. The word 'zest' comes to mind — somebody who is interested and aware."
>
> **SHIRLEY SHARZER**

Shirley Sharzer's career as a journalist is punctuated with many "firsts." As associate managing editor of the Globe *and* Mail *in the late 1980s, she was the most senior woman in Canadian newspapers. Now retired, she keeps busy with her grandchildren and various mentoring activities. At the time of this interview, she was also a member of the board of governors of the University of Waterloo.*

As a child growing up in north-end Winnipeg during the Depression, I loved to read. I thought I might like to be a writer, but never considered journalism as a career, although I can now see that the seeds of my profession were sown around the family dinner table. My father was a "news junkie" who encouraged us to discuss current events and defend our respective positions over every meal.

I entered university at sixteen, and with hindsight have concluded that I was emotionally unprepared for higher learning. After finishing my second year of arts, I decided to work for a year to earn some money. One Friday afternoon in 1945, I arrived at the *Winnipeg Tribune*, one of the city's two dailies, looking for a job. Any job would do. I was told to return Monday, but over the weekend the printers went on strike, and since my family was pro-labour, I wouldn't cross the picket line. A few weeks later I volunteered to work for the weekly newspaper started by the striking printers, which isn't as odd as it might sound. Those old-school printers who set type and caught errors knew more about journalism than some journalists did.

The job didn't pay a salary, but I was given a public transit pass. I covered the city — in the morning the police station, followed by the courts, then on to city hall, and possibly the legislature in the afternoon. If I encountered discrimination during this time because I was a female, I was too naive to be aware of it, although doubtlessly I was treated differently from my male counterparts. When the police court testimony became racy, the chief would distract me by inviting me to his office for an interview. I never complained. After freely confessing my quite astounding ignorance, I'd be rewarded with lessons in the relevant subjects from people like the city clerk who took me under their wing. I think they were responding to my youth and the fact that I was female. If they were patronizing, I didn't notice. I felt it was an advantage to be a woman because I received so much help and support.

Like other women in an all-male workplace, I developed a deaf, dumb, and blind reflex that carried me through awkward situations — I didn't get the vulgar jokes exchanged in the press room. I *did* get, from the reporters at the other papers, carbon copies of stories they were turning out daily. In those days, I assumed they were motivated by kindness, but now I'm inclined to think they were so generous because I posed no threat. I learned how to write stories by copying the more experienced reporters and, with time, gained the confidence to put my own stamp on the material I gathered.

I still don't know where I, a middle child with two older sisters and one younger brother, got the gumption to do some of the things I did. In later years my parents confessed that my daring often mystified them, especially since I'd been an extremely shy child — a trait that, after working in the business for so long, I've concluded many journalists share. Journalism offers the opportunity to be a spectator rather than a participant, and this serves as a kind of protective armour. I think my determination to accomplish things may have its roots in the fact that I was bit of a loner. I never felt any need to keep up with the crowd, but I can't tell you why. Basically, I established my own rules about what I wanted to achieve, which were quite different from those of my girlfriends. I was a feminist in the sense that I expected to be able to do whatever I wanted, and my father, who among other things, never indicated that he felt boys were superior, contributed to my self-confidence.

After I'd been working at the printers' paper for a year, I accepted an offer to join the Winnipeg bureau of the British United Press, an ultra-conservative, Catholic-run news agency that specialized in lively copy. Those were heady days and I felt like a seasoned reporter, but unfortunately, my joy was short-lived. When the head office in Montreal heard about this seventeen-year-old female who had actually been given the title "day editor," they hit the roof and ordered that I be let go. After hearing the news, I went home, settled on a pile of furnace logs in the basement, and cried my heart out.

Following a stint writing advertising copy for The Bay, I went to work for the newly launched *Winnipeg Citizen*, a daily newspaper built on the foundation of the old printers' weekly. There weren't many women in the newsroom, but Margaret Laurence, who wrote poetry in those days, was the labour reporter. None of us suspected she'd become one of Canada's greatest writers. I met my future husband, Myer Sharzer, at the *Citizen* and subsequently, we both quit the paper over an issue of principle — the use of the front page to run editorials that proclaimed the point of view of the publisher smack in the middle of the news.

Myer, the city editor, was fourteen years older than me and quite a change from the more callow medical students I was dating intermittently when we met. He immediately became an all-important support to my career. He was the best-informed, best-read person I knew, and he taught me the basics of being a good journalist. Years later, long after he had left workaday journalism, I continued to consult with him on almost everything.

Having quit the *Citizen*, I moved over to the *Winnipeg Free Press*, where I became the first woman on a major Winnipeg daily to cover city hall and, later, the legislature. There weren't many women in the *Free Press* newsroom, either, as in those days the few women journalists worked mostly on the so-called society pages.

I loved my time at the *Free Press*, but was happy when I became pregnant at age twenty-six. The city editor didn't think it was appropriate for a pregnant reporter to be running around in public, so we agreed that I'd try a stint on the copy desk. It's amazing to me now, but I don't recall being angry. I quit work about week before my son, Stephen, was born and, since there was no maternity leave in those days, left the paper with no thoughts of the future.

By the time I went back to professional work, we'd lived in Montreal, moved to Toronto, and I'd spent ten years working at home and producing a second child, my daughter, Jacqueline. I was very caught up in raising my children, but I think I would have returned to the workforce sooner if we'd stayed in Winnipeg because I really missed the newspaper business. After being turned down by the *Toronto Star*, I got a job on the picture desk at the *Toronto Telegram* on the recommendation of Percy Rowe, who had been my former city hall competition at the *Winnipeg Tribune*. I didn't even know what a picture desk was and was the only woman in the news desk set-up.

I moved around the *Telegram* and had some interesting jobs, including responsibility for page seven, the op-ed page, where the columns of opinion, interpretive articles, and so on appeared. My pages were "put to bed" early; but sometimes news events would break overnight and the news editors would grab my pages for the fresh stories. I learned to stand up for myself and insisted that I be phoned, even at three a.m., if they planned to intrude on "my" territory. I don't know how I acquired the guts to fight some of these guys, who were a pretty tough and seasoned bunch — maybe because I was defending my pages, my writers, not myself.

One day Andy MacFarlane, the managing editor, asked if I'd like to move to the news desk, another exclusively male domain. He told me there was opposition to my appointment. One news editor, Max Crittenden, was particularly distraught because he thought I'd be too emotional and would cry when I was stressed. He was also concerned that I wouldn't be able to tolerate the strong language. I pish-tushed that notion and accepted the job, which made me the first woman on a news desk at a major Canadian daily.

The hours were tough. Many early mornings, my car made the first tire prints on the snow that had fallen on the Don Valley Parkway overnight. My husband or the come-by-day housekeeper would get the kids off to school. Fortunately, my office day ended early enough that I could be home before the kids returned from classes. Yes, I did cry, but only once, at the wheel of my car at the end of the day. The news editor, although competent at his job, was a manic man who seemed determined to hassle me. Earning his respect was a challenge, but I finally did it.

Juggling office and family responsibilities required a certain amount of organizational skill, but I was fortunate that my children enjoyed good health. Once — and only once — I stayed home with my daughter when she ran a very high fever. I phoned the office and explained why I wouldn't be coming in. The next day Andy MacFarlane — and I want to emphasize that he was an early feminist, bless his heart — called me in and suggested that if this happened again I should simply say I was sick. I think he was trying to protect me, as some of my sexist colleagues might have used this as an excuse to create sentiment that motherhood was interfering with my job.

When the *Telegram* folded in 1971, I went to the *Toronto Star* to help set up their new Insight section, which *Time* magazine later called one of the best such sections in North America. Then, in 1972, my life changed dramatically. My husband died suddenly after a summer cold developed into bronchitis and full-blown pneumonia with complications. My children were in their teens and it was a rough and difficult period for all of us. In the longer run, I suppose I buried myself in my work and waited for time to undo some of the grief we felt.

After Myer's death, I started getting job offers from all over. The most tantalizing came from my old mentor, Andy MacFarlane, who was putting together a prospectus for a new Graduate School of Journalism at the University of Western Ontario. He asked me to head up the print program. When I resigned from the *Star* in 1974, I was happy that Martin Goodman, the editor, was away on holiday. Martin had been particularly good to me, but even he couldn't move me beyond the glass ceiling that fixed me firmly in place as features editor and ended my youthful attitude of expecting to be able to do whatever I wanted.

Eventually, I became assistant dean at the journalism school. When I was doing admissions I was the only woman on the faculty, and that year more than half of the students were women. One of the professors saw fit to comment that once a woman handled applications, the number of female students increased. It pleased me enormously to inform him that I never looked at the gender of applicants. The fact that women were being admitted in greater numbers indicated that students were being assessed on the basis of ability, not gender, which obviously had not been the case in the past.

Although I was ostensibly tucked away in an ivory tower in London, Ontario — a pretty but parochial city — I continued to receive job offers. It was flattering but also stressful, because I didn't treat these offers lightly. One evening in 1979, at eleven p.m., I received a call from Ted Moser, managing editor of the *Globe and Mail*, asking if I was interested in becoming the *Globe*'s assistant managing editor. After some deliberation, I accepted the offer — what journalist could resist an invitation from Canada's best newspaper?

I was thrilled to be at the *Globe*, but was turned off by the apparent smugness of some of its long-time employees. A few men clearly resented the fact that I was parachuted into the job. I was female, Jewish, and didn't have a *Globe* background. Yet I don't think anti-Semitism affected my career in any significant way. Initially, I was the only woman in the daily news conferences, and the male bonding that usually took the form of locker room humour and the photo chief's delight in passing around lurid sexist photos was hurtful. I bit my tongue and decided to win the respect of my male colleagues by making the right news decisions, encouraging good writing, and going to bat for conscientious and fair journalism.

People used to say that if you wanted to get ahead you had to hang out at the press club. If you're a mother, that's difficult to do. I never tried to become one of the boys by boozing it up with my colleagues. I kept my personal life separate from my professional life to the point that one colleague commented on my ability to "compartmentalize." Now, I see that this was necessary to preserve my mental health. The way we practised journalism then was all-enveloping; it could take over your life. The need to fill daily pages was always on your mind.

Although I did many other things, during my eleven years at the *Globe and Mail*, staff training and development became my specialty. I hired and/or oversaw some of the best columnists who ever wrote in Canadian newspapers.

I guess my chief satisfaction was in finding new talent, and I knew I had an advantage at the *Globe* because the best people would always choose it over other papers. I was called a den mother, which bothered me because it sounds so sexist. But nurturing is part of the skill of being a good editor — male or female.

After my first appointment as the *Globe*'s assistant managing editor I was promoted to associate managing editor and finally deputy managing editor. On each of these two occasions, I was passed over for the top newsroom job of managing editor, even though in later years editor-in-chief Dic Doyle told writer Susan Crean that hiring me was "one of the most brilliant decisions" he ever made. When I think about the past, I wonder about the factors that affected my career at the *Globe*. My friend, journalist June Callwood, once told a writer that my "management style" was at fault. She felt that my "conciliatory, respectful, and warm approach to people" was seen as a weakness in the male world. I remained at the *Globe* until the major bloodletting of the late 1980s when the publisher, Roy Megarry, moved to get rid of both Norman Webster, the editor-in-chief, and Geoff Stevens, the managing editor, who were both burrs under his saddle. Norman might have accepted the job he was offered as a roving correspondent, but when his buddy Geoff was peremptorily fired and offered a demeaning, fuzzily defined position, Norman quit. Geoff sued and I, number three in charge, left after being offered the job of publishing the *Globe*'s west coast magazine.

I left the *Globe* in 1989. I was sixty-one years old and had to start yet another career. In the brutal 1990s this isn't an unusual story, but the territory was unfamiliar for me and loaded with pain. Again, I received job offers, which I found flattering. I ended up working for the Southam Newspaper Group, conducting a survey of training and development needs at their seventeen daily papers, where, among other things, I learned that the status of women within Southam was a serious concern. I then became part of a task force to survey women's needs, and somewhere along the way joined the full-time staff with the title coordinator of editorial training and development.

For most of my career I was a feminist by deed — by going where women had not gone before and by helping to bring along women after me in journalism. However, my involvement in the task force at Southam made me much more aware of the issues affecting women in the workplace and determined to make more changes. Gloria Steinem has said that women become more radical as they get older because life is a radicalizing experience for women, and I can see the truth in that.

Four years after joining Southam, I retired. I keep busy at a variety of emeritus-type activities, plan to "do" fiction, and thoroughly enjoy my grandchildren and the stories they are already putting into the computer. The most wondrous thing to me is that I am still mentoring. I have allowed myself the luxury of large telephone bills so I can discuss at length matters of import to former students, staffers, and colleagues across the country.

Throughout my career I was often aware that I was being discriminated against. I often went home seething, but I think I tolerated a lot because I was working so hard. I concentrated on my job, and I didn't have time to be introspective. Although I didn't want to be one of the boys, they were my peers and colleagues and in a very deep way it hurt to be excluded by them. But given the big picture, these are minor concerns. I really did enjoy my career and there's nothing I regret about all those years.

These are not the easiest times. But the difficult times are not confined to journalists, and that makes the job of record-keepers all the more important. Although technology is an amazing resource, it can't talk directly to the victims of genocide or to hungry street people or poverty-stricken kids. That, for me, is the job of journalists, and that sense of mission has always given my job special meaning.

"The sports world is one of the last bastions of masculinity. Women get the message: do not apply, get out of our locker room, get out of our life."

JANE O'HARA

Jane O'Hara started playing tennis at the age of eleven and won her first Canadian Tennis Championship the following year. After several years on the women's professional tennis circuit, which took her around the world and to tournaments such as Wimbledon and the U.S. Open, in 1975 she became the first woman sportswriter at the Toronto Sun. *Three years later, she moved to* Maclean's *magazine, where she spent most of the following decade. In 1988, she was hired by the* Ottawa Sun *as Canada's first female sports editor. Subsequent to this interview, she returned to* Maclean's *magazine as a senior writer. There, among other achievements, she led the team that broke the story of violence against women in the Canadian military.*

Little did I realize, when my parents encouraged us to go outside and play ball — a natural suggestion for anyone with seven kids — that this kidding around would lead to two careers. By the time I was sixteen, I was playing on the national tennis team. When I retired as the number-one Canadian woman player at age twenty-three, my career in journalism had already begun.

George Gross, the sports editor of the *Toronto Sun*, often hired athletes to write first-person accounts. While I was still playing professionally, he asked me to write about my experiences on the tennis circuit. Then, in the early 1970s, I covered the Bobby Riggs–Billy Jean King match from the woman's perspective. Tennis was my primary focus at that point, but I was thrilled to be writing. I loved watching something, then producing a story, even though I didn't have the first clue about how to write for a newspaper.

In 1975 I was the number-one-ranked female tennis player in Canada, and was thinking about retiring. I'd devoted a big chunk of my life to tennis, and although I'd had many good times, I'd had some bad ones, as well. The dynamic of the tournament favours winning, so when you're on a losing streak — and I'd had them — it's devastating. Often you're alone in a strange place with no one to talk to. You can't tell the other players, "My backhand is really off," because you might play them the next day. Armed with that knowledge, they'd hit every shot to your backhand.

One day, when I was playing tennis with George, he asked about my plans for the future. I said I'd either go back on the circuit, which didn't appeal to me, or take a fifth year of university, which was equally unappealing. I was both surprised and ecstatic when he made me an offer: "If ever you want a job, come to me." My response was immediate. "Great. Consider it done."

It was 1975 and I was the first woman staff writer in sports at the *Sun*. My initial assignment was to write a first-person piece about playing in the Canadian Open Tennis Tournament. Once I lost, I'd cover the tournament. I drew Australian Margaret Court, then the number-one player in the world, as my first opponent and was immediately eliminated. That plunged me into part two of my assignment, which was problematic. As long as I was writing about myself I was fine, but covering the rest of the tournament was disconcerting because I had no idea what to do.

Luckily, a friend, Nora McCabe, who covered tennis for the *Globe and Mail*, came to my rescue. I didn't have the foggiest notion about reporting, who you talk to and so on. I asked Nora for help and I've never forgotten her generosity. "Follow me," she said. So everywhere Nora went, I went, too.

I quickly concluded that I had to get a handle on this writing stuff, which was now a job and serious business. I was too embarrassed to go back to the office and tell people I didn't know how to write a news piece, so essentially I started studying the format of newspaper stories. Nobody ever sat down with me and said, "This is what you do," but it doesn't take a rocket scientist to recognize there's a lead, then a quote, and usually some background.

I had a BA with a major in English, so I knew what good writing was about and I was a quick study. My family background and experience on the tennis circuit also provided good grounding in how to deal with the situation. I grew up in a competitive household with five brothers and was used to battling with them. I was very determined and liked to win. When I played tennis, people said I had a killer instinct, although I don't remember that. But being on the circuit had taught me how to manage on my own. My success had come before the days of the entourage and I was often in Europe on my own, travelling from tournament to tournament.

I soon proved my worth as a writer and George sent me out on some big assignments, which miffed some of the more established guys. Sports reporting has two basic parts: how you're treated in the newsroom, and how you're treated in the world of sports. There were two great guys in the sports department of the *Toronto Sun* — Trent Frayne and Pat Hickey. I don't know whether they protected me, but they certainly befriended me. Also, I came to reporting as an athlete, and there's nothing these guys respect more. It doesn't matter whether you're a man or a woman — if you're an athlete, you're in a category that in some strange way is neither male nor female. Also, growing up with five brothers, I had spent so much time with men that I had developed ways of dealing with them.

But the wide world of sports was another story. There were lots of barriers back then, such as not being allowed in the locker room. Sexual harassment was also a big problem, although I never told anyone because it was so embarrassing and hard to manage. The worst harasser was a well-known and highly respected coach who would chase me around the desk whenever I went to interview him. I felt I couldn't tell anybody because I'd lose my job or be ridiculed. And what could I say anyway? I couldn't refuse to interview the coach of that team. My solution was to make sure I interviewed him in a public place.

In those days, problems like this were swept under the carpet because women weren't welcome in the sports world. We had to put up with this stuff or we'd likely be fired for not being qualified for the job. I felt that keeping quiet was the price I had to pay for being a woman sportswriter. It was my job to handle the situations that came up, but I felt very isolated.

It turned out I was a good writer, and I soon moved into features, which I found easier than straight, old-fashioned news stories since there's more flexibility in approach and style, and room for personal opinion. That moved me beyond the sports section. Then, in 1978, *Maclean's* called and asked me to write their People section. It was a chance to try magazine writing, and I knew I wouldn't be doing People for long. That was an apt assessment — I soon became a senior writer. Then I went to Ottawa to cover Parliament Hill. After that I was national editor and finally bureau chief in both New York and Vancouver.

I was supposedly on my way to Washington for *Maclean's* when I met the woman I now live with, who was based in Vancouver. Suddenly, out of the blue, George Gross called and said, "We're starting a new paper in Ottawa and we'd like you to be sports editor." That's great, I thought. It will be a lot easier to commute from Ottawa to Vancouver than from Washington to Vancouver. So I took the job.

They hired me to make an impact. They knew a woman sports editor would get a lot of attention from the media and they wanted to make a splash in Ottawa because they were going up against *The Citizen*. But I knew I'd have to prove myself all over again because I came from magazines and hadn't covered sports for ten years. The publisher, Hartley Steward, wanted a writer and a personality. He's a terrific guy and a great boss, so my rustiness didn't matter to him. But the guys in the trenches are very statistics-oriented and they weren't too taken with my feature writer approach, which focuses on the dynamics of sports.

I told myself I'd stay for two years. In actual fact, I stayed for five. After a while I got the hang of writing a sports column, which is very different from any other kind of writing. Good columnists are lively writers who are both highly opinionated and extremely knowledge-able. You have to be an insider and outsider. It's quite a trick.

Sports readers are a newspaper's most committed readers. They're a dedicated group of people who care deeply about sports. They're passionate about their teams and their loyalties are profound. But some readers didn't want a woman telling them what to think. I was fairly controversial because I didn't take the party line on sports. I often wrote about the business of sports and how fan loyalty is sold. My stand was often the wrong stand from the perspective of the traditional sports fan. Sports fans are very reactionary and I received a lot of hate mail.

Sometime in 1991, I started working on a book with Marjorie Nichols, a long-time political affairs columnist, first with *The Vancouver Sun* and then with the *Ottawa Citizen*, which kept me in Ottawa for another year. I knew Marjorie from Vancouver and we had lunch a few weeks after I arrived in Ottawa. I didn't hear from her for months, although I knew she'd been diagnosed with lung cancer. One day, completely unexpectedly, she phoned and asked, "How would you like to write a book with me?"

"Great," I said. "What's our subject?" When she replied, "Me," I quickly concluded she knew she was dying, because usually Marjorie would never consent to write anything with anybody. I think she realized she would need help with what would be her final record.

Working on that book with Marjorie was an amazing experience and it affected me profoundly. I watched her die over a period of about six months. The two hours a day that I gave her was an incredible commitment, since I was writing five columns a week — four on sports and one on politics. My job, essentially, was to transcribe her life for her, but I knew I'd have to do more than that because I never thought we'd finish the book together. Frankly, it would have been an absolute nightmare had she lived, because Marjorie would have strongly disagreed with some of my impressions. She certainly wouldn't have wanted to admit she was as lonely as she was.

Considering how many friends she had in the business, the absence of intimate people in her life was very scary. It made an alarming statement about women who devote themselves solely to their careers. Although it was troubling to see her dying with nobody around, I knew I couldn't get too close or I'd get eaten alive by the situation. If I didn't keep my distance as a reporter, I couldn't do my job.

It was an interesting time and a sad time. Basically, I had to come to terms with the realization that journalism had killed Marjorie in a way, by providing her with a worthy-enough pretext to destroy herself.

When the book, *Marjorie Nichols: A Very Political Reporter*, came out it was well received and I felt I had done something worthwhile.

I left the *Sun* in 1993. I had grown tired of the newspaper business and the never-ending work. Christmas, Easter, New Year's — when you think of how few days a newspaper doesn't publish, it's easy to see how the business devours people.

I'd also had my experience with Marjorie. Seeing somebody who put so much stock in her career, who viewed journalism as a calling and was destroyed by it, had helped to crystallize thoughts I'd been having for some time. Journalism provides an immediate hit. Your work goes out, gets a reaction, and the next day it all starts up again. It's a form of instant gratification, but in the end there's not much to show for it. Marjorie's stories are in the morgue somewhere — that's what she left behind.

Although working with Marjorie influenced my decision to step back from journalism for a time, I'd been thinking about it before. I think we in the media take ourselves too seriously. I can see how self-important some journalists are. I've certainly suffered from some of that myself. It's easy to read what you've written and think, Who could have said it better? Or to read your byline and feel great. But surely there are more important things in life than seeing your name in print.

In 1993, I got a Southam Fellowship to study ethics and popular culture for a year, and after that season in the land of thought — away from daily deadlines — I had no desire to go back to work. Out of the blue, Laurier Lapierre, one of the great characters of Canadian broadcasting, phoned and asked if I had any interest in becoming the Max Bell Professor at the University of Regina, a one-year teaching/mentoring appointment at the journalism school there. When I finished that, a job came up at the Ryerson School of Journalism, so here I am teaching.

Many people feel it's time for me to get on with my life and get back into the old swing. They think I've fallen off my big career track, but I'm actually happier than I've ever been. I've got time to enjoy my life, my home, my garden.

The most pleasurable part of journalism is being a detective. Short of hurricanes, few things happen randomly. When you get into society, or the worlds of politics and business, there's always some psychological truth behind events. The interesting part of journalism is getting beneath the surface, discovering why people do what they do — that's so fascinating. I won't say I always achieved what I set out to do, but I certainly enjoyed trying to get to the bottom of a story. Between tennis and journalism I've been all over the world and covered a lot of interesting events. I feel that I've had a very privileged life. I'm forty-four and in mid-career. I hope the best is yet to come.

"In the early 1970s, very little women's history had been published; like every generation of women, mine thought we were the trailblazers. It was very lonely hacking through the bush by myself. It would have been so much easier if I'd known other women had carved out a path before me."

KATHLEEN SHANNON

As head of the National Film Board's award-winning Studio D, Kathleen Shannon broke new ground by using film to bring women's issues to the forefront of public consciousness and creating an institutional climate where women filmmakers could flourish. Films made by Studio D collected three of the eight Oscars won by the board, and for her achievements Shannon received an honorary doctorate from Queen's University in 1984, the Order of Canada in 1986, and an honorary doctor of letters from York University in 1996, the year this interview was conducted. The following year, at the age of sixty-two, she died of lung cancer in Kelowna, B.C.

I don't think anyone really knows why Studio D got started. Different things came together largely because of increasing pressure on the National Film Board (NFB) from women outside, as well as those of us who worked there. One factor was the audience response to the "Working Mothers" series, which I had done. I don't think the Film Board realized there were so many women in the country, and they were astonished by how enthusiastically the films were received. Also, International Women's Year was on the horizon, and the prospect of money from that source was tantalizing. Moreover, the NFB had to do a report for government on the status of its women employees, so things were churning, and in August 1974, Studio D was announced.

Our original mandate was to be a studio like any other, with a special responsibility for women's film, or some vague statement like that. In the absence of a mandate, I later wrote one, after reading what came out of the 1975 Women's Forum in Mexico City. The mandate had five points. The first was to provide employment for women, particularly in the crafts of filmmaking, from which women had been systematically excluded. The second was to provide training. I could see that sometimes individual women were given opportunities with no training, and they'd end up demonstrating that women weren't very good. In a way, I was set up for that, too, but somehow it didn't happen — I think partly because by the time Studio D emerged, I'd worked on so many films that I knew what would — and wouldn't — work. The third was to make films that women audiences need, and the fourth was to create an environment where women could explore our creativity. A big piece of that was seeing what kinds of films women would make when we weren't fitting into the male definition, and learning how we'd work together when we weren't under the direction of men. Finally, and most important to me, we were to use the medium of film to bring the perspectives of women to bear on all social issues.

Somehow, I recognized that the studio wouldn't succeed unless we created a climate that fostered women, not just provided a place for them to work. The "Working Mothers" films had generated a tremendous amount of dialogue and I wanted to create something similar with Studio D — to bring people together and get everyone's ideas. At some point I discovered that if I put a dilemma on the table and we all talked about it, solutions would emerge that none of us could have thought of by ourselves.

By the time Studio D was established, I was a full-blown feminist, an evolution that began in earnest with the "Working Mothers" films. In the late 1960s, I was doing a lot of editing for *Challenge for Change*, a government-funded program intended to provide a voice for those who were voiceless and to open up communication between policymakers and those whose lives their policies would affect. I felt that work was important and exciting. In 1970, journalist Ian Adams published a book called *The Poverty Wall*, which devoted an entire section to women as an identifiably poor group. This was a startling revelation. Likely it motivated the committee to program a film about working mothers, probably because they thought that only poor women had to work. Since few women worked in the *Challenge for Change* program and I was the one with the most film experience — not to mention relevant life experience — I was the obvious person to make the film.

On the basis of my own experience, I approached the subject of women wage earners differently from the members of the committee. I decided to look at the widest range of women I could find — women who might be wives of the committee members, their secretaries and daughters, as well as women who were poor. Although someone else was nominally producing — he basically signed forms — I did everything else. I researched, wrote, directed, edited, and sound-edited. I also designed the titles and wrote the theme music. I was very much the *auteur*, except it wasn't that kind of project. I felt it was important to let the women speak and not allow cinema to get in the way of what they had to say.

Some of the most exciting work I've ever done involved working with audiences for those films. People were incredibly excited. They said they'd never heard women talk so honestly. I think part of their willingness to be honest evolved from the technique. Since women usually do at least two things at once, we shot them engaged in tasks like washing dishes, ironing, or sewing while they talked to the camera.

Between the time I started the research and the filming, a couple of things happened that validated, clarified, and expanded my vision. One day, heading out on a research trip to Ottawa, I stopped in a bookstore to get something to read on the train. For some reason I noticed a collection of essays called *Voices from Women's Liberation*. Since I didn't see myself as a "women's libber," which is how feminists were described in those days, I was about to sweep by — I thought things were hard enough for most women without a bunch of crazy radicals embarrassing the rest of us by burning their brassieres. However, I like to think of myself as broad-minded, so I decided to buy a copy. I should mention that I read it on the train with the cover turned back so nobody could see what I was reading.

That book changed my life. Although the introduction was a bit flowery, the ideas were very interesting and they gripped me. It wasn't until I got to the end of the introduction that I realized it had been written a hundred years earlier and originally introduced the classic six-volume opus *The History of Women's Suffrage*, of which I was totally unaware. Reading those essays changed how I saw the world. I had been taught that women who challenged the status quo, such as the suffragists, were embittered spinsters who wore funny clothes and embarrassed other women. But this excerpt from *The History of Women's Suffrage* made me realize we'd been lied to. I was transformed. I was angry and energized, and it was wonderful.

That same autumn, as part of my research, I drew up a questionnaire about employment, which I sent to women at the NFB. I figured they would provide a good sample since the federal government is the largest, but not the worst, employer of women in the country. I had no idea what I was biting off. Basically, I learned that a striking number of women were dissatisfied with their wages, their positions in the hierarchy, their child-care arrangements, and so on. They sent a clear message: they knew they were being discriminated against because they were women.

As a result of the questionnaire, all sorts of women began to talk to me at work. At that point I was one of those women who believed I didn't have much in common with other women, an attitude I inherited from my mother, who always implied that women only talked about housekeeping and diapers. Consequently, I'd spent my working life trying to be one of the boys. All of a sudden, I realized I had much more in common with women secretaries than with men doing my job. This revelation was amazing.

I had been working for the NFB since 1955, when I was twenty. By then I'd spent over four years at Crawley Films in Ottawa, beginning with a summer job cataloguing background music. When I decided to drop out of school in grade twelve, I told my parents it was to devote myself to music — I played clarinet. In hindsight, I recognize that school embodied impossible, conflicting demands for an intelligent girl who accepted the 1950s wisdom that being popular was far more important than doing well in school but who could never do less than her best.

Working at Crawley Films full-time seemed like a good solution. Gradually, I worked my way up to editing music and sound. I earned next to nothing, but I didn't mind because the job was a true apprenticeship, an excellent way to learn how films are made since there were no film schools in those days. Also, doing things like working through the night made me feel important and valuable.

My timing was good. I was a skilled sound editor when the NFB moved to Montreal and started to produce for television. Few people had my experience, and when the NFB offered me twice what I was earning, I jumped.

In those days Montreal was Canada's most vibrant city, but I can't say I was thrilled to live there. I rented a little apartment on the northern edge of the city, which was sort of accessible to the Film Board, which isn't very accessible to anything. Basically, I lived at work. That's pretty much how I continued for the thirty-six years I was at the NFB. I never really lived in Montreal because I was totally wrapped up in my work, and once I had my son, caring for him was equally demanding.

I married for a number of reasons. I was programmed by 1950s propaganda that you wouldn't feel like a real person unless you were married. Also, I was pregnant and not brave enough to have a child as a single woman. I'd had one abortion when I was in my early twenties, when it was illegal, and I didn't want to repeat that experience, although it wasn't as bad as what many other women endured. I was fortunate enough to find an immigrant doctor who was skilled but unable to officially practise without a certificate of registration.

The marriage shouldn't have lasted more than two years. My husband was a person who needed to feel he controlled his family, and I am a person who cannot abide anyone's attempts to control me. The fact that we remained married for six years reflected our residence in Quebec. If I had left him, I would have been guilty of desertion, which meant I wouldn't have gotten custody of my son. Sometime around 1963, I consulted a woman lawyer I had read about in the paper. She was supposedly sympathetic to women and she advised me to quit work, stay home, and sue my husband for non-support because he didn't earn enough money. He was an Eastern European immigrant trying to become an English-language theatre director and I was the principal breadwinner. Thank God I had the wit not to take her advice, and not only because I couldn't afford to. Even then I knew that quitting my job would have meant giving up the only part of my life where I existed for myself, the only place where I could be creative and make decisions.

In those days, there were very few women at the Film Board. Most of them worked in slide-sound and film strips, which is not a high-status branch of the media world. There were no female documentary directors or producers. After I'd been at the Board for seven years, I negotiated to become a picture editor. I was told I had to take a cut in salary until I proved myself. I later learned that was illegal, but I'd been executive producer of Studio D for two or three years before I earned as much as I would have if I'd never left sound editing. But that's the price I had to pay for moving into picture editing, which had higher status and was considered more artistic.

As a picture editor, I could be more involved with actually making film, which I loved, although I hadn't really acknowledged, even to myself, that I wanted to be a filmmaker. Like many women, I didn't have a sense of a career and I never consciously planned ahead. I just found my work very satisfying and was very involved with whatever I did.

When my son was six, my husband and I separated. I was my son's primary parent for another four or five years, and juggling work and parenting continued to be a challenge. At that point my former husband married a woman who had rather a lot of money. They had a fairly affluent lifestyle and took exotic holidays, which my son enjoyed, so he decided to live with them. I agreed to this because I knew I didn't have a chance of getting custody. Legally, fathers still owned their children, and I knew that being employed would count against me in court. Even so, I felt that I had abandoned my child and the experience was very painful.

During my marriage, I don't think I could have moved beyond being a picture editor because my husband would have found it too threatening. He saw himself as the creative one and I was the support person. I wouldn't have been able to upset that balance. Around the time my son moved in with his father, I moved into directing. I think it was more coincidence than anything else. I had gone to work for *Challenge for Change* and was offered the "Working Mothers" project.

By the time I was asked to head Studio D, I was capable of seeing how I as an individual, women as a group, and the studio itself were discriminated against. Although we were given a place in the structure and some technical resources, Studio D was not allotted any money to speak of. The NFB started a drama studio at the same time we got going, which in contrast was bountifully endowed. At one point I was so frustrated that I told the director of production I was going to spill the beans in a radio interview I was doing for International Women's Year. I was often intimidating, and although no one ever threatened to fire me, I could always be brought back into line because I feared that the wrath of the institution would come down and they'd destroy the studio. I didn't worry much about myself, but I wouldn't have done anything to threaten the studio's existence

There was a continuous struggle between Studio D and the rest of the NFB, and I must admit that at certain points I fuelled the flames — particularly in the early days. I think I got a little smoother and smarter as the years went on, but the unfairness of how the studio was treated always bothered me. When you considered that the NFB had made films for forty years without any women — except during the war, and those women quickly became invisible once the boys came home — in a way Studio D had the job of remaking their entire catalogue with a female perspective. Plus, we had to make our new stuff. By any criteria, we never had a fair amount of money.

Worse still, in the beginning we were treated as a joke. For instance, one man said he'd eat the first good film we made and added that luckily he didn't have to depend on that for nutrition or he'd starve. When a rather beautiful secretary was assigned to us, another man asked what she was doing with all of us rejects. There were so many snide statements that instead of feeling badly, I decided to collect them and display them with their sources attributed.

For a brief period, the contempt was overtaken by praise when we won an Academy Award for *I'll Find a Way*, a film about a little girl with spina bifada. This was the NFB's first Oscar since 1942, and suddenly we were treated like mascots, a sentiment that barely survived our second Academy Award for *Flamenco at 5:15*, on a flamenco class at the National Ballet of Canada school. By the time

If You Love This Planet, an anti–nuclear weapons film, won our third Oscar, the men at the NFB were getting pretty uncomfortable. In fact, that film almost didn't get made or released. It was one of the so-called feminist films that made people uncomfortable.

When *Not a Love Story* was released, the deep-rooted hostility surfaced again. The film was a hard-hitting look at pornography. It was highly acclaimed in some quarters and dumped on by others, but everyone knew about it and it was interesting to observe the various reactions. Soon after the film was released, I read Dale Spender's book *Women of Ideas and What Men Have Done to Them* and was fascinated to see how some of the same things had been said to discredit women three hundred years ago. For example, in the past, women writers were discredited by the implication they were "morally loose," whereas the makers of *Not a Love Story* were dismissed as "uptight." Phrases like "poorly organized" and "unfocused" crop up across the centuries without the critic ever noticing that the material is simply organized differently from the male model.

By 1986 I could see a pattern: the more we were praised from the outside, the more difficult things became internally. And the more successful we got, the less money we received. I also concluded there were irreconcilable differences between me and some of the powers that were. Things had deteriorated so badly that I felt management couldn't see the difference between me and the studio. After much soul searching, I finally decided that stepping aside might be the best thing I could do for all concerned.

By this time, I was also exhausted. I'd been running the studio for twelve years and it hadn't been easy. It was a constant battle with the bureaucracy, but at the same time, I was the target of a lot of hostility from women, particularly those with a perspective or experience that differed from our film portrayals. Moreover, any women who felt the NFB had treated them badly were directed towards the studio and, of course, we didn't have the resources to employ them all, which also created bad feeling.

Trying to create a feminist workplace was demanding as well. Technically, I was both mom and boss, and I put up with bad behaviour that I wouldn't put up with now. I invested a lot of time in trying to make things okay for people it will never be okay for. Now I'm a little clearer about what leadership is. I've learned that leaderless groups are extremely unproductive and exhausting.

I was also very lonely. I had few women colleagues like me, so there was no one to share experiences or discuss problems with. Now I understand, too, that it's much easier to do unproved things if you have a support person. In some ways the studio performed that function, but the sword was double-edged because keeping up the front that everything was perfect was so stressful. I was aware that if I let it be known there was any internal friction, that would be taken advantage of, so everything had to be kept under wraps.

Finally, I concluded I was no longer effective. I'd done everything I could think of except stepping aside. I'm not sure I could have made that transition if a couple of things hadn't happened. First, I caught a glimpse of a film in trouble and realized that all I wanted was to spend a couple of weeks fixing it. So I asked the woman who functioned as my right hand to take over the studio and went off to work on the film. I felt a great transformation as a result — even my body felt different. Second, I realized that I didn't need to do this to myself any longer. Somehow I'd had the feeling that I had to stay until the studio was secure and safe, but at that point I acknowledged that would probably never happen.

I stepped down as head of Studio D in 1986 and took a year's sabbatical. After my return to the NFB I worked in the studio until 1992, making a number of films. Then I moved to a big house in Nelson, B.C. Basically, I needed to heal. I'd been sitting on many emotions during the studio years, including rage left over from my marriage, as well as from other exploitive relationships.

I don't quite know when my problem with drinking began. I think I was inherently vulnerable to alcohol. It's a pattern in my family. During most of my time at the NFB, people rarely didn't drink. The genius destroying himself was a common heroic model emulated by a great number of film people. Certainly, drinking was a method for becoming one of the boys, which of course I had to be. At the time, the parameters of what one could be in order to be accepted were very limited, and I remember a number of people remarking that I was so much more fun when I drank. I was a shy person and those compliments — or what I perceived to be compliments — that I could drink like a man or think like one encouraged me.

For a long time I was able to keep my drinking under control. It's hard to put a definite time on when that ceased to be the case — when I began to get really sick and feel horrible most of the time. It was probably around the first few years of Studio D. Although I felt ill most days, I functioned. At one point, some women associated with the studio attempted to confront me, but the timing wasn't right. Later, another three delicately and very lovingly raised the issue. They said, "This is what you're going to do. We'll take you to a clinic we've heard about." That initiated the process of healing.

The clinic experience is significant in that I determined there must be better ways for women to get help, and that led me into becoming a counsellor. I bought my house in Nelson to some extent because I wanted to create a kind of sanctuary for other women — what I felt I could have used when I was at Studio D. Often, I wanted to get away to the country, but I didn't want to go to a resort, where there would be stresses like having to dress up for breakfast. In Nelson, people can be informal. They can rest, read, walk, enjoy the fresh air, or whatever.

If I could live my life over again, I'd like to do it with the wisdom I've scraped together and the sense of entitlement I have slowly acquired. It must be wonderful to have a sense of who you really are before the age of thirty-five. From the age of five to thirty-five I lost the sense of who I was because I was so bent on being who I was supposed to be.

I will say that I'd always wanted to change the world, and film was the medium I happened to choose. I'll also say that where I am now is better than life ever was before — in fact, each decade of my life has been better than the one preceding. That's something I'd love to communicate to younger women. I wish someone had told me that when I was scared about turning thirty.

"In the late 1960s, I was working on my Ph.D. at the University of Toronto. One day, a young journalist interviewed me for a story she was doing for the *Toronto Star* magazine. It was called "Pretty Hip Dames — PHDs" and the idea was that her subjects were pioneers because we were working on our doctorates while married, raising kids, and knowing how to wield an eyebrow pencil. The young journalist was Barbara Frum, and reading that article will give you a very clear picture of how far we've come."

MARIAN FOWLER

A recipient of the Canadian Biography Award, Marian Fowler published her first book, The Embroidered Tent, *in 1982, when she was fifty-two. For many years she was a stay-at-home wife and mother; she began her career as an academic in 1970. Noted for the depth of her research and her insight into the lives of nineteenth-century women, Marian Fowler broke new ground by challenging the stereotypical images of her female subjects and revealing their discomfort with the restrictions of femininity, which they hid behind the polished veneer of their social roles. Her book* In a Gilded Cage *was short-listed for the 1993 Governor General's Award for Non-fiction.*

In 1963, when I read Betty Friedan's *The Feminine Mystique*, it changed my life. By that point I'd had ten years of so-called domestic bliss. I'd married a physician, had two lovely children, was active in the school, and entertained for my husband, who was on staff at The Hospital for Sick Children. I hooked rugs, smocked dresses for my daughter, and scraped down pine furniture for our country house. On the side, I did things like learning Italian and Spanish at night and taking courses in tailoring so I could make my own suits. I even took a course in hat-making! Although I was terribly busy, I was climbing the walls with boredom because I had nothing to focus my mind on. Betty Friedan's book, which documented women's dissatisfaction with the homemaking role, really struck a chord.

My kids were three and five, so I returned to university as a part-time student and in 1965 completed my MA in English. I had no thoughts of a career. I just wanted to challenge myself and get my brain working again. I was having so much fun I decided to do my Ph.D., but I still had no career plan.

In 1970, I finished my doctorate and decided to teach at York University. In those days, this was not the norm. When my husband and I went to cocktail parties, people would look at me as if I had two heads. The other doctors' wives couldn't understand my desire to work and study.

In 1977, after twenty-three years of marriage, I divorced my husband. My kids were in their late teens, preparing to leave the nest, and I wanted to live alone. As part of the divorce settlement, I got the country house, which was on twenty acres of wilderness. I soon established my lifestyle, teaching at York in the winters and spending the summers in the wonderful seclusion of rural Ontario. I'd sit for hours in my rocking chair on the veranda soaking up nature.

I started to keep a diary, which I wrote in daily. I lived inside myself for quite a while before I started writing. I needed the space and the silence to discover who I was.

I'd done my doctoral thesis on "Courtship Conventions in Jane Austen's Novels," although in those days I don't think I identified her as an underground feminist. I simply thought she was the greatest writer since Shakespeare. My interest in women's lives really grew out of my academic career. People were just beginning to look at Canadian writers and I started teaching about women such as Elizabeth Simcoe, Catharine Parr Traill, and Susanna Moodie. I could identify with their assigned role as accessories to their husbands. Mrs. Simcoe was dragged to Canada in 1792 when her husband became the first lieutenant-governor of Upper Canada. Catharine and Susanna were trying to write and earn money with children underfoot. I could understand their sense of female obligation. Like them, I received the message that, as a woman, I had to be selfless and live for others.

I grew up in Richmond Hill, a town just north of Toronto, in the 1930s. A colony gets the culture of the mother country one generation late, so I actually had a Victorian upbringing, like the ones I later read about in the courtesy books that told young nineteenth-century ladies how to behave. My role in life was to act like a scatterbrain, because if I let boys know I was intelligent, I'd never find a husband. And once I found him, I was to lead a totally selfless existence devoted to making him and my children happy.

Most of the women I knew, like my mother, followed this model. But I had one older cousin, Jane, who never married and was the principal of a school in Toronto. I thought she had the most exotic life. She'd go to Europe every summer and bring me unusual presents. In summer she wore big picture hats and lots of jewellery. She was an Auntie Mame figure and I thought she was wonderful.

One day, I was waxing eloquent on the subject of the "ladies" I was teaching. One of my colleagues, the critic and novelist Peter Such, suggested I write a book about them. I looked at him aghast. "I couldn't write a book — I'm not a writer," I protested.

Peter assured me I could, and spurred on by him, I started writing. I'd show him my chapters and he'd say, "Oh yes, they're wonderful. Keep going." They weren't wonderful. They were terrible, and I stuck them in the bottom drawer of my desk.

Sometime later I heard that the Association of Canadian Studies was awarding money for proposed biographies of Canadian figures. It took me a while to muster the nerve, but eventually I submitted a proposal on Sara Jeannette Duncan, the pioneering Canadian journalist, novelist, and world traveller. Much to my surprise, I received one of the awards. That sparked requests from several publishers who wanted to publish this book, which I hadn't even started to research! One was from Jim Polk at Anansi, who said he'd noticed that the press release mentioned a book in my bottom drawer called *The Embroidered Tent*. He found the title intriguing and wanted to see the manuscript. I took it down to him and he made an offer to publish.

I had two years to research and write the book on Sara Jeannette Duncan and to finish *The Embroidered Tent*, and I was still teaching.

But writing gave me such a sense of satisfaction that I wanted to do it for twenty hours a day. I guess I'd been storing it up for so long, I had a lot to say. *The Embroidered Tent: Five Gentlewomen in Early Canada* came out in 1982, and *Redney, A Life of Sara Jeannette Duncan* was published the following year.

It took me quite a while to begin to think of myself as a writer. I wrote those first two books on the dining-room table, clearing it off at meal times because I couldn't commit to a proper study. Jim Polk was an inspirational editor. I don't know what he saw in those first chapters. "Get rid of the scholarly claptrap and let these women speak in their own voices," he'd say. "Tell it like you feel it."

The first time I really felt *The Embroidered Tent* coming together, I was in the country working on the chapter on Elizabeth Simcoe. I remember thinking, This is great stuff, which was a new feeling. I got up and looked out the window. It was a misty, rainy day and two gorgeous deer were standing in the field. That was a real moment of clarity. I finished the chapter and sent it to Jim. "This is terrific," he said. "It's far ahead of anything you've done before."

The creative process is a mystery and ideas just pop into your head, so I can't identify the source of my thesis for *The Embroidered Tent*. I was reading all the time, and the idea that the Canadian wilderness liberated these proper English gentlewomen from the rigid sex roles of their upbringing just came together. I'm sure my love of nature entered into it. One of my great joys as a child was to go off bird-watching by myself. As a writer, I was using nature as a set of emotional metaphors for myself.

Every book must come from the centre of the writer. I've written about twenty different women in my books. I've looked at their lives and their problems and I have great empathy for them. These are important lives — the women who went out to India with their viceroy husbands, or the American girls who married into the British aristocracy — and we shouldn't trivialize them.

Despite my moment of epiphany in the country, I didn't have that much confidence in myself as a writer. When the first reviews of *The Embroidered Tent* came out, I remember thinking, Gee, I fooled all these people. They think I'm a writer. It took about three books before I could say, Yes, I *am* a writer.

I was fifty-two when *The Embroidered Tent* was published, which I consider quite an accomplishment in itself, since society tends to assume that women's lives are finished when they reach fifty. Looking back, I really resent all those years I wasn't writing. I should have started in my twenties. Alice Munro was writing when she was housebound with little children and I could have done that, instead of making the clothes, the hats, and the hooked rugs, but it never occurred to me.

I can see how the social restrictions of being a woman delayed my birth as a writer, but even so, I love being female. I think there are some women achievers who wish they'd been born male, but not me. I wouldn't have wanted to miss having children, which I found very enriching, and I love being feminine. Unlike some women, I don't believe that fashion is restricting. In fact, for me, clothes are very creative. For years and years before I was doing anything else, I was sewing all my own clothes, not to mention all the curtains and upholstery in the house. I think my creativity came out that way. Now I hardly sew at all because I've found a more legitimate channel for my creativity.

I didn't know I was going to be a writer, but I've always had a writer's sensibility — standing back and observing things with an irreverent, ironic point of view and able to see the hypocrisy in social situations. Whenever I went to a party of medical doctors and their wives, I was Jane Austen, observing. That detachment is what allows writers to write. I think every writer has that kind of hard edge, the ability to see through conventional wisdom.

In 1982, I decided to leave York University. Actually, there wasn't much to give up. Like many women, I was teaching on contract and outside the tenure stream. I had a full-time course load and was being paid about half of what the mostly male faculty received, even though I knew I was as good a teacher and had published more than some. All the women were aware of the inequity and we were very resentful.

Living in England appealed to me because I had a very British upbringing and England was my cultural mother country. I ended up spending seven winters there, researching, and in the summers I'd come back to my lovely house in the country to write. For about ten years, I was incredibly driven. I felt I was so old. I had so few years to make my name and I was very ambitious. Then, gradually, I felt I could take a breath.

I'd like to be more financially successful than I've been, but other than that and starting earlier I can't think of much I'd change. That's the thing about writing — somewhere along the way you discover that the rewards aren't in appearing on television or radio or getting your name in the papers. The reward of writing is in writing. The process of doing it is so satisfying. If I had to pay somebody to be allowed to write, I would.

I feel very happy about how far women have come in my lifetime. There's no reason women should go on hold for twenty years until their children are grown before they can do something. It's a good thing that selfless women who devote themselves to their families are on the wane. It's hard for me to believe they've had a fulfilling life. I think there's another life they haven't tasted.

"I had a destiny, to become an Acadian writer when the culture was in shreds. I was very aware that I had to write something that had never been written before. I knew I could not let the voice of my people die without a last cry."

ANTONINE MAILLET

Almost single-handedly, Antonine Maillet created Acadian liter-ature, making the rest of the world aware of the culture of this unique group of French-speaking people who began to settle eastern Canada in the early 1600s and were cruelly uprooted and deported by the English in 1755. She began writing in the 1960s, while still a teacher, and published numerous plays and novels in French. She came to the attention of a broader audi-ence in the 1970s. Her novel Don l'Orignal *won the Governor General's Award in 1972 and was translated into English, and her beloved character la Sagouine began to tour Canada and Europe in the person of the actress Viola Léger. In 1979, Maillet became the first non-European to win France's most distin-guished literary prize, the Prix Goncourt, for her novel* Pélagie La Charette. *She currently lives in Bouctouche, N.B., where she grew up, and in Montreal, on a street christened in her honour, Avenue Antonine Maillet.*

One day when I was eleven or twelve the teacher told us to take out our books and write a composition entitled "My Own Funeral." As always, we were to write in English. I didn't care about funerals, but the idea appealed to me because I found it amusing. For the first time, though, it struck me that we shouldn't be writing in English. In New Brunswick, English was the official language, even in my town, Bouctouche, where ninety-eight percent of the town were French and the other two percent were Irvings of the oil company. For some inexplicable reason I felt compelled to stand up and ask the teacher in what language we should be writing.

"In your language," she replied. "In the language of the country, in the language that will be the language of your work when you grow up." She was very sweet about it. Fortunately or unfortunately, depending on your point of view, I wasn't interested in being placated.

"But English is not my language," I proclaimed. "I don't want to work in English. I don't want to earn my living in English when I grow up."

Surprisingly, the whole grade eight class stood behind me and said they wouldn't write in English, either. Once I realized I had incited something along the lines of a student strike, I became frightened and began to worry about how my father would react. He wanted me to learn in French, but I don't think he wanted me to create a revolution. The teacher sensed my fear and emphasized that writing in English was for my own good. I think I understood that something stronger than my being was speaking through me, because I continued to insist that writing in English was not for my own good. Finally, the teacher got mad and told me to sit down and do as I was told. But I wouldn't; I couldn't. Exasperated, she asked in an ironic tone, "And what are you going to do for a living in French when you grow up?"

There was only one thing I could say, because it was coming from my gut: "I'm going to write."

I remember her mood changes during this exchange very clearly. First she was nice, then she was mad, then she was ironic. When I told her I was going to write, she inquired sarcastically, in French, "Where? In *L'Evangelaine* or *Le Revue des Fermiers*?" These were, respectively, the French-language newspaper in New Brunswick and the farmer's magazine, neither of which was held in high regard. The moment I felt the irony, I knew I was winning, so I stayed my course and I won. We wrote our composition in French, and at that moment I committed myself to becoming a writer.

I also have a vague memory of another event that took place not long after, when the school inspector visited our class and he asked us to write a composition — in French. I remember very clearly the title

La Pomme de La Fontaine. Jean La Fontaine was a seventeenth-century French writer who is best known for his *Fables*. The next day, the inspector returned with the marked compositions. I remember his comments written in red ink: "*Chère mademoiselle*," mine began. (I was more impressed with the "*mademoiselle*" than anything else, because it was the first time I'd been called that.) "*Si vous continuez à lire et à écrire, le succès vous attend!*" (If you continue to read and to write, someday you will be a success.) His comments kept me going for many years. Every time I doubted, every time I wondered how I could be so daring as to believe I could be a French-language writer in a place where there was no college for French-speaking girls, no French universities, no French libraries, no French publishers, no books, no role models, I thought of the professor's note. I also thought of the teacher who tried to stop me — that gave me an extra kick in the back.

In the end, my desire to be a writer was stronger than me. I think I had accumulated stories and characters, almost through my genes, from womb to womb, from great-great-grandmothers to great-grandmothers to grandmothers to my mother to me. That was my legacy. After many years of thinking about it, I've come to the conclusion, more or less, that memory can be transmitted genetically — a bit like Jung's collective unconscious. One day I was lecturing in Vichy, France, and in the course of the lecture I mentioned that I'd been born with a birthmark on my left thigh. Afterwards a woman came up to me and said, "I'm a Maillet and for four centuries no one in my family has ever gone to America. You might be interested to know that three members of my family have the very same birthmark on the left thigh."

I thought this was preposterous so I insisted that she show me her birthmark, which did in fact exist. If we can transmit a birthmark from France to North America through four centuries, why can't we transmit other things, like memory, language, or images? I'm not a prophet, I'm just proof that there's truth beyond what we see.

I was one of nine children born right by the church in the middle of the town of Bouctouche, New Brunswick, on May 10, 1929. Both of my parents were teachers, but after they wed, as a married woman, my mother couldn't continue to teach. In any case, she was soon fully occupied raising her family, which, by the way, wasn't large by the standards of Bouctouche. My father went to work for the Irving Oil company since he couldn't support all of us on a teacher's salary, but for us he was always a teacher, kind though somewhat strict. He had a very open mind, so I wouldn't say he was a nationalist in the negative sense of the word, but like my mother, he wanted us to remember who we were. They wanted us to have memories of our past, to identify ourselves through our culture, and to speak good French. In many very positive ways, I owe to my parents the side of me that fought for the Acadian culture to survive.

I grew up knowing I was a Maillet, I was Acadian, and I was French. My father wanted us to understand that our French was not a second-class language, as many Acadians believed. I belong to the generation that discovered we did not speak poor French. Acadian French was not a dialect, not a *patois*; it was ancient French, very picturesque and very poetic. Instead of speaking with concepts, we spoke with images. My father wanted us to imagine that we could make not only a life, but also a living, in French, which was a revolutionary concept. Now I recognize how privileged we were as a family because of our parents.

I was lucky, too, because I was among the first group of Acadian girls who could study in French. In 1943, Mère Jeanne de Valois, whom I wrote about in my book *The Confessions of Jeanne de Valois*, founded the first college for French-speaking girls in Acadia, and in 1945, I was ready to go. She was my teacher at the school, then became my Mother Superior when I chose to enter the convent. I think she could have been prime minister of Canada. She had everything it took: the guts, the vision, the intelligence, the power, and the strength. She was my role model, my mentor, both in my personal life and in my professional life.

I attended the University of Moncton, which was the only French-language university outside Quebec. While I was studying there I became a nun. In Acadia, it's not a big deal to enter the convent. The only way I could teach literature was to teach in a college for girls that was run by nuns, so I thought it was a normal thing to do. Of course, I didn't become a nun just to teach. I thought it offered an appropriate future for a young girl who was writing and teaching and who wanted to help young women to be free and to learn. But the moment I realized I did not have to be a nun to do these things, I left the convent.

I was the first person to get a master's degree at the University of Moncton. I went to see the president and asked to do my master's in literature. He told me it was impossible because the university didn't grant graduate degrees. I said, "You're going to start now and give one to me because I can do it." "Of course you can," he replied. "But how are you going to do it? We don't have the classes." I told him he had one student and he had professors, and he gave in.

I suppose that took a lot of nerve. I think I got that from my mother. My father had the wisdom, but my mother had the guts. She was visceral and stronger than my father, who was more thoughtful and intellectual. My mother used to discuss things with the priest, which was very daring. Unfortunately, she died when I was just four-teen. In one sense, it was a tragedy; in another, it forced me to fly with my own wings.

I did my doctorate at Laval because I wanted to study with M. Luc Lacourcière, who was French Canada's greatest ethnologist and specialist in Acadian oral culture. I went to Paris to write my thesis on the sixteenth-century French writer Rabelais and how his work fit in with the Acadian tradition. Although the Acadians came to Canada in the seventeenth century, they took the sixteenth-century culture with them. They also came from the same regions of France as Rabelais, who was from the middle class and of the world of artisans, not the aristocracy. He wrote the story of my people, living in those same regions of France, just before we came to Canada. All his words, proverbs, images, traditions, and legends relate to Acadian traditions.

For many years I combined a career in teaching with writing. I started to publish with Quebec publishers in Montreal, and my third novel was published in France. My first book to be published in English was *Don l'Orignal*, which won the Governor General's Award in 1972.

While I was living in France, in the late 1960s, I started sending stories weekly to Radio Canada in Moncton. They were vignettes about funny things I saw in France. When I returned to Canada I continued the practice of writing about anything and everything that interested me, but I soon realized this wasn't fulfilling me as a writer. I knew I was writing to earn a living, and I wasn't happy with that. One day I decided to write something that came from my heart, not my head, so I closed all the doors of my brain and I listened. *La Sagouine* is what came to me. I wrote it as if la Sagouine, a seventy-two-year-old charwoman, was speaking to me in her language, old *Acadien*. That was the first time that Acadian French was written down. I remember saying things and realizing I didn't know the word. The words came with the expression of the emotion. Now, I recognize that when I write I remember words I don't consciously know.

It took me a day or two to complete the first chapter, then I sent it to Radio Canada. I felt either it would be a terrible flop — nobody would accept the language — or it would go very far. I knew there was no middle ground. The next day I got a phone call from the CBC telling me they wanted more.

If somebody had asked me to write the story of a typical Acadian woman as a symbol, never, on my soul, never, would I have written *La Sagouine*. She was a poor woman, she was the underdog, she was kneeling down, she was the symbol of some kind of servitude. I didn't want Acadians to be that. And yet, la Sagouine was speaking about more than her misery. She was also looking up at the stars and dreaming. So she *was* a typical Acadian.

Eventually, *La Sagouine* became a play and a television series, and people began to see the character as the new Evangeline, the antidote to Longfellow's romantic heroine, whose quest for her lost Acadia becomes a search for her lost lover. If I had known la Sagouine was going to become so famous, that she would be seen as the archetype for Acadia, I'm sure I would have made her far more noble. Now I recognize that you should never ask a writer to give you an archetype. We do it wrong. Fortunately, we don't do what we want, we do what we can. La Sagouine is absolutely right as a symbol of Acadia. She's a woman, an underdog, a member of a minority who is struggling for more than survival. She's fighting for her place in the sun and her right to be a full-fledged citizen.

By the time *La Sagouine* was performed, I had built a body of work, but I wasn't sure I could make a living as a writer. Then *Don l'Orignal* won the Governor General's Award, and in 1975 I decided to quit teaching and write full-time. Of course, I had a few moments of doubt, but I've never regretted that decision. Only when my novel *Pélagie La Charette* won the Prix Goncourt in 1979 did I begin to enjoy some financial security. The financial prize is not very big, but the award is highly publicized, so you sell many books. Over a million people have read *Pélagie* and I sold the film rights. In terms of impact, I don't think there's an equivalent award in English — I suppose the Booker comes closest.

La Sagouine and Pélagie are both very strong women. La Sagouine is a visionary. She has something to say and she has a way of saying it that makes you believe her. I speak of her as if she is some kind of heroine who has little involvement with me because I do feel she's beyond me. So I'll allow myself to be very unbiased in favour of her. She has a wisdom, a way of speaking truths, that we know but didn't realize we know. Pélagie, on the other hand, is not a philosopher. She's a leader, a woman with a vision. Pélagie has spent fifteen years in exile in Georgia since the deportation. One day she packs up her oxcart and begins a ten-year voyage back to Acadia because she understands that if she stays in Georgia, she will lose her culture and her soul. In time, the LeBlancs will become Whites, and that will be the end of Acadia.

Some Quebec writers — very few — were disappointed that the first Goncourt awarded to a non-European didn't go to one of them. A small number even expressed their displeasure directly to me. They felt their culture was superior because it was more sophisticated and intellectual. Who was this Acadian who wrote in an ancient dialect about rustic characters and the roots of tradition? I pointed out that the Acadian culture is every bit as rich as theirs and at least as deserving. Where were they when Rabelais was writing? Acadian traditions come from a time when many people who call themselves French had not yet joined the family.

I've also been criticized because I'm not a separatist. I believe that having a small pocket of independent French-speaking people in the huge mass of North America would further endanger the French language and culture. I think our culture has a better chance of surviving and flourishing as part of Canada.

I suppose some people might think I'm boasting, and I don't want to do that — I just say things as they seem real to me. From the time I decided to become a writer, I never had any serious doubts about my choice. Like all writers, I have doubts about individual works, but ultimately, I don't think the decision to become a writer was mine to make. As I said, everything was decided for me. I had a destiny.

"When UBC awarded me an honorary doctorate, I said this wasn't new to me since my culture also bestows honorary names on white people. I feel strongly that other cultures should be recognized and valued."

DOREEN JENSEN

Doreen Jensen was delivered by a medicine woman on May 13, 1933, in Kispiox, B.C. She won her first award for art at age eleven and describes herself as "a traditional Gitksan artist," noting that the designation also encompasses her work as a teacher, historian, community organizer, mother, grandmother, and political activist. Her carvings are in various public and private collections across Canada and much of her work has involved promoting better awareness and understanding of aboriginal culture. Her honours include an Honorary Doctorate of Letters from the University of British Columbia, the YWCA Woman of Distinction Award for Arts and Culture, and the Golden Eagle Feather, the highest award of the Professional Native Women's Association.

I was twenty when I became vocal about the need to change the way First Nations people were treated. It was 1953 and my eight-month-old son, Rick, had been admitted to the Hazelton hospital with bronchial pneumonia. The next morning I phoned to see how he was and was told he was fine but he "got into some warm water." Since that didn't seem right, I rushed to the hospital, where I learned he'd been scalded. They'd been steaming him with a hot plate and a jug of hot water, and I guess he got up in the morning and fell out of the crib into the boiling water.

It was a horrific accident. I call it an accident, but I really think it was neglect on the hospital's part because he was a native child. I'd grown up in Kispiox, a little community about 750 miles north of Vancouver. Although I'd spent two years at a United Church residential school, where among other things I had to scrub floors until I could see my reflection, I didn't get a real education in racism until I began working and moved to Hazelton. In those days, native people were segregated. My husband, Vergil, isn't a native, and when we went to the movies on our first date we didn't know what to do because the natives sat on one side of the theatre. At Vergil's suggestion we sat on the native side. The hospital was segregated, too. The non-native part was very different from the native ward. Natives had to enter through the back door and line up in the hallway. It was more like being processed than receiving care. Seeing my baby suffer because of these attitudes turned me around. After my son's hospital experience, I decided something had to be done to right these long-standing wrongs.

Not long after Rick's scalding, I joined the museum association in Hazelton. The only other native person on the board was an elderly man, who said, "This is a place where our treasures are going to be. Don't call it a museum because our culture isn't dead. It's only sleeping." So we called our museum the Skeena Treasure House. I spent a lot of time working there, and eventually that involvement led to construction of the 'Ksan Village, a living museum depicting the Gitksan culture, which opened in 1969. When I started, I never saw it as a mammoth undertaking — which, with hindsight, it was. I just did one thing at a time as it needed to be done.

Although I was doing a lot of art myself, I really didn't think about whether I was an artist. I just did what I enjoyed doing in the way I felt it should be done. I also helped to raise funds for the village, organized classes in wood and silver carving, and coordinated performing arts groups who were reviving our ancient songs and dances. I travelled to Toronto to buy gold and silver for our jewellery classes and learned how to silk-screen. I did all the silk-screening for 'Ksan Village while we were getting ready to open and also taught silk-screening myself. In the early 1970s, I completed a two-year carving course at the Kitanmax School of Northwest Coast Indian Art, which is part of the 'Ksan Village museum. Only one other woman took the course and tourists were very curious to know how acceptable it was for a woman to carve. I told them there was no difference between men and women. Carving was art and I was learning how to do it just like everybody else. I felt comfortable with carving because I'd grown up hearing about a woman from my father's old village who was an excellent and very sought-after mask carver.

That period was such a busy time for me, it now seems like a blur. I got married when I was sixteen and started raising my family when I was eighteen. I have four children, so I combined my art and my voluntary activities with looking after them. When they were growing up I did a lot of my work at home, in addition to all the parent-teacher things like taking them to skating and piano lessons and reading to them every night when they were little.

We left Hazelton in 1972 when my husband, who was an electrician and heavy duty mechanic for B.C. Hydro, was transferred to Vancouver. By that time I was quite knowledgeable about native art, including the technical aspects. Although I continued working with 'Ksan Village, I started learning about aboriginal cultures on the Lower Mainland and became a buyer for the Canadian Indian Marketing Service, an Ottawa-based federal government program to develop a market for Canadian arts and crafts. During this period I was travelling a lot and met many established native artists and artisans across the country. The travel made managing my family a little difficult. By this time the kids were teenagers and we made sure one of us was always there, even though coordinating activities wasn't easy. Vergil has always been very supportive of what I do and very helpful in many ways. We'll be celebrating our fiftieth wedding anniversary in the year 2000. Our kids are all grown up and doing well, and we have six grandchildren who are a great source of joy.

In 1978, I went to Adelaide, Australia, to speak at a conference on the effects of museums on indigenous peoples. There I met Silver Harris, exhibitions manager for the Adelaide Festival Centre. She was totally mesmerized by the ceremonial robe I wore and said, "We must have an exhibition of these." I said yes, we must. About five years later, the phone rang one Sunday afternoon and it was Silver calling from Australia. She said, "I finally got some money for that exhibition of ceremonial robes. Can you do it?" This was pretty typical of how my life unfolded. I never stop to think about how much work these things will involve, because they're such learning experiences. Others gain, but so do I.

In 1983 that show travelled to six venues in Australia, then returned in 1985 to the Museum of Anthropology in Vancouver and travelled to four additional venues across Canada. The catalogue, *Robes of Power: Totem Poles on Cloth*, was published by UBC Press in 1987. Between 1982 and 1987, I also organized several exhibitions of northwest coast art and coordinated the Aboriginal Women Artists Retreat held in Coquitlam, B.C., which focused on recognizing women artists and the importance of preserving traditional women's arts. In 1988, I curated and coordinated an exhibition and festival at Sterling University in Scotland. These are just some of the things I've done to create a climate so that the culture of my people can be appreciated and valued.

I never experienced a conflict between having children and being an artist, but as I became more and more involved with promoting First Nations culture I found my activities consumed time I wanted to spend doing my own art. Yet it was difficult to say no, because there was such a need to create a climate that encouraged other artists to come forward, and quite often I was in a position where I could do something. I participated as long as the work was connected with art, because I felt I was still doing art in a different way. When I started, even totem poles weren't acknowledged as art. Now there's some recognition. But I've paid a price for all the labour. The demands of society — people wanting me to speak, people wanting me to write or to organize events — have kept me from my own work.

Art was always important to me. I grew up hearing about the wonderful masks that our carvers had made. People spoke so clearly about them that they became real in my mind. The masks and the fabric art had all been taken away from us — or our people had burned them — but the oral history was so vivid that I could see the artifacts in my mind's eye.

I had a happy childhood in Kispiox. We could run and play and do whatever we wanted. My parents and grandparents were very proud of our Gitksan culture, and even though it was frowned upon, I grew up learning the language, songs, legends, and customs of my people. However, we couldn't feast. The feast was actually a court of law at which wonderful food was served, but since white society felt this was a waste, the ceremony was banned from 1884 to 1951. We still heard about it, though, because my family made a point of teaching us about our traditions, which has made me proud of my Gitksan heritage. When I went to the two-room Indian day school I started to notice other things, like the fact that we were not allowed to speak our language. The teacher had a long pointer and she'd tap us on the head, prompting us to speak English. We were not heard unless we spoke English. I didn't think that was right, so for my whole first year of school I said basically nothing. I'm fortunate, because in their own quiet way, both my parents were very strong and I definitely had their support. As I got older I realized that, like me as a school child, native people didn't have a voice — we couldn't say no. That's why I've devoted so much of my time and energy to ensuring that others could speak in their own voices.

In my first or second year of school we had an art class and were told to draw stick people. Not only did I not want to draw stick people, I found it offensive. I had a different idea of what art should look like — totem poles and masks. However, I was scolded for not being like everybody else. One day I'd had enough, so I asked if I could go to the bathroom. Instead, I left school and went home. "You're home early," my mother said. She cuddled me and gave me something to eat, and eventually I told her about my problem. She laughed and said, "I went to school only for three years, but much of the time I'd leave school and lie on top of the woodshed and look at the clouds. Now I wish I had gone to school." That was all she said. The next day I went back to school and mastered stick figures.

My first memory of art-making is of playing hopscotch. The game became an art form because everything had to be perfect — finding the most beautiful piece of glass and so on. And, of course, we had totems in Kispiox, which I visited every day. I didn't think of them as art, but as very interesting and exciting forms. Sometimes I'd lie on the ground and look at them to get a different perspective. Last year, Vergil and I were visiting Kispiox with friends and I told them to lie down on the grass so they could see how wonderful the totems were. So this group of adults lay on the ground looking at the poles. It was a magical moment.

Unfortunately, we bury that childlike excitement, which exists inside all of us. Our child self is the source of our desire to create and it gets lost as we collect diplomas and degrees and become focused and narrow. That doesn't mean that art can be separated from politics. Still lifes may seem innocuous, but if you choose to paint one it raises underlying issues, such as who picked the apple, who made the bowl?

I really think fairness is just a matter of educating people. I don't think people want to be racist or to dominate other groups. At one time that was how it was, but today we'd just like to live in harmony with one another and with nature. In order to do that we've got to work together, although at times people still find it difficult to hear things.

Now, I'd really like to spend a lot of time doing my art. At one point, I was on ten different boards. Last year I resigned from all but two. When I first started carving, I'd work until four o'clock in the morning and Vergil would yell at me to get to bed. I'd like to be able to carve all night again.

"Margaret Laurence said it was given to her to write. I don't know if it was given to me to paint, but I had to do it, in spite of all the obstacles that were put in my way."

HELEN LUCAS

A highly regarded painter, Helen Lucas grew up in Saskatoon and graduated from the Ontario College of Art in 1954. She has exhibited widely in Canada and the U.S. and has illustrated two books of her own, as well as the children's book A Christmas Story *by Margaret Laurence. The recipient of numerous awards, including the YWCA Women of Distinction Award, in 1991 she was accorded an honorary doctorate from York University.*

I remember 1975, International Women's Year, as the first time I was able to meet and get to know a lot of interesting women. It was also the first time I realized my urge to paint wasn't unrealistic or neurotic. The feminist movement had a very positive influence on me and my work because it allowed me to discover a world where my creative self was accepted.

I'd grown up in a traditional community of Greek immigrants, where I was always told that my desire for self-expression was inappropriate because I was a woman. In 1962, after my first show, the Greek Orthodox priest told my father-in-law to order me to stop painting. The doctor, who was a god in the community, went even further. Since I was painting nudes he said I was promiscuous and must be having affairs with men. I was painting gentle lovers embracing. They were nude because that's what I'd been taught in art school — I hadn't learned to put clothes on people yet. But I was made to feel I had done something very, very wrong and I'll never forget how guilty and ashamed I felt.

All around me the world was saying, "Don't do that." In response, I started to paint icons. Surely, I surmised, my detractors would approve of art that decorates churches. I bought some books on the art of icon painting and learned these religious artists were not allowed to have an ego. Not only were icons never signed, they follow a rigid set of rules. The nose and eyes must form a cross. The eyes must be completely dilated to indicate that the holy figure sees everything. The mouth is small because holy figures don't eat or talk, nor may they show any emotion. With hindsight, I can see I was putting myself into a strait-jacket, but I worked away. After completing numerous icons, I called Paul Duval, the only art critic I had ever met, and invited him over to see my work. He had given my first show a great review, but he liked only one of my icons. It was the first one I had done and I had painted it from my memories of icons, before I'd read the books. A Madonna was holding a child and her eyes were shut — really shut. It was a very violent mother and child, which I have since destroyed. At the time I didn't realize why he felt it was good, but now I see it was the only icon that expressed anything of me.

I suppose my vision of the Madonna and child was a nightmare because my marriage was so awful and my husband was so threatened by my painting. Like most Greek men, he was raised to believe that the man is the centre of attention in the family. My painting drew attention to me and it was very hard for him to cope. Now, I don't blame him because I've since realized that his ego is very fragile.

My painting icons lasted a couple of years, and of course they weren't satisfying, so I started doing heads and figures. For a long, long time I painted only in black. Black is the colour of death and it's quite a prevalent colour in the Greek community. When my third sister, Mary, was born I remember letters edged in black arriving from Greece. What a tragedy for a family — a third daughter and no sons! My dear middle sister thinks I'm melodramatic, but our legacy was to end up as Greek women wearing black. In Greece if a parent dies, the little girls wear black until they grow up. And, of course, when your husband dies, you must go into mourning. When my father died, my mother refused to wear black. She wore grey and blue. In spite of how traditional she was, she was also feisty. I guess my sisters and I got our determination from her.

After my father died, my mother learned to drive, but she never learned to put the car in reverse. One day, after she'd been driving for about eight years, travelling back and forth to work every day, I told her she must learn how to back up. "I'm not concerned with where I've been, only where I'm going," was her response. Isn't that a wonderful statement? In many ways, I think she wanted her daughters to break out, but she was trapped by the restrictions of her world.

I grew up in Saskatoon. At the time, the Greek community in Saskatoon was very small — about seventy people, most of whom came from the same village in Greece. Basically, a young man arriving in Canada from Greece would get on the train and keep going until he found an area that needed a little restaurant. I have no idea why men picked restaurants — possibly because they could be their own boss. A little lunch counter made you independent. My father followed the pattern. He bought a little hotel with a lunch counter, and after achieving a certain level of success, he heard about my mother, who was from the same village in Greece and who had been brought to Chicago by her elder brother. She met my father and they married, with my uncle providing the dowry and paying for the big wedding.

Greek culture in Canada was very insular and competitive, probably because people came with so little and it was so important for them to succeed. Growing up, my reality was that it was strange to be born in Canada, yet not to be Canadian. The one thing I cannot forgive my parents for is not letting me have friends. In my small community there were no other Greek girls my age, and I think my parents thought that if I had girlfriends, sooner or later I would want to do what Canadian girls did — wear lipstick, date, and be outspoken. Of course, I could have nothing to do with boys. The expression was that girls must never become *petaxti*, which means like a butterfly — that is to say, we must never be noticed. Girls must be quiet, subservient, and speak only when spoken to. When we went to the social gatherings, I had to sit neatly with my hands folded and eat very little of what I was offered. A good girl could be starving and would only speak when spoken to. If people perceived that you were like that — subservient and without any needs of your own — word would get out that you were good marriage material. Marriage, of course, was a girl's only real objective in life.

I was so unhappy. When I graduated from high school I was vale-dictorian because my marks were good, but I couldn't stay for the party afterwards. I remember a few nice things that happened at school, but for the most part I didn't want to be there. As a result, I did a lot of day-dreaming and tuning out, and I think that's why I became an artist. I studied a lot because I had nothing else to do, and in grade school I started doing little drawings — copies of artists which I took to school. The teacher would admire them and put them up on the board, and that gave me the pat on the back I never got at home. I learned very early that drawing was one way to get the attention I needed.

In the Greek community, girls married at sixteen, seventeen, eigh-teen. If that didn't happen, university was a way of saving the family's esteem. I had a female cousin who was a doctor, and since I had no marriage prospects, my parents thought it would be great if I became a doctor, too. I enrolled in pre-med but soon realized my heart wasn't in it. Also, my father died the year before I started university and I was terribly unhappy. I made up my mind to find a way of getting out of pre-med and getting to Toronto. One of my great joys was putting my ear to our floor-model radio and listening to the CBC — The Fletcher Markle Stage Series plays, the Lux Radio Theatre, the Metropolitan Opera. Drama and music triggered some-thing in me and I remember thinking I had to get to Toronto, which I perceived as the source of this beauty.

By then, I had made some kind of decision to become an artist. I didn't even think "try to become." I just assumed you went, you studied, you became. That's also the time I starting twirling. My mother would be in the kitchen and I'd clench my hands and twirl until I fell. A couple of times I vomited. The Greek community could control my will and my behaviour, but they could not control my body. Twirling was the only resource through which I might gain my independence. I thought if I could make myself look sick, I could make them realize that I had to get out of Saskatoon. It's the kind of thing a twelve-year-old does, but I was seventeen. I wasn't really sick. I was play-acting. Twirling was a very manipulative, very infantile tantrum, which I repeated again and again as a statement of my desperation. Finally, my mother was so upset she didn't know what to do. "What do you want?" she asked. I said, "Let me go to Toronto. Let me go and study painting."

By then my middle sister had finished high school, so my mother got into our old car and drove us to Toronto. My sister went into restaurant management at Ryerson, and in the fall of 1950 I started at the Ontario College of Art. That's how I got away from home. Except I didn't get away. In the first week I met my future husband, who had changed his name from Loukides to Lucas. I thought, "Oh good, he wants to be Canadian, just like me." We started dating and four years after we met, we married. Then, the two children came. It was twenty more years before I got out of what became the traditional marriage I thought I would never have. We both went into our programming and did everything that we hated, but we were stuck.

Throughout my marriage I kept drawing and painting — even if a corner of the kitchen was my only work space. Once, all I had was a walk-in closet. Eight years after I married, I started exhibiting. I painted because I had to. I can't explain it. Completing a drawing gave me a great high, which I wanted to repeat. At first I think my husband found it kind of cute, but the more serious I became, the more difficult it was for him. He was programmed to have a wife who cooked and looked after the kids, and there I was, saying, "Oh, good, I'm going to have a show." My first exhibition and all the criticism it generated within the community was very traumatic for us both. That's when I realized the marriage wasn't there. My husband couldn't even talk to me. He whispered. The marriage was a celibate one for over twelve years. He did his thing and was rarely home. When the children went to school, I'd go into the studio, and when he was home, we tiptoed around each other. Although I preferred it when he wasn't there, I was much too timid to think about a divorce. It terrified me. I knew of nobody in the Greek community who had been divorced.

Both sides of the family had bought us a house on Warren Road in Forest Hill. One morning sometime around 1963, without even consulting my husband, I called a real estate agent and put the house up for sale. By the end of the week, it was sold. My in-laws were horrified. I think my mother was upset, too. I gave the money to my husband to start his own business. I knew he was involved with somebody by then. He could have taken off, and I think that's what

I wanted him to do. I felt very guilty because of the reaction to my first show, and I think giving him the money from the house was a way of absolving myself.

Slowly, I started getting out of the Greek community because I was so ashamed of all the criticism I was receiving and my husband's behaviour was so humiliating. In 1973, the year my divorce came through, I began a new chapter in my life. A friend told me about a feminist psychiatrist, Mary McEwen, whom she had found very helpful. I had come across the word *feminism* in things I'd read, and realized I was a feminist because I wanted equality for men and women. Mary, who loved men and reinforced that they are not the enemy, helped me to see my part in my divorce and to move on. My mother gave me $30,000, which was quite a sum of money in those days, for the downpayment on a house where I could have a studio. I also started teaching at Sheridan College, which gave me a great sense of emotional independence. I was so grateful to have that job, but by 1979, after eight years, it was very tiring. I really wanted to do my own work.

When I was growing up, mother always had a flower garden, and every year she won prizes in the local garden show. Because I was the dreamer, the one who wasn't much good for anything else, I helped her in the garden. I hated it because I'd see the kids from school going off to movies or parties and I'd be working in the garden with my mother, but obviously that experience is deeply connected to my work.

For many years, I painted exclusively in black. Sometime around 1980, tear stains, forms that were almost inverted petals, started to appear on the faces of my black-and-white figures. The more I worked with the tear stains, the more they wanted to become petals. One Good Friday I did a series of crucifixes, one of which was covered with flowers. They were very abstract flowers, done by dipping a rag into turpentine saturated red, but for me they were a breakthrough because they had colour and were flowers. Suddenly, I realized that the flowers could actually be my subject matter, that I no longer needed to paint the painful images that had occupied me for so long. After so many years of black and white, I'd found a reason for painting in colour.

Around the time I started painting flowers, I met my second husband. By then, I had done a lot of work on myself. I'd been divorced for seven years and Mary McEwen had helped me to see that the male population is as important as the female. I was reading women writers and I was embracing everything that had to do with women and enjoying the company of all the wonderful women I had met. But males remained unknown. Growing up with sisters, I never learned very much about boys and I didn't know if I could have a good relationship with a man. I had a few relationships after my divorce, but they were really quite neurotic. I was attracted to one man because he drove a Mercedes and another because he was an opera singer. I soon realized that whatever he had to give, he gave when he was performing. I was very lonely, especially after I gave up teaching and Andrea, my second child, was ready to leave home. That's when I met Derek.

A friend, Margo Lane, was doing some research on personal advertising for a CBC television program and she suggested that I put an ad in the *Globe and Mail*. I was shocked. I said I wouldn't be caught dead doing that. But Margo had been so enthusiastic that, as I was painting, I found myself thinking about what I'd say. To make a long story short, I submitted an ad. Four days later I received a package of letters and the first one I opened was from Derek. The first man I met was Derek. I think we both wanted something to happen, and about six weeks later he moved his record collection in. He wasn't a successful businessman or a moody artist who wrote great novels or sang in a wonderful baritone. He was a graphic artist, who from the age of twelve saved his money so he could go to chamber music concerts. He was divorced, with no children, and he was lonely. Becoming involved with Derek was very selfish on my part, I suppose because I didn't have to compromise very much. He fit right into my life and my friends and my lifestyle and he loved my painting. His ego wasn't threatened by my work. He was very content with himself and I think that's what creative women need. Creative men have always had women to look after them and tell them how wonderful they are, but the same isn't true for women who are similarly inclined.

When my mother died in 1984, she left us some money. I told Derek that we could put the money in the bank and not have to worry, or we could move out of the city and build the studio I'd always wanted and he could have his heart's desire — a large garden.

We moved to the country. The interesting thing is, I was imagining a studio that resembled a double garage. Derek's belief in me resulted in the magnificent studio I have today. We had seen Ken Nolan's studio — he's a contemporary American colour field painter — in *Architectural Digest*, and Derek's response was, "If Ken Nolan has 1200 square feet, you'll have 1500." Derek also wanted the studio to be high. I kept thinking, I don't need the height — it will cost a lot to heat, but Derek disagreed. The ceiling is twenty-eight feet and his belief that I deserved a big studio is what built that beautiful space.

Derek took wonderful care of me, and that's when I really flourished as an artist. I think having a partner who is supportive is a great gift. I don't expect that I will ever want another man in my life. There could never be anybody as compatible as him. He died almost two years ago and I'm still grieving because I am very loyal to what we had.

No doubt, the devaluation of women in the Greek community played a big part in making me want to achieve. The images in my life have evolved as I have: from the letters rimmed in black at the birth of a sister, to the black-and-white paintings, to the big, beautiful, powerful, and colourful flowers I paint now. I think the flowers have to be large because they're a political statement. Women have always been told to think small. I don't paint flowers; I paint what they mean to me, which is joy and celebration. They represent everything that is positive. I recently rediscovered the word *praise*, which I love. It is very spiritual. The word *joy* is another beautiful word. I have since learned, with my present grief, that joy and grief are very connected; you must know one to understand the other.

I think my mother would be proud of what I have achieved, but she wouldn't really understand it. She was pleased that I painted, but she had no frame of reference for it. When I started teaching at Sheridan College, she would say, "This is my daughter, the teacher." She understood that, but she didn't understand what it meant to be a painter. If I sounded tired when she phoned, she'd ask what was wrong. I'd say I was tired because I'd been painting all day, and her response was, "I wish you could win a lottery and never have to paint again." She didn't understand when I said, "Mother, if that happened I would paint all the more." She could never comprehend the need to create.

Now I have my work and my friends. Finding that community of women in the mid-1970s was the first time I found support for myself as a woman who wanted to achieve, and it was such a bonus in life. For the most part, the women I'm close to have gone through the struggle of finding their own voice and then achieving the excellence that voice demands. It's our common bond and from them I get the unconditional love I thought only mothers give. Derek also gave me that.

AFTERWORD

In their own way, all the women included in this book qualify as "extraordinary," and herein lies a cautionary tale. Inspiring as they are, they are the exceptions that prove the rule. Evidence of unequal treatment notwithstanding, their achievements may be used to suggest that the door is wide open for all women. Actually, great strength of purpose and a solid sense of self are prerequisites to challenging the status quo, and a sense of destiny provides valuable support. The fact that these qualities do not comprise the common core of female upbringing contradicts the myth of unlimited opportunity for women.

Unlike men, women cannot assume that equal opportunities are open to them, based on their skills and abilities. Most women are still worth less than men — in monetary terms, 73 cents on the dollar — and the struggle to right this wrong continues. Carol Lees didn't succeed in getting a question on unpaid work included in Canada's census until 1996, and she risked going to jail for her efforts. In 1998, a study commissioned by the federal and provincial ministers on the status of women concluded that if women who work in the home are accounted for, women's earnings would decline to 52 cents on the dollar.

While small in number, a few women have risen to the rank of CEO. However, in the higher echelons of power, women lack "bench strength," the critical mass — about thirty percent, say sociologists — necessary to have impact as a group. According to a 1998 study by Ronald Burke, a professor at York University, only six percent of the seats in Canadian boardrooms are occupied by women. A study which included Crown corporations, released in 1999 by Catalyst, a highly respected non-profit research group, upped that figure to 7.5 percent, but noted that almost 60 percent of Canada's largest companies still operate without female representation on the board. Quite simply, there is no valid reason for this degree of underrepresentation. Another 1998 study, partially funded by the Conference Board of Canada, suggests that male bias is at the heart of this discrepancy. The study identified major gaps between women's perception of their performance and that of their male bosses, who felt that a significant percentage of women lacked the characteristics necessary to succeed in top jobs.

Change is a painful process, particularly when it challenges deeply embedded attitudes and beliefs. Tokenism — and its likely result, the co-opting of female tokens who are cautioned to disassociate themselves from advocacy of female equality since any hint of radicalism could damage their careers — has contributed to the cycle of two steps forward and one step back that characterizes women's progress throughout the ages. In today's climate of anti-equity backlash, it's all too easy to overlook the battles women waged in the ongoing struggle for equality and the price that many have paid to ensure that young women enjoy many opportunities denied to them. By writing this book, I hope to have played some small part in ensuring that some of those milestones are remembered and that women trailblazers become part of history, too.

INDEX